Jewish Workers in the Modern Diaspora

D0863185

Jewish Workers in the Modern Diaspora

Edited by

NANCY L. GREEN

with the collaboration of

PATRICK ALTMAN

EDGARDO BILSKY

DAVID CESARANI

DAVID FELDMAN

LUDGER HEID

SELMA LEYDESDORFF

DANIEL SOYER

JACK WERTHEIMER

With translations

from the Yiddish by Daniel Soyer
from the German by Thomas Kozak
from the Dutch by Wanda Boeke
from the French by Lisa Greenwald and Nancy L. Green
from the Spanish by Rick Francis

University of California Press

BERKELEY   LOS ANGELES   LONDON

University of California Press
Berkeley and Los Angeles, California

University of California Press, Ltd.
London, England

Library of Congress Cataloging-in-Publication Data

Jewish workers in the modern Diaspora / edited by Nancy L. Green; with the collaboration of Patrick Altman . . . [et al.]; translated from the Yiddish by Daniel Soyer; from the German by Thomas Kozak; from the Dutch by Wanda Boeke; from the French by Lisa Greenwald and Nancy L. Green; from the Spanish by Rick Francis.
    p.   cm.
    Includes bibliographic references and index.
    ISBN 0-520-20127-2 (cloth : alk. paper).—ISBN 0-520-20128-0 (pbk. : alk. paper)
    1. Working class Jews—History—19th century—Sources. 2. Working class Jews—History—20th century—Sources.   3. Jews—History—1789–1945—Sources.   I. Green, Nancy L. II. Altman, Patrick.
  HD6305.J3J49   1998
  305.5′62′089924—DC21   97-34835
                                    CIP

Printed in the United States of America
9 8 7 6 5 4 3 2 1

The paper used in this publication meets the minimum requirements of American National Standards for Information Sciences—Permanence of Paper for Printed Library Materials, ANSI Z39.48-1984.

Contents

Preface

The comparison of Jewish workers around the world has also been the occasion for a gathering of Jewish academics in the modern Diaspora. This has been a collective project, from the collection of documents to the extensive translations involved. We nevertheless each take responsibility for our respective geographic areas of expertise: New York—Daniel Soyer; London—David Cesarani and David Feldman; Paris—Nancy Green and Patrick Altman; Buenos Aires—Edgardo Bilsky; Germany—Jack Wertheimer and Ludger Heid; Amsterdam—Selma Leydesdorff.

As general editor, I would especially like to thank Edgardo Bilsky for having initiated the project, Daniel Soyer for being an unflagging contributor, translator, and advisor, and Selma Leydesdorff for having organized our working meeting and conference in Amsterdam; we all thank the Van Leer Foundation for its funding and the Joods Historisch Museum for its hosting of that meeting. The Memorial Foundation for Jewish Culture as well as the University of California Press provided much-needed support for the translations. And I would personally like to thank Douglas Abrams Arava for having been so patient and encouraging.

A note on the transliterations: We have followed the YIVO guidelines for transliteration from the Yiddish except where proper names have another recognized spelling.

Ellipsis points that are enclosed within brackets indicate that material has been omitted from the original text; ellipsis points that appear without brackets are part of the original document.

Introduction

"How did you spend your leisure time?" the interviewer asked.
"Who had leisure time?"
        Interview with Polish-Jewish immigrant woman

In 1889, the Jewish unemployed in London marched in protest through the East End to the Great Synagogue. In 1907, Jewish immigrant women on the Lower East Side demonstrated against the rising cost of living. By the interwar years, Jewish Bundists, Communists, and Zionists around the world were debating everything from politics to the use of Yiddish, while immigrant parents and their children navigated the shoals of generational conflicts against the background of Americanization, Anglicization, Gallicization, and so on.[1]

The Jewish worker remains an anomaly. Ignored at worst, seen as ephemeral at best, the Jewish cap makers, shoemakers, diamond workers, and tinsmiths of the turn of the century have all but faded from memory in a history of modern Jewish social mobility. Only the Jewish tailor remains an emblematic if somewhat folkloric figure of a Jewish working class.

In the last few decades, several books have brought to the fore the lives and working conditions of the men and women, garment workers, butchers, metal workers, and peddlers who peopled the Lower East Sides, the East Ends, and the Pletzls in the major Western cities of the early twentieth century.[2] Our purpose here is both to provide some of the key documents pertaining to their stories and to confront the different experiences of Jewish workers in the West. By publishing some of the primary documents that have been the building blocks of recent scholarship, we propose an inside view of the early Jewish neighborhoods through the multiple voices of the workers themselves and of some of their observers and critics. However partial or partisan, these newspaper articles, memoirs, and literary accounts help us reconstruct the lives and identities of Jewish workers and the Jewish poor. They let us see the communities on their own terms and explore the diversity and even divisions within the Jewish neighborhoods.

At the same time, these documents provide a sorely needed comparative perspective on the Jewish worker. This collection of documents from six different countries helps us go beyond the single-country approach so familiar to Jewish and general history. These stories—from Buenos Aires to Amsterdam, from London to New York, from Paris to Germany—ask important new questions about the comparative nature of Jewish settlement. To what extent have Jewish workers been alike the world over? How have local conditions shaped the experience of Jews in the modern Diaspora? And how did Jewish workers help internationalize national labor movements?

The term *workers* is used here in its most ecumenical form. When a Jewish workers' group in Paris in 1898 proclaimed that the "Jewish proletariat" was the most proletarian in the world, it did not bother to define its terms. The group argued that the double burden of class and "nation" (ethnicity, as we would say today) distinguished the Jewish proletariat, and that this alone merited the attention of the French socialists, to whom it appealed for support.[3]

In the documents that follow, we too have emphasized class and ethnicity in our presentation of the Jewish worker. And, as will be clear, these two aspects of identity generated much debate within the Jewish workers' communities themselves. At the same time, however, we use the term *worker* in its widest sense, encompassing the various lower strata of the Jewish communities under study from the late nineteenth century to the 1930s and stretching to the "entrepreneurial proletariat" engaged in the ubiquitous subcontracting system. Women and men, peddlers and petty merchants, tailors and seamstresses, diamond workers and furniture makers, small-time bosses and self-employed contractors—all populate a story that examines laboring conditions as well as unemployment and the endemically seasonal nature of many of the "Jewish" trades.

The modern Jewish Diaspora to which we refer was the mass migration from Eastern Europe. The Jews were not alone in moving westward in the nineteenth century; Italians and Poles also left their homes in vast numbers at the end of the century. The Jews, like the others, were pulled by the image of a *goldene medine* (golden land), but they were also pushed by tsarist anti-Semitism, local pogroms, and stifling economic conditions in the Pale of Settlement (western provinces of the Russian Empire to which the Jews were confined), and pulled by visions of liberty. The modern Wandering Jew often began his or her trek by simply moving within the Pale to a larger town. Eventually four million Jews went westward between 1830 and 1925, heading to North America and South America, to Northern Europe and Central Europe as well as to Palestine and South Africa. In this perspective, even Paris and London were a "new world" for the Eastern European immigrants. With the exception of Amsterdam, the Jewish poor in the period under study were thus for the most part also immigrants.

We begin the story of migration at the point of arrival, greeting the immigrants in New York, London, Paris, Buenos Aires, and Germany and comparing the Jewish immigrant workers there with the more indigenous Jewish working population in Amsterdam. Our time period starts with the beginning of the mass migration from Eastern Europe (1870s to 1880s) and goes through the 1930s.

Although this period of Jewish history was punctuated by sporadic and, later, steadily escalating xenophobia and anti-Semitism, we have chosen to focus on the internal social history of these working and immigrant neighborhoods. Jewish history has often been defined, with good reason, as a reaction to anti-Semitism, and Jewish immigration history has largely been defined with regard to native-immigrant relations. We have sought a different emphasis in order to suggest the richness of intra-community differences in a comparative perspective. We have thus chosen documents that represent: daily life, labor, and leisure (chapter 1); the organizations created by the workers and immigrants (chapter 2); the politicization that marked all of the Jewish communities and brought diversity to the national working-class movements as well (chapter 3); and the debates over acculturation and Jewish identity (chapter 4). Through published and unpublished memoirs, letters, archival reports, newspaper articles, printed reports, and novels, we can see the diversity of the Jewish workers' experience through their own eyes and as mirrored in a variety of sources, many of which have remained inaccessible until recently.

Our survey, like any survey, is not exhaustive. The experience of Jewish workers can be examined from many perspectives—as a conflict of natives versus immigrants, rich Jews and poor, immigrants and the state—some of which have been treated in monographs, some of which remain to be explored in greater depth. Other cities—Brussels, Jerusalem, Johannesburg, Chicago, Leeds, and Manchester, for example—still need to be brought into the comparative picture. We hope this book is a suggestive starting point for further comparative research on the social history of modern Jewish communities.

In order to situate the following documents, we can begin with a brief introduction to the history of Jewish workers in each area. The specific local contexts, the timing and pattern of migration, the economic fortunes of the garment industry or the diamond trade, for example, had an effect on the lives and livelihood of the Jews in different places. From the Lower East

Side of New York to the East End of London, the Jewish worker confronted different political and legal environments, different social contexts, and different customs.

NEW YORK

Between 1870 and 1914, some two million Eastern European Jews immigrated to the United States, the largest East-West transfer of those under study here. A large majority of these newcomers settled in New York, where the Jewish population rose from an estimated 80,000 in 1870 to almost 1.5 million people (over a quarter of the city's inhabitants) by World War I. Immigration fell drastically during the war, and the restrictive immigration laws enacted in 1921 and 1924 put an end to the era of mass immigration. Nevertheless, another 400,000 Jews entered the United States between 1915 and 1929. Jewish immigrants and their descendants constituted some 26 to 29 percent of the city's multiethnic population in the interwar period.

The Lower East Side of Manhattan, long a center of immigrant life in the city, became New York's first, and for decades its most important, Eastern European Jewish neighborhood. In 1890, three-quarters of New York's Eastern European Jews lived there, although by the turn of the century other sections of the city had also become home to large numbers of newcomers: Brownsville and Williamsburg in Brooklyn, and Harlem in uptown Manhattan. In the interwar period, Jewish immigrants and their offspring moved to new neighborhoods in the Bronx and in Brooklyn, until these boroughs became the most Jewish in the city. Jews made up 45 percent of the population of the Bronx in 1930.

The immigrants concentrated, here as elsewhere, in specific industries. New York was already the major center of a booming ready-made clothing industry when the Eastern European Jews started arriving in the 1870s and 1880s. This industry underwent tremendous growth in the late nineteenth and early twentieth centuries and became a major employer of these immigrants. Some 50 to 60 percent of Jewish workers in New York City in 1890 were involved in some aspect of the *shmate* (literally rags, clothing) business. As the Jewish population grew and became diversified, and other immigrants came to the sewing machines, the percentage of Jewish workers involved in the industry declined, but it remained an important center of Jewish economic activity. Large numbers of Jewish workers also worked in food preparation, the building renovation trades, printing, metal and jewelry work, and tobacco production.

Religious tradition continued to be an important part of immigrant life, even as new forms of secular Jewish culture arose. There were twenty-nine Jewish congregations in New York in 1872. By 1914, there were eight hundred, an astonishing rate of growth almost entirely due to the Eastern European Jews. *Landsmanshaftn*—hometown associations—were created, visible testimony to patterns of chain migration.[4] And the Yiddish press played an important role in the lives of immigrant workers. The socialist *Forverts*, or *Jewish Daily Forward*, founded in 1897, was unquestionably the dominant newspaper of the Lower East Side. Under the leadership of its brilliant and strong-willed editor, Abraham Cahan, the paper's popularity spread well beyond the New York immigrant neighborhood. Combining socialist politics and didacticism with a lively and popular style, it had the largest circulation of any socialist daily in the country or of any Yiddish daily in the world. Yiddish theater was also one of the most popular pastimes of the immigrant community, and the audience, passionate and unruly, played an active role in establishing the character of the Yiddish theater.

Jewish workers built several influential unions and other labor organizations, but many also felt a strong desire to leave the shop for the middle class. Over time, Jews in New York experienced a relatively high rate of social mobility. The prospect of access to greater material wealth was, in fact, one of the central promises of America, even to those who remained within the working class. In the context of the growing New York economy, several avenues were open to those aspiring to higher social status. Education, popularly seen as the most widespread road to success, was of importance primarily to later generations rather than to first-generation immigrants. Becoming a boss in the garment industry was a more likely option for the immigrant, as was becoming a proprietor of a small business such as a grocery or cleaning store. Many of these undertakings were precarious, and many individuals moved back and forth between business and workshop. But, in the course of a generation or two, the Jewish working class gradually disappeared as the immigrants, their children, and especially their grandchildren moved into the middle class.

LONDON

Between 1880 and 1914, approximately 120,000 Eastern European Jews moved to Britain, about half of whom settled in London. Approximately 80 percent (48,000) of them gravitated to the East End, where foreign and native Jews together constituted 45 to 50 percent of the population before World War I. In addition, 150,000 to 200,000 transmigrants passed through

London during this period, staying a few days or a few years before heading on to North America, South America, or South Africa. For many, the Poor Jews' Temporary Shelter was their first and only residence in London. By 1921, approximately 184,000 Jews lived in the inner London boroughs.

Immigration was halted earlier in England than anywhere else. The Aliens Act of 1905 marked the culmination of a long campaign against Polish-Russian Jews. This law gave the British government power to expel aliens and greatly dissuaded new immigration. The later laws of 1914 and 1919, instituting registration, brought immigration to a virtual halt.

In the meantime, however, the East End had become the center of a vibrant Jewish working-class community. David Feldman argues that emigration actually led to proletarianization rather than upward mobility for many Eastern European Jews who left behind self-employment in petty commerce and industry to become wage-earners in the London inner city.[5] As elsewhere, Jewish men and women were overwhelmingly engaged in tailoring. As workers in the workshop trade, the immigrants became the focus of a Royal Commission inquiry and of social scientists' speculations as to whether or not specifically Jewish characteristics were the cause of "sweating." As in Paris, the Jewish immigrants also became cap makers and cabinetmakers. But, more specific to London, Jewish men became boot and shoe makers, while many Jewish women went to work in cigar and cigarette factories.

After World War I, the Jewish concentration in these trades declined. Mechanization and de-skilling, the halt of new immigration, and the gradual movement of cabinetmaking, for example, out of the East End, all affected the definition of what had seemed to be "Jewish jobs." The Whitechapel market burgeoned as petty commerce reemerged as an important livelihood for the Jewish poor. Women moved into dressmaking as the dress trade overtook tailoring. New skills and new sectors appeared as Jewish workers became furriers, hairdressers, and barbers; women became shop assistants and typists and men became engineers. According to one estimate, 20 percent of East London Jews were owners or managers of shops, workshops, or factories.[6]

In the interwar period, post-wartime prosperity and better urban transportation led many Jews out of the inner city toward the northwest neighborhoods of Golders Green, Hendon, and Hampstead. Only 60 percent of London's Jews lived in the East End in 1929 compared to 90 percent forty years earlier.[7] As David Cesarani has shown, the changing geography, along with the anti-alien laws had an impact on culture and identity. With no new immigrants arriving to reinforce the earlier settlements and with many of the East Enders moving to the suburbs, "families became strung out along the bus routes and railway lines that stemmed eastwards and northwards from the East End. Parents and children were separated by language, education, culture, politics, and leisure-time pursuits."[8] The old Jewish working class moved into new occupations and new neighborhoods. Interwar Jewish working-class youth became socialized into English working-class institutions rather than their immigrant parents' friendly societies. They took up rambling to discover the English countryside, and they frequented dance halls, billiard rooms, and the racetrack. Young Jews flocked into sporting activities, and the Jewish boxer came of age. Generational polarization further diluted Jewish immigrant worker culture.

PARIS

Like London, Paris served as a way station for many emigrants on the trek westward. But jobs and freedom also attracted immigrants to the City of Lights. Two specific factors may have been decisive in the choice of settling in Paris: the image of Liberty, Equality, and Fraternity inherited from the Revolution, which had emancipated the Jews in 1790–91; and a liberal French immigration policy, which extended through the 1920s.

One of the paradoxes of the French case is that, in spite of the Dreyfus Affair, Eastern European Jews continued to emigrate to France. One explanation is that the critical years of the affair (1894–98) simply did not coincide with the peak years of emigration from Eastern Europe (1881–82, 1890–91, 1904–5). But it may be too that French anti-Semitism against a Jewish army officer paled in comparison with the pogroms of the Russian Empire, and that the ultimate denouement of the affair in Dreyfus's favor calmed passions and fears.

During the same period, and through the early 1930s, French immigration policy was in fact one of the most liberal in Western Europe. Seeking to "fill the void" caused by the nineteenth-century relative lag in French demographic growth as well as by the drastic losses of World War I, the French government actively recruited workers from abroad in the 1920s. While Jews were not among the mine workers and agricultural workers specifically welcomed, they nonetheless benefited from the general climate. As the United States quota laws went into effect in the early 1920s, Paris became the home for many Polish Jews who might have otherwise crossed the Atlantic. In the 1930s, however, under the double and related impact of the Depression and xenophobia, regulations began severely limiting the immigrants' right to enter and work in France.[9]

Between 1880 and 1914, some 35,000 Eastern European Jews settled in Paris. Another 150,000 came in the interwar period. They became cap makers and tailors, cabinetmakers and jewelers, peddlers, shopkeepers, and textile merchants. They organized Yiddish-language sections within the French trade unions and became Bundists and in even greater numbers Communists during the interwar period. The Yiddish union sections' umbrella organization, the Intersektsionen byuro, representing over a dozen Jewish trade-union sections in Paris before World War I, was followed by the Intersindikale komisie between the wars.

The Eastern European Jews first settled in what became known as the Pletzl (in the St. Paul neighborhood, or the Marais), alongside Alsatian Jews who had arrived there in the 1870s, after the Franco-Prussian War. As many of the Alsatians moved up the social ladder and out of the poor neighborhood, however, the quarter took on an increasingly Eastern European air. After World War I, a second Jewish working-class immigrant neighborhood developed to accommodate the Polish Jews arriving in the 1920s. Belleville, extending to the area around the place de la République, became the second major center of the Jewish working class in Paris until the wartime deportations and subsequent new immigration changed the composition and character of the quarter.

Besides the Alsatians and Eastern Europeans, two other groups of Jewish immigrants added to the heterogeneous nature of Paris Jewry: Sephardic Jews from the ex-Ottoman Empire and German Jews after 1933. Among the latter group there were few workers; the middle-class German Jews settled in a more dispersed fashion throughout Paris. The Sephardic Jews, whose own modern Diaspora merits a separate book of documents, became small shopkeepers and textile merchants around the Roquette and other quarters.[10] Our volume examines only the Eastern European Jewish workers in Paris, but the relatively more varied background of the Jewish immigrant population in Paris, compared with other cities, remains true to this day. From the onset of immigration by Russian Jews prior to World War I to the arrival of Polish Jews during the interwar period to the massive post–World War II arrival of North African Jews, the history of Jewish workers in Paris has often been that of a succession of different immigrant cohorts.

BUENOS AIRES

Until the late nineteenth century, there were few Jews in Argentina. Two factors encouraged settlement there beginning in the 1880s: a liberal immigration policy, which also brought massive numbers of Italians and Spaniards to the country until the Depression of the 1930s; and the concerted efforts of the Jewish Colonization Association. Founded by the Baron Maurice de Hirsch, the association had two major aims: relieving the population pressure and desperate material conditions of the Jews in Eastern Europe, and making the Jews more productive by training them to become farmers. The emigrants sent by the association to Argentina (as well as Brazil and elsewhere) first settled in agricultural colonies purchased for that purpose. However, many of the Jewish gauchos (cowboys) left the countryside for the city, while a parallel, spontaneous emigration headed directly to the urban areas. Buenos Aires, a city of immigrants (over 50 percent foreigners in 1914) and the center of the Italian and Spanish communities in Argentina, also became the focus of Jewish life. Approximately 50,000 Jews had settled there by World War I, and an estimated 135,000 lived there in 1936, representing by then 5.5 percent of the city's population.[11]

German Jews, French Jews, Dutch, Turkish, and North African Jews all formed part of the city's Jewish mosaic by the interwar period. But, as elsewhere, the Eastern European Jews were by far the predominant subgroup within the Jewish community. The term *Russian* became synonymous with *Jews* in Argentina, and the eleventh district, in the western part of the city's center, became known as the Russian Quarter. The descriptions of that neighborhood are not unlike those of Jewish neighborhoods in other cities: a teeming neighborhood of the modest or downright poor, colored by storefronts and posters in Yiddish and what are described as exotic costumes and customs. In the interwar period, other neighborhoods developed further to the west: Villa Crespo, Caballito, and Paternal.

While the Jewish farmers for a time made the occupational structure of Argentine Jews one of the most unique in the world outside of Palestine, the Jews in Buenos Aires worked in most of the same urban jobs as elsewhere in the modern Diaspora. Yet Jews of different origins worked in somewhat different occupational sectors. The Sephardic minority was especially present in ready-made clothing and the linen trade, while the Western European Ashkenazic "aristocracy" were active in the jewelry and export-import businesses. The poor Eastern European Jews were for the most part concentrated in the manual trades they had known in the East: in the clothing industry (garments, shoes, furs, caps, raincoats) and in furniture making. After World War I, textiles, leather, and knit goods became important, and there was a significant number of peddlers and small shopkeepers. In 1928, according to one source, one-half of the Jewish colony was engaged in some sort of (mostly petty) commerce, 27 percent were involved in manufacture, 14 percent in agriculture, and 4 percent had university degrees.[12]

At the other end of the socioeconomic spectrum, the Jews of Argentina became infamous for another "specialty": prostitution. The white slave trade, organized by Polish Jewish procurers and exploiting poor Jewish immigrant women, became the object of a vigorous campaign led by English and German Jewish women to eradicate the phenomenon. The Buenos Aires Jewish community itself became active in denouncing the problem, setting up associations for the protection of women and exiling the "impure." By then the latter had already set up their own synagogue and cemetery.

GERMANY

Even more than in Argentina, Eastern European Jews in Germany spread widely throughout the country. The key reason for this was the German structure for dealing with immigrants. Unlike laws elsewhere, immigration law in Germany was ruled by local—that is, state (*länder*)—rather than federal policy. And each state dealt with immigration through administrative rather than legislative measures. Police measures, such as expulsion, rather than laws and quotas, became the most common method of regulating immigration. One of the most important results of this system was the dispersal of Eastern European Jews throughout the German states. Thus, before World War I, although a Jewish neighborhood called the Scheunenviertel took form in Berlin, it could not compare with the major concentrations of Jews in the more centralized capitals of Europe. As Jack Wertheimer has noted, the immigrant Jews in this earlier period "failed to create a vibrant equivalent in Germany to the East European 'ghettos' that emerged in other Western lands. There were no settlements comparable to London's East End or the Parisian Pletzl, let alone New York's Lower East Side."[13] Thus, for Germany more than elsewhere, we need to look at the scattered localities where immigrant workers went to work and live.

Between 1905 and 1914, some 700,000 Eastern European Jews passed through Germany on their way westward via Hamburg, Bremen, or other ports. Of the approximately 70,000 Jewish migrants who were "settled" in Germany in 1910 (less than one-tenth of 1 percent of the country's population), many were transients: visiting intellectuals and writers, beggars, and university students who eventually moved on.[14] Since German administrative policy clearly favored the more well-to-do, there were many more merchants than manual craft workers among the immigrants. There were perhaps only 20,000 to 30,000 working-class Jews in the Reich before World War I.[15]

The Jews had a near monopoly on cigarette making in Berlin, Munich, and Offenbach until the expulsions of 1904–6. Jews from Austria-Hungary were in particular concentrated in the garment industry, although this trade did not become a "Jewish" industry to the same extent that it did in other countries. Eastern European Jewish women also became domestic servants for German Jewish women.

Perhaps the most striking departure from Jewish economic stratification worldwide occurred in 1912 with the project of importing Jewish men as seasonal mine workers in Upper Silesia.[16] It was rare for Jews to work in heavy industry in any country, but after the Silesian experiment, and as demand for workers increased under wartime conditions, tens of thousands of Eastern Jews were forcibly recruited to man heavy industry in Germany during World War I. Even after the war, some Eastern European Jewish men continued to migrate to unskilled jobs in construction, mining, and the steel and iron industries in the Ruhr. However, these experiments in employing Jewish immigrants as laborers in heavy industry were short-lived.

By and large, the Jewish immigrants in Germany were petit bourgeois and middle class. Merchants and traders dealt in everything from furs to the import-export of grains, textiles, and lumber. Small-time vendors sold eggs, used furniture, or secondhand clothes. In many ways, the occupational patterns of the Jewish immigrants resembled those of native Jews to a greater extent than elsewhere.

AMSTERDAM

The Jewish workers of Amsterdam are unique among our sample in two particular ways: they were largely Dutch rather than immigrant Jews, and they had a long tradition as workers and street peddlers. Although some diamond workers became rich, the history of the Jews in Amsterdam is more closely tied to that of Dutch workers in general.

There had always been many poor Jews in this city of burghers where Jews had been barred from all guilds and could enter only those trades that did not have guilds. The early Spanish and Portuguese Jews founded the new tobacco and diamond industries in the seventeenth century. But with Amsterdam's commercial decline in the eighteenth century, 54 percent of the Sephardim and 60 percent of all Ashkenazim—who dealt in secondhand trade and market selling—ended up living on charity.[17] At the turn of the twentieth century, poverty and unemployment were still important problems, although as Selma Leydesdorff has stressed, the Jewish poor would try anything, peddling or small jobs, before resorting to charity.[18]

From picklers to peddlers, cigar makers to clothing workers, diamond polishers by day and amateur musicians by night, Jews formed up to 13 percent of the population in Amsterdam in 1900. Several specifically Jewish organizations were set up to provide charity and perform other functions within the Jewish community. The Jewish workers in Amsterdam also believed in a wider humanity, beyond ethnic identities, and many of them turned to Social Democracy at the turn of the century.

The Jews were active in the Social Democratic Party from its founding in 1894. Amsterdam's first Jewish Social Democrat was elected to the city council in 1902, and the first Jewish Social Democratic alderman was elected in 1919. When the Social Democratic Party undertook the so-called *Gemeenteprogramma* (municipal project) in 1899, the party's emphasis on local initiative had an important impact on the Jewish working class in Amsterdam. Similarly, the Housing Act of 1901, which provided for cheap workers' lodging, benefited Jewish workers along with Dutch workers as a whole. This housing reform marked the beginning of the end of the Jewish neighborhood known as the "ghetto." An exhibit in 1916 already commemorated, in a nostalgic vein, the disappearance of this quarter. Nonetheless, in Amsterdam and elsewhere, as the Jews dispersed to outlying areas, they often moved together to certain streets or neighborhoods.

Jewish leaders played an important role in the Dutch labor movement as well, starting with the founding of the Algemene Nederlandse Diamantbewerkers Bond (ANDB—General Dutch Diamond Workers' Union) by Henri Polak and Jan van Zutphen during the strike of 1894. Indeed, the history of the Jews in Amsterdam is closely tied to that of the diamond industry, in which so many of them worked that it was simply known as "the trade." The industry's boom in the 1870s made some diamond workers very rich, but after 1880, recession and decline had a serious impact on the Jewish community.

The economic situation of the industry may also explain why more Eastern Europeans went through Holland—embarking at Rotterdam for points further west—rather than settling there. Yet the Jewish population of Amsterdam doubled between 1869 and 1920, due to natural increase and a small immigration of both Sephardic and Ashkenazic Jews. The native and immigrant Jews did not always get along, as memoirs from the period recall. Enmity if not fisticuffs divided the Dutch Jews from the Russian Jews they scorned, even if their children later grew up to be friends.

Although Jewish integration into Dutch society proceeded apace, with increasing intermarriage after World War I, this did not mean that the Jewish working class simply exchanged its old religion for a new (Socialist) one. The Jews adapted to the Dutch way of life without losing their identity, and adaptation worked both ways. Some Gentile Socialists used Yiddish words, while Dutch Jews transformed their Jewishness into a more modern, secularized version.

Harlem, Whitechapel, and the Pletzl are part of a vast modern "Jewish geography" which needs to be examined comparatively. New York garment workers, London boot makers, Paris cap makers, Buenos Aires furniture workers, German petty merchants, and Dutch diamond workers all attest to the wide range of experiences of the Jewish urban poor. There were Jewish tailors, seamstresses, peddlers and small shopkeepers everywhere, but their daily lives were not quite the same in Brooklyn, Belleville, or Golders Green.

NOTES

1. The source for the chapter epigraph is "New York City Immigrant Labor Oral History Collection," tape I-3, n.d., City College Oral History Research Project, Tamiment Library.

2. See Bibliography.

3. Karpel and Dinner for the Groupe des ouvriers juifs socialistes de Paris, *Le Prolétariat juif: Lettre des ouvriers juifs de Paris au Parti socialiste français* (Paris: Imprimerie J. Allemane, 1898), p. 8. The context for this letter was the Dreyfus Affair; see chapter 3 herein.

4. Daniel Soyer, "*Landsmanshaftn* and the Jewish Labor Movement: Cooperation, Conflict, and the Building of Community," *Journal of American Ethnic History* 7:2 (spring 1988): 22–45; idem, *Jewish Immigrant Associations and American Identity in New York, 1880–1939* (Cambridge, Mass.: Harvard University Press, 1997). See also Bibliography.

5. David Feldman, *Englishmen and Jews: Social Relations and Political Culture, 1840–1914* (New Haven: Yale University Press, 1994), pp. 155–65.

6. Nettie Adler, "Jewish Life and Labour in East London," in *New Survey of London Life and Labour*, vol. 6, ed. H. Llewellyn Smith (London: P. S. King and Son, 1934), p. 287.

7. David Cesarani, "The Remaking of the Jewish Immigrant Working Class in England," paper presented at the conference "Jewish Workers: Integration and Jewish Movements: A Comparative Approach," Amsterdam, March 27, 1992, p. 3.

8. Ibid., p. 18.

9. Vicki Caron, *Uneasy Asylum: France and the Jewish Refugee Crisis* (Stanford: Stanford University Press, forthcoming).

10. Annie Benveniste, *Le Bosphore à la Roquette: La communauté judéo-espagnole à Paris, 1914–1940* (Paris: L'Harmattan, 1989); Edgar Morin, *Vidal et les siens* (Paris: Seuil, 1989).

11. The Italians and Spanish represented 20 percent and 19 percent, respectively, of the city's population in 1914 and 12 and 13 percent, respectively, in 1936. Guy Bourdé, *Urbanisation et immigration en Amérique Latine, Buenos Aires (XIXe et XXe siècles)* (Paris: Aubier, 1974), pp. 190–91.

12. Study by Arturo Dab, cited by Edgardo Bilsky, "Ethnicité et classe ouvrière: Les travailleurs juifs à Buenos Aires (1900–1930)," *Le Mouvement social*, no. 159 (April-June 1992): 39–56.

13. Jack Wertheimer, *Unwelcome Strangers: East European Jews in Imperial Germany* (New York: Oxford University Press, 1987), p. 115.

14. Claudie Weill, *Etudiants russes en Allemagne, 1900–1914* (Paris: L'Harmattan, 1996).

15. Wertheimer, *Unwelcome Strangers*, p. 117.

16. Ludger Heid, "East European Jewish Workers in the Ruhr, 1915–1922," *Leo Baeck Institute Yearbook* 30 (1985): 141–68.

17. Philo Bregstein and Salvador Bloemgarten, eds., *Herinnering aan Joods Amsterdam* (Amsterdam: De Bezige Bij, 1978), p. 13.

18. Selma Leydesdorff, *We Lived with Dignity: The Jewish Proletariat of Amsterdam, 1900–1940* (Detroit: Wayne State University Press, 1994), p. 152.

Chapter 1 Daily Life and Work

Everywhere the Jews settled at the turn of the century, they generally settled together, whether for religious, economic, or purely social reasons. They created Jewish neighborhoods, not as the imposed ghettos of old, but rather as voluntary settlements. Synagogues, mutual-aid societies, and work opportunities drew Jews to each other, which in turn engendered more synagogues, mutual-aid societies, and work opportunities within the ethnic quarter. Cafés, saloons, and coffeehouses became the new meeting places for the secular Jews.

In this chapter, we look in on the Jews as they arrive and settle, as their neighborhoods are formed: the Lower East Side of New York, the East End of London, the Pletzl of Paris, the "Russian Quarter" of Buenos Aires, the Scheunenviertel of Berlin, and the already existing "ghetto" near the Waterlooplein in Amsterdam. Poverty within the tenements, social life on the streets, work, and leisure—all form part of the early-twentieth-century Jewish workers' communities. The neighborhoods were the locus of family life, of visiting relatives, of more long-term boarders, and even of prostitution. They could be reassuring, stimulating, or stifling.

In a daring parallel, we could suggest that the garment industry, like prostitution, was a strategy of survival as much as it was a trade. Both were in large part a result of the migration process. It was easier to migrate with a trade in hand than with capital and a clientele. Contracting, home work, and sweating became identified with Jews from London to New York to Paris to Buenos Aires. Yet in addition to small-scale manufacturing, petty commerce was the other identifying characteristic of the Jewish communities. As peddlers, street merchants, and small shopkeepers, Jews were visible in the poor neighborhoods of the early-twentieth-century cities. Even in Germany, where they were more spread out, Jews were also prominent in certain petty trades, and they became grain and cattle dealers.

By the 1930s, the Jewish neighborhoods had changed considerably, however, in all of our cities. Congestion had led to further dispersion, as many immigrants sought better housing. In New York, London, Paris, Buenos Aires, and

Amsterdam, this movement spawned areas of secondary settlement in more outlying neighborhoods. The Bronx, Hampstead, Belleville, Villa Crespo, and Transvaalbuurt were among the expanding Jewish neighborhoods of the interwar years.

NEW YORK

First Impressions

Bernard Weinstein came to New York in 1882. In his memoirs, the future secretary of the United Hebrew Trades describes the first time he ventured beyond the immigrant reception center at Castle Garden into the city itself. To get to the immigrant Jewish quarter on the Lower East Side, he and his companion first passed through the Wall Street financial district, where they were impressed by the crowds of well-dressed Americans. But the teeming "ghetto" was not far away.

We two greenhorns go for a walk in the Golden Land, where, they told us at home, people make heaps of money. We walk along, but do not see a single penny.

We are led to Pike Street, and shown the way to Orchard. We enter from Division and see before us a narrow street. We approach Hester, with its tall red buildings. The street is terribly dirty. There are barefoot children and masses of pushcarts, with fruit, fish, and what-have-you. The peddlers call out their wares loudly in English. Because of the narrowness of the street, it seems to us that the tenement houses are very tall. You have to crane your neck to see the roof of each tenement. . . .

Bernard Weinstein, *Fertsig yohr in der idisher arbayter bavegung: bletlekh erinerungen* (New York: Verlag Veker, 1924), p. 23.

Tenement Life

Bessie Mischaloff arrived in New York in 1914, joining her parents and other relatives already living on the Lower East Side. In her autobiography, Mischaloff describes the family's initial difficult efforts to set up house in the New World. As her husband began to earn more money as a garment worker, the family's standard of living rose and eventually the Mischaloffs went into business for themselves.

My parents lived here in three rooms on Rutgers Place. We arrived in New York three days before Rosh Hashanah. The heat was terrible. The rooms were small, and there were ten of us altogether. So people slept on the floor and on the fire escape. The next day we went to look for some rooms. We took two rooms on Madison Street, for which we had to make an immediate deposit of ten dollars. My husband had six dollars and fifty cents in cash. But my brother-in-law had twenty-five rubles. So my husband borrowed twelve rubles from him, and we paid the rent. We hired a pushcart and took all of our packages and the big trunk full of things and set out. When we moved in we immediately asked the janitor if she knew where we could get some old beds and a carriage for the child. She brought us right down to the cellar and sold us two old iron beds and an old carriage that had been left by previous tenants. We moved, with fortune, into the rooms. When I sat down on our big trunk (we didn't have any chairs yet) and contemplated the rooms a bit, my heart sank. The walls were painted dark green and spread gloom. But I did not have much time to think. I immediately went to work on the children. There was no bath, of course, so I immediately heated some water on the old gas burner which we had bought from the janitress for small change. I washed the children and put them to bed. My husband attended to the packages and bags. And that is how the day passed. [. . .]

When my husband brought home his first six dollars in pay, we decided that we had to buy a table and a few chairs. Peddlers were very much in style then, so we bought a table and several chairs from such a peddler. We bought a table and four chairs on installments. So from each pay envelope, we paid fifty cents a week for the furniture. Altogether it came to ten dollars, and since we paid very promptly, we were all paid up in twenty weeks. But the peddler pretended not to notice and came as usual for his fifty cents, because, as they say, "habit becomes nature." He had gotten into the habit. But when we showed him that we were fully paid up, he had to stop coming whether he liked it or not.

YIVO Institute for Jewish Research, Collection of American-
Jewish Autobiographies (1942), RG 102, #11, Bessie Mischaloff,
pp. 21–23, 25–26.

In the Sweatshop

New York was already the major center of a booming ready-made cloth-ing industry when the masses of Eastern European Jews started arriving. The immigrant contractor, often recently a shop worker himself, would rent a loft or tenement apartment, acquire a couple of sewing machines (or make the workers supply their own) and hire teams of workers to assem-ble precut material into a given number of garments per week, for a fixed

*price. Labor leader Bernard Weinstein describes how this "task system" led
to endless hours of work at the shop or at home.*

The wave of immigration in 1882 brought with it a large number of tailors
from Russia. In addition, many of the newly arrived immigrants learned to
operate sewing machines on men's cloaks. These workers worked at the
cheapest sort of tailoring. The Hungarian and Galician workers, who had
already been good tailors in the old country, did not want to have anything
to do with the "Columbus tailors," as they called the semiskilled artisans.
As a result, the cheapest sort of tailor was exploited in the worst way. They
worked only in the sweatshops run by small contractors who received work
from the big warehouses.

These "sweaters" then introduced the accursed "task system." The basis
of this system consisted of the week's work of a "set" or "team," which consisted of a baster, a half-baster, an operator, a helper, a finisher, a half-
finisher, and a trimmer, as well as bushelers and pressers. They were all paid
weekly, unless the contractor ran off with the payroll. In return, the set had
to produce a predetermined number of cloaks each day. The boss normally
provided a large portion of cloaks. The limit on the better lines was fourteen cloaks a day, but it went as high as eighteen or more. If the set was not
finished with the day's work by ten in the evening, the workers slaved away
until midnight—or for as long as their strength held up. When they arrived
in the shop at four the next morning, the set had to finish the previous
day's work. This often took until noon. During the busy season, the tailors
thus labored six days and six nights a week, but only completed three and
a half days' worth of work. Since the best operator's wages then amounted
to eighteen dollars a week, he received only twelve dollars for four "task
days" (in reality six full days of hard labor). Those workers who were supposed to earn eight or ten dollars a week used to take home five dollars. The
tailor bosses took advantage of the fact that there was no union, and continually added more cloaks to the daily quota.

> Bernard Weinstein, *Fertsig yohr in der idisher arbayter bavegung:
> bletlekh erinerungen* (New York: Verlag Veker, 1924), pp. 98–100.

Many workers were brought into shops by relatives or landslayt *(compatriots from the home country), while others resorted to the infamous "pig
market" in Seward Park at the corner of Hester and Essex Streets.*

The "Pig Market" in Hester Park

Along with all the peanuts, home remedies, and the other sweet treats that are sold for nearly nothing on Hester Street, you will find one sort of merchandise that can stand a whole day without going sour. It is not sold by the pound, the gallon, or the yard, but by the piece. Besides, this particular merchandise is sold very cheaply—more cheaply than the poorest sort of merchandise in the "pig market." [. . .]

This merchandise appears to consist of a tremendous mass of two-legged creatures with mournful faces, emaciated bodies, and long, bony legs. In reality, however, these are operators, pressers, finishers, and all kinds of helpers in the men's clothing trade. [. . .]

The park is especially crowded with tailors at [word illegible] o'clock in the morning. Then everyone expects to find a job. The whole world is there in the morning. It is as tumultuous as a fair. A dozen little bosses stand among the many tailors, and the workers make "contracts" with them. One worker names a price. The little bosses laugh at him, and a second worker gives a cheaper price right away. The bosses will not hear of this cheaper price either, and they try to clear a path through the throng. They already know which of the unfortunate "exchange tailors" to approach. You can depend on them. They will certainly find proper goods at bargain prices. But God in Heaven forfend that the little bosses leave without their "tradesmen!"

"Der khazer mark in 'Hester' park," *Forverts* (Jewish Daily Forward), September 29, 1907.

Sweatshop Poets

The so-called sweatshop poets decried the misery of the shop and expressed the bewilderment of immigrants unaccustomed to the industrial system of production. One of the most famous of these is Morris Rosenfeld (the only one who actually worked in a shop), who, after leaving his hometown near Suwalki, Russian Poland, first for London, and then for New York in 1886, worked for many years as a presser in the men's garment industry.

The Sweatshop

So wild is the roar of machines in the sweatshop,
I often forget I'm alive—in that din!
I'm drowned in the tide of the terrible tumult—
my ego is slain; I become a machine.
I work, and I work, without rhyme, without reason—

produce, and produce, and produce without end.
For what? and for whom? I don't know, I don't wonder—
since when can a whirling machine comprehend?

No feelings, no thoughts, not the least understanding;
this bitter, this murderous drudgery drains
the noblest, the finest, the best and the richest,
the deepest, the highest that living contains.
Away rush the seconds, the minutes and hours;
each day and each night like a wind-driven sail;
I drive the machine, as though eager to catch them,
I drive without reason—no hope, no avail.

The clock in the shop, even he toils forever:
he points, and he ticks, and he wakes us from dreams—
a long time ago someone taught me the meaning:
his pointing, his waking, are more than they seem.
I only remember a few things about it:
the clock wakes our senses, and sets us aglow,
and wakes something else—I've forgotten—don't ask me!
I'm just a machine, I don't know, I don't know!...

But once in a while, when I hear the clock ticking,
his pointing, his language, are not as before:
I feel that his pendulum lashes me, prods me
to work ever faster, to do more and more!
I hear the wild yell of the boss in his ticking,
I see a dark frown in the two pointing hands;
I shudder to think it: the clock is my master!
He calls me "Machine!" "Hurry up!" he commands.

But when there's a half-hour lull in the uproar,
at noon, when the boss turns his back on us, then—
oh, then the sun slowly arises within me;
my heart reaches out—and my wound burns again;
and tears that are bitter, and tears that are seething,
soak into my thin little banquet of bread—
I choke on the food—I can't swallow a morsel!
Oh bitter to be neither living nor dead!

At lunchtime the shop's like a grim field of battle:
the cannon are resting. I look all around—
wherever I turn I see nothing but corpses;
the blood of the innocent shrieks from the ground!
One moment, and soon an alarm will be sounded:
the corpses awake, they return to the fight;
the dead rise to battle for strangers, for strangers;
they strive, and are stricken, and sink into night.

I look at the bloodbath with rage and with horror,
with grief, with a vow to avenge what I see;—
at last I can hear the clock rightly—he wakes us:
"An end to enslavement; an end let there be!"
He ticks back to life my emotions, my senses,
and points to the hours that are hurrying past:
as long as my lips are sealed up, I'll be wretched;
as long as I am what I am, I'll be lost.

The man who had slept in me slowly awakens;
the slave seems asleep, that was wakeful in me;
the hour, at last the right hour is striking!
an end to misfortune, an end let there be!
But in comes the boss with his whistle: his bugle;
I'm lost—I forget what I am, what I mean—
such tumult! such battling! my ego goes under;
I know not, I care not—I'm just a machine . . .

> English translation by Aaron Kramer, in
> Itche Goldberg and Max Rosenfeld, eds.,
> *Morris Rosenfeld: Selections from His
> Poetry and Prose* (New York: YKUF
> [Yidisher Kultur Farband], 1964),
> pp. 26–28.

Upward Mobility

Jews experienced a relatively high rate of social mobility compared to other immigrant groups. For the immigrant generation, the most common avenues of advancement included becoming a boss in the garment industry or the proprietor of a small business. After working as a hatmaker, M. Havelin opened his own manufacturing concern.

In 1909 my wife had another daughter. Then I decided that working for someone else would not do. So I left with two other men from the shop, and we took a place on Bond Street for twenty-five dollars a month. We had three hundred dollars. Each of us invested one hundred dollars. [. . .] We divided up the work: one was a cutter, the other an operator. I was given the honor of being the businessman—the buyer, the salesman, and the bookkeeper. To make a long story short, by the beginning of 1910 we had quite a large shop on Cooper Square with ten machines.

> YIVO Institute for Jewish Research, Collection of American-
> Jewish Autobiographies (1942), RG 102, #21, M. Havelin,
> pp. 25–26.

Even the Socialist Forverts's *popular advice column, the "Bintl brief" (bundle of letters), debated the propriety of a union giving its former delegate a gift to help him become a manufacturer.*

Worthy editor of the *Forward!*

Please print the following letter in your "bundle" and give your opinion.

I have been a member of the Children's Jacket Makers' Union of Brooklyn for the last 28 years, and never before has such a mistake been committed as now. I have really been very demoralized by the union's recent actions.

For the last 19 months we have had a certain walking delegate. Several weeks ago, while a delegate for our union, he bought a shop. Now he had one foot in business and the other in the union. This made me and several other active members very angry, and we protested at a well-attended meeting. A debate arose, and one member stood up and made a motion to support him with fifty dollars. I tried to convince them that it did not make sense to use union funds to support a person who was in the process of becoming a boss. Our funds are only for strikes and aid to the unfortunate and the needy. I demonstrated that many former active members, even secretaries, of the union are today the worst tyrants as bosses. They try to break the union at every opportunity. Seeing Comrade Weinstein of the United Hebrew Trades at the meeting, I asked him through the chairman to give his opinion. Comrade Weinstein said that it would make very little sense for the walking delegate to ask the union for money. Since there were only fifty members left at the meeting when the resolution to give him fifty dollars was voted on, it passed.

Now, Mr. Editor, please give your opinion on this question.

In Solidarity,
A member of the Children's Jacket Makers' Union

[Answer:]

It is not worth stirring up discord in the union over this. Those who voted to give the fifty dollars have their own honest reasons for doing so. They are convinced that the walking delegate was very loyal and devoted to the union, and provided it with much worthy service. They think that if he had gone into another business—a store, for example—no one would have objected to the union helping him out of fraternal recognition. The question only arises because he is becoming a boss in the same trade. [. . .]

We don't think that a union should use its own money in
unusual cases like this to help someone become a boss. But it is not
necessary to introduce dissension in the union over it.

"A bintl brief," *Forverts* (Jewish Daily Forward),
November 24, 1909.

Despair

*Isidore Wisotsky was fourteen years old when he arrived in New York
around 1910. He later became a member of the editorial board of the Yiddish anarchist publication, the* Fraye arbeter shtime. *In his memoirs he
evokes the informal nature of neighborhood networks. He also describes
one method of coping with adversity that is little acknowledged in most of
the immigrant literature: suicide.*

In those days, if anyone had trouble, the most common expression was:
"Take the gas pipe." And many did. During the middle of a summer night,
when quiet and calm reigned over Suffolk Street, the peace was disrupted
by many voices calling: "Gas, gas, gas smells!" We'd jump out of bed and
half-dressed run into the hallway from where the noise came. There we
found many other tenants with sleepy eyes, bewildered, some in night-
gowns, some in bathrobes, some shabbily dressed. All were looking for the
apartment from which the poisonous gas was leaking.

The awful smell led to the fourth floor, the apartment in which the Gdaley family lived. The door was locked. Knocking on the door did not help.
Finally a policeman came and with the help of several others, broke in the
door. Nearly all of us fainted from the wave of the poisonous gas that hit
us. We were gasping for air. The windows, shut tight, were broken. Some
fresh air came in. We were shocked by what we saw in the kitchen. Gdaley,
a middle-aged man, dressed but unshaven, was lying on a folding bed near
the gas stove, with the gas pipe tied with a handkerchief to his mouth. He
was dead. No one else was in the apartment. Women started to cry, and
clasping their hands, were chanting: "Oh, a broch, Oh, a broch" [a tragedy].
An ambulance came and took him away. No one went back to sleep that
night. "What happened? What happened? It shouldn't happen to a dog,"
said Mrs. Rosenberg, his next door neighbor. He did not work for five
months. He couldn't get a job in his trade. He was a pocketbook maker. He
tried some other work, but it didn't last. He even tried to peddle with fruit
on a pushcart but he couldn't make a living. He had a wife and two small

children, one three years old and one a year old. He owed the landlord for three months' rent. He paid only ten dollars a month, but he didn't have that much money. Yesterday he got a notice from the landlord that if he didn't pay his rent, he will be dispossessed. So he sent his wife and children to her sister and for himself he took the gas pipe.

YIVO Institute for Jewish Research, Collection of American-Jewish Autobiographies (1942), RG 102, #288, Isidore Wisotsky, pp. 27–28.

Escaping Summer Heat

But all was not only hard work and hard times on the Lower East Side. On hot summer days, residents of the sweltering tenement district sought out cooler spots: rooftops, small local parks, bridges, Central Park, or Coney Island.

The hot, stuffy, breathless summer evenings were spent on the Williamsburg Bridge, better known on the East Side as the Delancey Street Bridge. It spanned the East River and was only blocks away from our house. The people came there to cool off in the breeze from the East River. They played games, sang songs of their native lands. Some came with balalaikas or guitars. The elders discussed world affairs.

On hot scorching summer weekends, the East Side made an exodus to Coney Island for a breath of cool fresh air, a swim in the ocean, or a rest on the beach. Some started their two-hour journey by streetcar Saturday night and slept on the beach to be the first on line at the City Baths, where, for ten cents, they got a locker for their clothes and a free shower after bathing. Most, however, came at dawn to Delancey Street to catch a seat on one of the streetcars. Those cars were so jammed that some even rode on the roof.

But it was all worth it, after taking a dip in the ocean. I went together with our four boarders and Mother. Dad did not care for Coney Island. "It's a crazy house," he used to say. "Too many people. I got to look for my own hands," and stayed home. He bought all the Jewish newspapers and a cold, sliced, sour watermelon, one of his delicacies. That's the way he spent his Sunday summers. "Nothing better than home," he exclaimed in a loud triumphant voice. Mother, too, did not care for the congestion, but she loved the water and was a good swimmer as she had lived during her youth near a large river in the Ukraine. For the trip she used to provide us with pumpernickel, two herrings, a dozen hard-boiled eggs, sour pickles, onions, and some fresh fruit. We all carried something . . . wrapped in our bathing suits and paper. [. . .]

[. . .] On our homeward trek, we traveled with many other people from the East Side . . . jolly, refreshed, tired.

YIVO Institute for Jewish Research, Collection of American-
Jewish Autobiographies (1942), RG 102, #288, Isidore Wisotsky,
pp. 22–23.

LONDON

A Boot Maker's Reflections on Immigration

Earlier than anywhere else, England sought to put a stop to foreign immigration. As in the United States, the first step was the creation of an investigating commission. The Royal Commission on Alien Immigration, appointed in 1902, focused almost entirely on Russian-Polish Jews, who were the primary target of the subsequent Aliens Act of 1905. In the following excerpt, Mr. A. tells of his first coming to London and of his work in the shoe and boot trade, and now, thirteen years after his arrival, he takes an anti-immigration stance himself.

3416. What happened to you then?—When the foreigners came round to me they saw I was a greener because I had my parcel under my arm, and they began to ask questions as to where I had come from and what I was. I told them where I had come from, and I told them I was a bootmaker by trade. They took me round to a finisher in the same street. When I came to the finisher's place there were about four or five people working in the place, so the finisher asked me what tradesman I was. I told him I was a bootmaker by trade, so he turned round to me and said, "Have you got any money?" So I put my hand in my pocket and I showed him the money which I had, which, as I stated before, was 38 pfennigs. The finish of it was he gave me no answer when I showed him my money, and some men took me round to Leman Street—I recollect it very well—No. 84, Leman Street, where I had lodging and grub free.

3417. At the Jewish Shelter? [Poor Jews' Temporary Shelter]—Yes. [. . .]

3458. Had you got relations of yours here asking you to come over?—No, I have not got any relations of mine here. I have got relations at home. I have got a little letter here which I hold in my hand. I found it in an old pocket. It is a letter in which my brother is absolutely begging for me to send for him to come over here. He is hard up. The letter is dated 1899. My answer was only one answer. I said: "If you have got a potato and a cup of tea to it, stop where you are, because people coming over here, if they are foreigners" (I am a foreigner myself, but I am going to speak the truth) "cannot make no fortune." It is absolutely a hard job to make a living. I know people what I call foreigners in the East End of London who sent for their own relations, their own landsmanns [sic, fellow countrymen], who had bad reputations in their own country, and they were sent for by big manufacturers here to work for them.

3459. You told your own brothers not to come?—Certainly.

3460. You said they had better stay where they were?—They had better stay there than come over here, because I was working 12 years among foreigners, and I told them how many hours I worked and how I was paid. I am working now for an Englishman, and now I begin to see that I was absolutely 12 years in Siberia during all those 12 years I worked amongst foreigners. I am working now for an Englishman, and have been for 12 months, and I begin to see there is a difference. I begin to see what a cruel life I had when I was working amongst the foreigners. [. . .]

3499. Have you noticed any change in your trade in the 13 years you have been here?—The first change is this: from the first beginning when I came over here I remember from eight to nine months during the year it was busy, and between three and four months in the year it was slack, as I stated before, only in the slack time there was always a chance to get a bit.

3500. Something or other?—Yes; and the prices were fair. Now I can say there are only four months in the year busy, and eight months in the year slack, in my trade.

3501. Your special trade is the lady's dancing shoe making?—Yes.

3502. What do you attribute that change to? What is the reason of that in your opinion?—In my opinion the reason is that there are too many people in the trade. The trade mostly lies in foreigners' hands, and there are too many hands in it, and they are coming over every day, and when the busy time commences they are absolutely working day and night, and, of course, the work cannot last very long. [. . .]

3512. What do you say is your remedy for this?—My remedy is, we should not allow them to come over.

3513. Not in such numbers?—No. [. . .]

3545. If that had been done 13 years ago, that have stopped you?—I would not be sorry.

Royal Commission on Alien Immigration, 1903, pp. 119–25.

Rothschild Buildings

The Rothschild Buildings, opened in 1887, were designed as a model tene-ment block. They were constructed on capital raised by Jewish philan-thropists and businessmen led by Nathan Rothschild. The investors were promised a return of 4 percent on their investment, lower than was customary among companies providing model dwellings. The units could thus be rented at a low rate of five shillings per week. The following account, from an interview conducted by Jerry White, is by Mrs. J., who moved into the Rothschild Buildings with her family when she was eleven years old.

When I was a child my 2 brothers slept in the bedroom and I slept with my mother on a couch. For years we didn't even have a sideboard; we had a wardrobe, a drawer, table, chairs and utensils to eat with, I suppose. Oh no, we didn't have armchairs; what would we do with armchairs? My mother worked; I was always in trouble doing the wrong things looking after the boys, so what would armchairs be any use to us? On the walls we had enlargements of my family; my father, my mother. They were photographs taken in Russia, but they were enlarged because we had somebody in the family that was a—used to go round the houses, take photographs and enlarge them—and he enlarged them for us. (What did you have on the floor?) Floor. Nothing, till we started work, till my brother and I started, and then I remember we bought red lino. We had the big sideboard—that's when we grew up and everybody had sideboards, so we managed to get one after I went to work, my brother went to work. [. . .]

Well, my mother was a very very ambitious woman, although there was nobody to help her ambition. So she worked. My mother was more or less, when my father died, what you'd call now a home help. Then she went into tailoring. But after a couple of years she borrowed a few pounds and became a tally* —(Where was she a home help?) For a maternity hospital, but it was in the East End of London, Underwood St. And when a woman had a baby and she had to have somebody to come to house to see to the woman, the baby, and do all the other work that the woman managed to leave behind till the baby was born, so that the so-called home help would do. And that was like the big sum of a pound a week.

Jerry White Transcripts, Tower Hamlets Local History Library,
Mrs. J.

Our Street

Willy Goldman, born in the East End before World War I, was one of the first writers to depict the sweatshop environment realistically. His unsparing portrait of Jewish life in Stepney and Whitechapel was first published in 1940.

---

*A tally is a door-to-door salesman (often a woman) selling items on credit.

Our street, like the larger world, was a "divided" community. The divisions were merely not so fundamental: which means, in plainer words, that somebody as respectably well placed as a bank-clerk would have turned up his nose at us all. In their innocence, however, this didn't prevent various inhabitants turning up their noses at each other. Class identity is something people only recognise when it is forced on them by a class catastrophe. Ordinarily each man likes to think there is some one on a lower step in the social ladder he can look down upon. [. . .]

My father was really not very differently placed from the ordinary sweat-shop worker: it is a commonplace that the market and sweat-shop worker mutually envy each other largely through ignorance of each other's trades. My father was always harping on the stability of people with a "real trade in their hands"—irrespective of the fact that at the time there were close on two million of these people with "a real trade in their hands" signing on at the Exchange. The sweat-shop worker talked perpetually of "the adventure of trading." Yet before him too was the spectacle of "adventurers" who hadn't moved an inch in a dozen years from their pitch in the gutter.

There was a stigma attached to the poorly flourishing market worker that the equally poor sweat-shop worker somehow escaped. It can only be explained by the brutishness of the market worker's job: the kind of habits he indulged in followed as a consequence. He was irreligious and undomesticated. His own family bored him. He preferred the rough talk and manners of his friends in the Yiddish restaurants. These places took up the market worker's leisure; and because of the irregularity of their hours and work market workers had quite a lot of leisure. [. . .] During the War we were prepared to believe he was there discussing "business"; but in the absence of any real business since, we could only regard it as blatant loafing.

Willy Goldman, East End My Cradle (1940; London: Robson
Books, 1988), pp. 147–50.

Gender and Conflicts in the Sweatshop

Like Willy Goldman, Simon Blumenfeld's work represents the "proletarian novel" of the 1930s, which sought to show another side to the usually embellished folk memory of immigrant beginnings. In Blumenfeld's first novel, Jew Boy, *first published in 1935, he described divisions within the workplace between worker and boss but also among workers themselves.*

A dozen automata bent over the garments, sewing, machining, pressing, at top speed. Speed! Speed! That was the keynote. No time even to wipe your nose, the coats must be kept flying about the workshop, on the move all the while. Speed! Speed! The quickest worker set the pace.

The machinist ran down a couple of seams and threw them to the presser to be pressed open. The presser soaped the seams, clumped the hot iron over them till they were glued down flat, then threw them at the machinist's feet. Without taking his eyes off the work before him, the machinist leaned sideways, scooped up the garments with his free hand, and put them on the table. Snip, snip. A piece of silesia barbered into shape became a breast pocket. Over to the presser. Over to the tailor to baist in canvas stiffening. Back to the machinist, the presser, the girls, the boss. Round and round, and round again, till Harry, the apprentice, got busy with his bodkin, and pulled out the baistings for the last time.

Then the garments said good-bye to the dusty floor, where they'd been knocked about for days, where they'd been trodden on, spat on, thrown about like rags, and graduated to wooden hangers, from which they were suspended on a shiny rail, high up. High up in a place of honour. [. . .]

The presser struggled with a coat, cursing silently. At last, unable to make it set right, he tore it from the sleeve board and threw it angrily at Janey's feet.

"I'm a presser," he growled, "not a magician. Look at the way you've baisted those armholes!"

Janey [the chief tailoress] picked up the coat and examined it. Disdainfully, she threw it back to the presser.

"It's not my fault," she said tartly. "It's the machinist. Notice how the sleeves are sewn in."

The machine stopped suddenly. Max jumped up, excited from his stool . . . "What! . . . What!" He pounced on the coat, peering closely at the sleeves, stretching the seam with his long, bony fingers. Then he held the garment at arm's length in front of him.

"These sleeves bad?" he shouted towards the boss. "What! These sleeves are badly sewn in? Look at the way they hang. I ask you, guv'nor, look at them. Perfect! Perfect!"

The boss was silent. He didn't want to interfere, not if he could help it. He hated rowing between workers, it clogged the run of the work, it was a free entertainment, made the girls drop their jobs and look up to see what was happening; besides, he was the only one he liked to hear shout in the workshop. Max took it that the boss agreed with him. He turned to Janey and flung the coat under her stool.

"There!" he said, "Don't blame me for your rotten work, you dried up old nanny goat!" [. . .]

"I may be a nanny goat," she snapped, "but I do know my work. You should ask the apprentice to sew the sleeves in for you, if you can't do them yourself. Four-eyes! Get another pair of glasses!" [. . .]

The boss went over to Janey and looked closely at the coat. He put it in her lap, and showed her what to alter. It was the machinist's fault after all, but Janey could put it right with a couple of stitches. Janey. It was always Janey. She was the only reliable one. Max took offence so quickly. He might put on his hat and coat and run off in the middle of the whole damn' rush, and good machinists were hard to find. He whispered soothingly in her ear, and squeezed her arm gently.

Janey looked up at the boss, then shrugged her shoulders grudgingly. Oh, all right! There was still a whole lot she owed Max, but she'd be a lady, she wouldn't say anything. Let him choke, the long skinny bastard!

> Simon Blumenfeld, *Jew Boy*, 2nd ed. (London: Lawrence and Wishart, 1986), pp. 12–13, 16–19.

The Unemployed Protest at the Synagogue

Unemployment was a particular hazard due to the seasonal nature of so many immigrant occupations. On March 16, 1889, a Jewish Unemployed Committee organized a march to the Great Synagogue to protest Chief Rabbi Hermann Adler's tepid attitude toward the sweating system (see chapter 3). In February 1894, another march was held protesting the principles of poor relief administered by the Jewish Board of Guardians.

The Unemployed Agitation

DISORDERLY BEHAVIOUR IN THE GREAT SYNAGOGUE.

In response to a "manifesto" issued on Thursday week by the Jewish Unemployed Committee, calling on the unemployed Jews in the East End to take possession of the Great Synagogue in Duke Street, Aldgate and remain there as a protest against their starving condition, a crowd of between 200 or 300 persons assembled on Friday evening outside the synagogue. The Sabbath eve service commenced at the usual hour, the Rev. Hast and the Rev. Gordon officiating. The congregation was not large, but nearly 100 constables of the City police were stationed in a building attached to the synagogue. [. . .] At the conclusion of the service the great majority of the congregation left the building, but about 300 remained in their seats. The clergy retired, but Mr. A. Rosenfeld, the warden, and some members of the Board of Management and the officials remained. The men were frequently requested by the warden to leave, but refused to do so. Mr.

Rosenfeld addressing a group of persons, said, "Now, I ask you to leave. We cannot assist you here, but the Jewish Board of Guardians will meet on Monday next, and will do all they can for you." A Voice: But that will not find me a lodging for to-night. I have walked the streets for three nights. Another Voice: My wife and family are starving. Mr. Rosenfeld: I cannot discuss matters here. After some persuasion, a number of the men were prevailed on to leave the building but about 100 still refused to stir, and commenced a violent discussion. Meanwhile a body of constables had closed round the malcontents, and after every other means of removing them had been tried an order was given to clear the building, and those still remaining were bundled out without much difficulty. No resistance worth mentioning was offered, and no arrests took place. Outside the crowd was kept on the move, and prevented from assembling in the vicinity of the synagogue. [. . .]

THE CHIEF RABBI ON THE QUESTION

At the New West End Synagogue on Saturday the Chief Rabbi devoted his sermon to the question of the distress existing in London through want of employment. Taking his text from Prov. xxix., 7, "The righteous considereth the cause of the poor, but the wicked regardeth not to know it." Dr. Adler traced the causes of the present distress to the general depression of trade [. . .] Dealing with the present distress the Chief Rabbi advocated carrying into effect the conclusions of the Mansion House Committee which recommended the strengthening of the existing other charitable organizations, and while leaving the idle and loafing to be dealt with by the Poor Law, to treat all others in distress, from no fault of their own, with every degree of gentleness and sympathy. [. . .]

The following constituting

SUGGESTIONS OF "JEWISH UNEMPLOYED"

to the Executive Committee of the Board [of Guardians] on Jan. 22nd, 1894, was laid upon the table:—

(1) That the Jewish Board of Guardians should immediately relieve those cases of the Jewish Unemployed which are now in distress.

(2) That a Bureau should be established for the registration of the Unemployed.

(3) That the Jewish Board of Guardians should supply work in lieu of charity.

(4) That a Conference be called together of employers of Jewish labor, with a view to take some action to reduce the hours of labor, and by that means to reduce the number of Unemployed.

(5)   That the Jewish Board of Guardians should approach Jewish members of Parliament, with the view of urging the matter of the restriction of shorter hours of work, upon the House of Commons.

(6)   That an Inspector of Factories and Workshops, who is able to speak "Yiddish," should be appointed by the Government.

(7)   That a member of the Committee of the Unemployed should accompany the Investigating Officer of the Board, in the investigation of cases of the Unemployed in need of relief. [. . .]

FULL TEXT OF THE REPLY

Resolved that the delegates be informed:—

(1)   That the first function of this Board is to relieve after investigation persons who are in distress through no fault of their own, especially those *bona fide* workers who are out of employment through no fault of their own, which function they have always discharged to the best of their ability; and having regard to the distress now existing they are applying the funds at their disposal with as much liberality as the extent of their funds will permit.

(2)   That the Board is unable to concern itself with the establishment of labor registers, which appear to the Board to come rather within the province of the workers themselves.

(3)   That the Board adheres to its resolution frequently arrived at that it is undesirable if not impossible, to establish a labor yard or other means of supplying work in lieu of charity.

(4 and 5)   That the Board is unable to concern itself with general economic labor questions that are absolutely outside its scope.

(6)   That it is inexpedient to ask the Government to reconsider its decision not to appoint a Yiddish speaking Inspector of Factories and Workshops.

(7)   That the Board while always prepared to receive any information from all reliable sources considers that it has in its own officers, and a large band of visitors, a sufficient means of investigation.

The Jewish World, February 2, 1894.

Prostitution

Prostitution occurred in almost every center of Jewish immigrant settlement, a function of the disruptive process of migration and the marginality of the Jewish immigrant trades. The Anglo-Jewish figures, such as Claude Montefiore, who played a leading part, along with German Jews, in the international Jewish struggle against prostitution, depicted Jewish women as the victims of "white slavers." But a certain number of women took up prostitution as a survival strategy, a point made by Morris Winchevsky in the following poem.

Three Sisters

In England there's Leicester—the city;
in London there's Leicester—the square;
and daily three sisters, three pretty
young sisters, are known to be there.

The youngest is out selling flowers;
the second cries "Laces!" all day;
the oldest comes by in dark hours
and bargains her body away.

The younger ones look at their sister
not hatefully, not with a frown;
all three curse a world that is twisted;
all three curse the street and the town.

And yet, when those two—after hours—
return to the hole that is "home,"
they moisten the laces and flowers
with tears that will never be known.

Aaron Kramer, trans. and ed., A Century of Yiddish Poetry
(Cranbury, N.J.: Cornwall Books, 1989), p. 43.

The Depression

When unemployment became particularly severe during the Depression, young Jewish men tried to "kill time" as best they could. Some tried to get work at the docks, although few Jews were hired there. Others went to the movies or the public baths to while away the hours.

You don't feel unemployment so badly in the first days. A late and leisurely breakfast helps you to see things in a philosophical light and the sight of other lads "in the same boat" when you step into the street tends to strengthen that view. [. . .]

That was how things were the first days. Saturday gave you a jolt. You realised you were stale and restive. You recalled the old feeling of exhilaration at the end of a week in the workshop. There was nothing now to make you feel it was the week-end. You couldn't even change into another suit of clothes. If you were so lucky as to possess a "new" suit you would have been wearing it during the week and it didn't make a change putting it on on Saturday. [. . .]

Your "freshness" is a mere memory with the opening of the second week. You begin to hate the sight of the streets. You know the programme before you start. You get up later in the mornings if you can. You are now desperately out to kill time.

I think it was worse for us under-sixteens. It was not only the money we missed. We were afraid we might be long enough out of work to forget the little we had learned. [. . .]

When you get resigned to unemployment as a chronic fact you try and take the edge off the week by going to a film matinée on Monday. [. . .]

There are also the "commentators" everywhere. These are usually housewives, for Monday is "forgetfulness day" for them as well as for the unemployed. They love discussing the film during its progress. Mostly it is a drama that sets them off—they try predicting the various situations before they arrive. They do it with a great sense of triumph. They consider themselves very clever, like people who work out a crossword puzzle.

They were unbearable during an interesting film. Yet shifting from them might only be an exchange for a seat adjoining a peanut crackler or orange squelcher. [. . .]

Later we learned the trick of whiling away an afternoon at the Public Baths. [. . .]

[. . .] Week-day custom was sporadic and confined mainly to three types of patron: unemployed youngsters, old Jews and turbaned Indian pedlars. The youngsters were least businesslike in intention. Washing was a consideration secondary to that of "having a good time": this comprised unsolicited solos from various unmusical people and sporadic outbreaks of community singing. [. . .]

You got into a kind of unemployed rut—equivalent, but without the advantages, to the rut you had previously got into as a worker: you were always doing the same things.

Willy Goldman, *East End My Cradle* (1940; London: Robson Books, 1988), pp. 104–10.

PARIS

Arrival: Advice to Griner *(Greenhorns)*

Beware of charlatans! Getting started in a new town is always hard, but informal immigrant networks have always helped newcomers get settled.

In 1910, Wolf Speiser published a Kalendar *in Paris with information, instructions, and warnings to the newly arrived.*

Warning to Those Who Have Lived Only a Short Time in Paris

A certain gang who call themselves lawyers have recently settled in the Jewish quarter. In reality they know absolutely nothing of this profession, but only how to take money. People run to ask advice only once they have already fallen into their clutches. It would make more sense if they asked for advice first instead of afterward. They would avoid the loss of money and the inability to accomplish anything, because in Paris any ignoramus has the right to put on his card "avocat-conseil," that is, attorney-counselor. [. . .]

In order to avoid these daily scandals, the publisher of this *Kalendar* has decided to provide an information section in which the newly arrived will find everything that they might need to know at the start. The wayfarer will know where to turn and what to do. Anyone who wants to stay will know where to turn in time of need, where to look for work, and, finally, where to find people who share his ideas. [. . .]

The first thing that the new arrival should do if he does not have anybody here is to inquire for rue des Rosiers. That is the center of the Jewish quarter. (It is most practical to take a cab, in French a *fiacre*, which costs from about one franc and twenty centimes to one franc and fifty centimes.) As far as possible, do not change money at the train. If you have to change money, make it as little as possible (whatever you need right away). On rue des Rosiers, go into Rosenstrauch's Restaurant, or Landau's Restaurant. You can also go into Speiser's Bookstore. In these places you will have the opportunity to meet with the most varied people. You can meet *landslayt*, fellow tradesmen, etc.

Wolf Speiser, *Kalendar* (Paris: n.p., 1910), pp. 24–27.

Baruch and the Immigrant Network

The immigrant network served as employment agency, housing office, and information bureau for newcomers. In the autobiographical novel L'Epopée de Ménaché Foïgel, *the colorful Baruch is a one-man, multiservice broker who helps immigrants write documents in French and find jobs, apartments, and even friendly philanthropists.*

Baruch then had an ingenious idea. He decided to make lists, a kind of secret file containing all the addresses of Jewish men and women known for their generosity, indicating their preferences, manias, shortcomings, and even silly characteristics that could be exploited for charitable purposes. Some were known for their predilection for large families; others were only interested in orphans; others in pregnant women; others in needy old spinsters, etc. Baruch had noted all of these specialties on his cards and used them, almost unfailingly, to steer his clients to the right person. His phenomenal success soon made his little business into a veritable information agency for professional moochers. He was able to indicate to each person the benefactor who suited him best and, furthermore, took care of writing up the request, peppering it with citations from the Torah and with subtly chosen Talmudic moral tales. Little by little, he expanded his scope to job ads. His agency became a placement office. The cap makers of the Saint-Paul district gladly turned to him to recruit workers. But his own and inimitable specialty always remained his card file of the charitable Jews of Paris.

> André Billy and Moïse Twersky, *L'Epopée de Ménaché Foïgel*, 3 vols. (Paris: Plon, 1927–28), 2:28–29.

The French Concierge

Adapting to Paris went beyond material concerns, however. It also meant adapting to that quintessential French institution, the concierge.

The immigrant suffers from the fact that, once 10:00 P.M. rolls around, he must tell his name to the concierge [to be let in], must not make noise in his apartment, and must respect the rest and the tranquillity of his neighbors. He doesn't understand why, after 10:00 P.M., you can no longer sing without the neighbors complaining—those self-satisfied petit bourgeois, who furthermore want to enjoy their sleep in peace and quiet. [. . .] The "large" and romantic soul of the Russian adapts with difficulty to this daily discipline.

> Jacques Tchernoff, *Dans le creuset des civilisations*, 4 vols. (Paris: Editions Rieder, 1936–38), 2:86.

Place de la République

During the interwar period, the immigrant Jews of Paris lived in two neighborhoods: Belleville and the vicinity of the Marais. The place de la République was an important meeting point thanks to its cafés, which served as gathering places for political and union meetings, or more simply, for having tea on Sunday. The Café Capitaine Thénint remained the

*meeting spot for the elderly Jews of the neighborhood until the early
1990s, when it was bought out by a Tex-Mex restaurant!*

Place de la République

THE HEART OF JEWISH PARIS

*Report from the well-known Yiddish writer who writes under the
pseudonym Rémi*

Three Jewish tribes have pitched their tents around the place de la
République. To the east, the Jewish worker of Belleville sits in utter misery.
To the south, the older Jewish quarter between rue des Archives and rue du
Temple sleeps on a soft bed of promissory notes. And to the north, on the
hills of Montmartre, the rag dealers fight with the diamond dealers in the
societies. As a rag dealer from the *marché aux puces* [flea market] says:

—There is no difference between rags and diamonds as merchandise; it
is up to God to send prosperity. Rags can make one person rich, and diamonds can make another poor.

It is clear that when the three tribe-quarters have to meet, or when one
has to look for a living among the others, their paths have to cross at the
place de la République. [. . .]

Its real name is Café Thénint, but we call it by a more Yiddish name—
Café Taynen [Café Complaint], because that is where the Yiddish actors
gather every evening to complain to each other, and to spell out their complaints about the world, the audience, the director, the critics, and their dark
and bitter fate in general. The only person they do not complain about is
the Frenchman who owns the café. He has gone so far as to defend his café
by serving sandwiches on soft kosher bread. The first thing you notice
when you enter the café is the arrangement of tables and benches. In all
other cafés, for example, each table stands separately. Here, however, they
are pushed together lengthwise along the wall, and the guests, with one
heart and soul, sit pressed together at the long tables like the guests at a
Hasidic wedding, or at the banquet of a Talmud society. You have no idea
where the romantic lead is sitting, and where the comedian, where the
prompter, and where the owner of the theater-buffet are. It is one big family here in the Café Complaint. And not only here, but all over the world.
Special telegraph lines run here from New York and Buenos Aires, Warsaw
and Riga, and Kiev and Moscow, carrying the latest news of colleagues in
those places: who is playing what role, who is doing good business, and who
is doing bad business. On the other hand, they talk very little about love
affairs and gossip from behind the scenes, as do the goyim, because, as is

well-known, any Jacquot [*zhako*] from the Pletzl can learn something about family life from the Yiddish actors. [. . .]

Suddenly, someone calls out over the whole café, "Hush!" And as one, everyone becomes quiet for thirty seconds, only to start up once again. The only one who sits there silently the whole time is the prompter. And this is only natural, because when Jews complain, they do not need prompting. They already know what to say on their own.

Pariz, April 12, 1935.

Bakers and Waiters

In Paris, as elsewhere, many Jewish immigrant workers were tailors. They were also cap makers (a Jewish specialty) and woodworkers (in the faubourg St. Antoine), all producing for the Parisian market. Certain jobs, however, served the immigrant community first and foremost. Butchers, bakers, and waiters in kosher restaurants all catered to their own, but not without both labor conflicts and appeals to community solidarity.

On the Jewish Bakers' Strike

And this we learned from the Jewish bakers' strike: that the Jewish bakery bosses, like the Jewish bosses in many other "Jewish" trades, consider it their privilege to pay their workers wages and keep them in working conditions that would send shivers down the spine of even a . . . French boss. [. . .]

Every Jewish worker, and every friend of the Jewish workers, should know that Jewish bread from Patatski's and Zubritski's bakeries is made of the sweat and blood of Jewish bakery workers who have been transformed into slaves and strikebreakers . . .

With the organized material and moral power that the Jewish worker possesses in Paris, we will eventually succeed in doing away with the Jewish bosses' "privileges," and turn our "green" friends into red ones.

Der idisher arbayter (The Jewish Worker), July 5, 1913.

Garçons (Servers in Restaurants)

The Jewish public thinks of us, *garçons*, waiters, as people without a distinct occupation. That is, they do not consider us skilled workers. Our work has no value. Many even think of us simply as beggars, because who else sticks out his hand for two sous as often as the garçon. These people do not give much consideration to the reasons that force us garçons to ask the customer for two sous. The French waiter lives a very sad life. But we Jewish waiters working for the Jewish restaurateurs live in even worse conditions, because the French restaurateur would not take the liberties that the Jewish restaurateurs take. When one of us takes the liberty of protesting somewhat the bad conditions, he is immediately replaced with someone else. Moreover, our places are taken by greenhorns, not tradesmen. On the one hand, the restaurateurs demand that we be good, quick young workers and experienced waiters. And on the other hand, they always threaten us by saying: "A greenhorn can take your place. I could make him into a good waiter in two days." Under these circumstances, we end up working for very low wages. Without tips from customers, we would not be able to survive at all. One restaurateur recently took the liberty of demanding that his garçon pay him for letting him work in his restaurant on the pretext that very good customers eat there and one gets higher tips. [. . .]

Some of them declare openly that they do not want to deal with our organization. In order not to surrender to us, they want to discredit us in the eyes of their customers. They invent all kinds of lies about us. They call us nothing but robbers, thieves, swindlers, beasts, gamblers, etc. All of this for no other reason than that we organized without asking them. [. . .]

Unfortunately, many of us were used by our bosses. We used to feed the customer scab bread. There are still many, only a few of whom get bread at the cooperative. The rest get it from Zubritski, Kenig, Mendel, and others. We waiters have to show our bread-givers that our interests are the same as those of the bakers, tailors, and hatmakers. We also hereby inform the working-class clientele that they should not stand by as our bosses replace our union members with strikebreakers.

Der idisher arbayter, February 7, 1914.

The Strikebreaker

Strikes broke out in the Jewish trades (see chapter 3) which pitted Jewish bosses against Jewish workers. But they also ruptured relations among workers in the shops, affecting daily life for the striker as for the strikebreaker.

The Strikebreaker

Deadly still is the workshop, nobody is there,
The tools and machines—closed up tight.
In the air above hovers a terror concealed,
For the diligent bees are on strike.

They strike and demand their share of the honey.
To reach their goal, onward, they try.
An oath they have sworn—Oh, but one has proved faithless,
Betrayed them has he on the sly.

He works on in secret, away from the light,
He starts at a human being's voice.
The master has woken him up from his sleep,
And promised him double the price.

The house is unheated. The children are bare.
The little one through the night cries.
He thinks not of himself, but of his poor lambs—
His wife—in confinement she lies.

And he made the decision his oath he would break,
His suffering brothers would sell.
And it gnaws at his conscience: An Esau are you—
For a potful of lentils to swill!

> Yudl Yafe

> *Der idisher arbayter,* November 29, 1913.

Shop Workers and Home Workers

A great many Jewish workers suffered from tremendous economic insta-bility in jobs related to the garment industry (leather work, tailoring, the fur trade, knitting, shoe manufacturing). Whether a salaried worker in a workshop, a more or less independent home worker, a jobber, or an arti-san, all of these designations had different meanings depending on the state of the economy or the vicissitudes of the legislation aimed at foreign workers.

Shop Workers and Home Workers Must Fight Together

We return to the question of workers, home workers, and *façonniers* [inde-pendent workers], which was discussed with such tolerance and reason in *Der veker* some time ago. In light of the opinions expressed then, we extend the idea of a socialist artisans' organization among the Jewish artisans in Paris.

The four articles that appeared in *Der veker* were written by Jewish arti-sans toiling in various trades. They may not know each other personally, but they all came to the same conclusion: that the *façonnier* and the worker both suffer from the same economic and social pressures and no improve-ment of the situation of the Jewish working class is possible until the work-ers and the *façonniers* unite for common economic action.

This discussion is an encouraging development in our Parisian Jewish world, where a young community is being raised on lies and empty illu-sions by a leadership of shopkeepers and busybodies.

What difference does it make to them, these society presidents, if a dull and undeveloped mass emerges with little true concept of life? What do they care about the cannibalistic war which the Jewish workers and *façon-niers* are forced to wage against one another over a piece of bread? What do they know about the physical and emotional suffering that comes from a life without free time for physical and spiritual rest? Of broken family-lives, and badly raised children? Of the degeneracy which must emerge from such a social life, and which is nauseating to everyone? They have only one answer to this: philanthropy and oafish nationalism.

Where can we now find the kind of comfort and guidance offered by leaders like those who were so closely connected to the laboring masses at the beginning of the Jewish immigration to America fifty years ago? The couple of voices that have been raised in favor of unity with the workers and a socialist artisan's union form a new phase in our life, together with *Der veker*, which has allowed them to be heard in public. This is the first protest against the influence of the Jewish bourgeoisie. It is the awakening of class instinct among the Jewish artisans.

Der veker (The Wakening), May 27, 1933.

For the Forty-Hour Week

During the Popular Front in 1936, Jewish workers joined French workers in calling for the forty-hour week.

48[sic]-Hour Workweek—The Demand of the Hour

The CGT [Confédération Générale du Travail]'s main slogan this May Day, and the most pressing question around which the CGT is now mobilizing the working masses of France, is the struggle for a forty-hour workweek.

Strengthened by the unity realized by the addition of hundreds of thousands of new members, and with the support of the Popular Front, the trade-union movement will certainly carry out the tasks assigned to it by the Toulouse Congress.

At this moment, when the CGT is carrying on the struggle for a shorter workday, we Jewish workers and home workers must ask ourselves:

Will we, Jewish workers and home workers, who are in France under the protection of the French workers, continue to work late into the evening, thereby obstructing the struggle of our French comrades?

We know that when one asks a home worker to work less, he answers that he cannot do so, because he must work longer hours to earn his bread.

But when you take a look at the situation in the Jewish trades, this is what you see:

> Thanks to the Jewish home workers' long workday, the season is shortened and the firms do not have to keep any "stock."
>
> Thanks to the long workday, home workers' wages have fallen 50 percent—even more in some trades.
>
> Thanks to the long workday we are putting ammunition in the hands of the anti-Semitic French Fascists, and they use it to direct the anger of the French unemployed against us.
>
> Thanks to the long workday we are in danger of remaining isolated, at a time when, more than ever, we need the help of the French working class in order to fight for the passage of the law that will make it possible for us to stay in this country without being at the mercy of the administrative authorities.
>
> *Der yidisher arbeter* (The Jewish Worker), May 1, 1936.

BUENOS AIRES

A Report on the Eastern European Jews in Buenos Aires

Rabbi Halphon, rabbi of the Israelite Congregation of Argentina, was sent to Argentina from France in 1906 by the Consistoire and the Jewish Colonization Association (JCA). From the time of his arrival, he endeavored to reinforce the community's institutions and to improve their image in the eyes of the Argentinean authorities. His regular reports to Paris were critical of the behavior of the Central European Jews and of the immigration situation in general.

Eight-tenths of the Jewish population of Buenos Aires [estimated at 40,000] is of Russian origin. The oldest and today also the richest among them are former members of our association [the JCA]. The other Jews may be classified as follows: approximately 3,000 Turkish, Arab, and Greek Jews; 1,000 Moroccans and Italians; and 1,500 French, German, English, and Dutch. The latter are all merchants and generally represent the top businesses here. Among Moroccan and Turkish Jews, there are also many rich merchants, but the large majority are only poor secondhand storekeepers, hawkers, and peddlers. As for the Russian Jews, while many of them are engaged in trade (there are at least 6,000 *sucuentanicks* [from the Yiddish *kuentenik*, peddler] alone, and the cigarette and match peddlers are all

Russian), there are also a very large number of workers and artisans in all sorts of manual trades. [. . .]

MATERIAL CONDITIONS

Even though in Buenos Aires there are a large number of rich Jews, even some very rich ones, today in the flats there are also many poor Jews who only manage to earn a living with great difficulty, especially since general conditions have declined. It is hardly unusual today to encounter, among our coreligionists from here, many families who find themselves in poverty and often even in dire necessity, needing to turn to public charity. To understand this, it is enough simply to visit the many Jewish *conventillos* [slums] of the capital, where poverty and misery are spread out in all their horror.* [. . .]

OCCUPATIONS AND TRADES

The majority of our coreligionists in Argentina are above all merchants. One can even class them, except for a few rare exceptions, by specialty according to their country of origin. The Russians generally deal in furniture, the Turks in notions, the Moroccans in fabrics and clothing, the French, German, Dutch, etc., in jewelry. Many of these traders, it is true, are very rich, but the large majority of them are only petty merchants. There are also a certain number of employees and a few others who have careers in the liberal professions. Finally, among the Russian Jews, there are also a large number of workers engaged in all sorts of manual labor. Unfortunately, as a general matter, neither the Israelite merchants nor artisans understand how to keep up a good reputation; some because they have too few scruples, others because of their revolutionary theories. [. . .]

Let us now turn to Israelite workers. One thing is certain, that they easily find work here, and they are appreciated from a professional point of view for they generally know their trade. That which has largely harmed

---

*A little while ago we visited one of these *conventillos* with Mr. Veneziani. What especially struck us was the general filth and crowding that we observed among the 50 Israelite families (approximately 460 people) who lived in this courtyard. They were, moreover, families of workers who earn their bread completely honestly. In leaving this site, we thought that it would be a great humanitarian deed to find a practical way to save such Jewish families from these two dangers that constantly threaten their physical and moral health: the lack of hygiene and the unfortunate crowding. If low-cost housing were constructed in neighborhoods outside of the city (like Flores, Floresta, Bella Vista, for example), an honest worker could easily manage, after a certain number of years with only the cumulative sum of his rent (which is very high here—$40 to $50 per month for one room), to pay the price of the house of which he would become the owner. In fact, commercial companies have already tried this here with excellent results. [Footnote in original document.]

them in the eyes of employers has been their revolutionary tendencies. In effect, both in the workshops and during public protests made by the working class, our coreligionists are always the first to preach strike actions and to put forward their revolutionary theories. When May 1 or any other occasion arises, the red flag that waves higher than all the others in the marches is the distinctive one of the Jewish workers. Naturally, the local newspapers pick up on this and comment and even often show photos of this Jewish flag. These photographs then spread throughout the Republic in hundreds of thousands of copies. It is easy to understand the [effect] that such propaganda has throughout the country with regard to our working class. And so, in many of the factories and workshops, many employers will accept only reticently or refuse altogether the Russian, in other words, the Israelite, artisan.

Even now, the corporation of cabinetmakers and upholsterers is on strike here. And Mr. Glaser, an English Israelite and owner of an important furniture factory, assured us that in his workshops, the first workers who struck and who convinced their comrades to follow them are especially Russian Israelites. Our coreligionist was all the more outraged because these workers had been in his employ for a long time, and, not long ago, when several of them had been arrested by the police during the recent anarchist attack, he had done his best to get them out of prison on his own guarantee. Mr. Glaser told us, moreover, that in a meeting held recently by the furniture makers of the capital, the director of the large manufacturing house, Thompson & Co., spoke very harshly on the subject of the Russian Jewish workers. He denounced the danger that they represent if, while still foreigners and ignorant of the language of the country ("gringos"), they succeed in corrupting their comrades.

S. Halphon, *Rapport adressé aux membres du Conseil de l'I.C.A.*,
July 29, 1910, pp. 171–73, 184–85, and 206, in Archives of the
Alliance Israélite Universelle, Paris.

Main Characters of the Rio de la Plata

This fragment of the first Yiddish anthology of stories published in Buenos Aires shows both the desire of the immigrants to preserve the Yiddish language as well as the process of acculturation they were undergoing.

Our Environment and Our Character

Yoysef Mendelson

The Jewish colony in Argentina is still young. Not more than twenty-seven or -eight years have passed since the late Baron de Hirsch showed the masses of Jewish emigrants the way here. His intention was to realize his dream of creating a "promised land" for the Jewish people on the fertile fields watered by the two mighty arms of the River Plata—the Paraná and the Uruguay. Twenty-seven or -eight years is a very short time for anything to be forged concretely into a distinct and definite shape beyond outline form.

In such a short time as this, only a few barely noticeable features could be added to the old, crystallized forms brought here fully forged from the Old World by the masses of Jewish immigrants. These new features have a purely local character and are, to a certain extent, as new as the local conditions for the masses of Jewish immigrants. These new features, the "banks of the Plata features," as I call them, have not changed the old picture entirely. But they have added color and given it a new appearance. [. . .]

[. . .] the reader will thus certainly recognize Ethel, the boss's daughter, as the long-familiar bourgeois girl of the old country, who seldom lifts a finger except to do homey crafts; who sits and waits for a bridegroom because her dowry is already taken care of, thank God; and who quietly engages herself to the neighbor without her parents' knowledge. She has changed somewhat here under the hot Argentinean sun, becoming a bit more careless, a bit more passionate. But these changes are barely noticeable. The author has, in passing, with only a few strokes, portrayed her as she appears here. He has left for the reader to compare her picture to those of her sisters in the old Yiddish literature, and to see the difference and changes brought about by the Rio de la Plata. And what about the dreamy Fanny, or the simple Bertha, who does not think deeply into things, taking with a smile whatever life brings her, without superfluous questions and without speculation? Because of these qualities she is the opposite of the friend with whom she lives, and whom she does not understand after all. And what about Khaym—the crude and somewhat comical, but good-hearted, Jewish youth who loves Fanny so much? He suffers when she treats him so coldly, so contemptuously, even as she suffers with Bunin. Are they not old familiar figures from Yiddish literature? They are old, but they are also new, because the Argentinean-Jewish milieu in which they are situated is new. Buenos Aires, with its sun-drenched streets, with its houses and rooms, with its patriarchal and exotic "mate" [local herbal tea], is new to Yiddish literature. All of these Argentinean concepts, nuances, and traits are new to Yiddish literature. Unnoticeable, they lie scattered here and there in this story, as they do in all our stories and sketches written on the banks of the Plata. They constitute the new which we have here amalgamated with the old.

Not new, for example, are the carpenters depicted in the several "workshop sketches" and in the story "Nokhum":

They came here as adults, with fully formed characters and outlooks on life. And yet, life here has given the carpenters something new that they did not possess in Russia, Poland, or Lithuania. Its lines are barely noticeable, yet here and there they alter the old picture, often completely transforming its appearance. A guest from abroad would not sense these nuances, however strong his powers of observation. But a local person who carries traces of the new within himself senses the new, and comprehends its features in a purely intuitive way.

The Jewish *taller* [workshop] depicted in these stories is itself distinctively Argentinean, and bears a distinctively local stamp. It is not the American "shop," with its hundreds of workers, in which the interests of "labor" and "capital" truly collide. But neither is it the familiar Jewish workshop of the Old World, where the work was carried out in the old-fashioned, good-spirited, genteel way; where needs were small, and earnings even smaller. The *taller,* in the Buenos-Aires-Jewish sense of the word, is yet another amalgam, a melding of the small-town Russian workshop and big-city exploitation, such as it is. The boss works together with the workers because he has not yet had time to work his way up. He often suffers as much as those he "exploits" and who "struggle" against him. They are both equally interested in finishing the furniture suite as quickly as possible, and therefore work through the night. Otherwise they will have nothing to eat ("The Conflagration"). And yet, their interests are different, because new features and new lines have been added to the familiar old picture. Tragicomic situations arise from this. The workers often feel instinctively that they should fight against the "boss," that they must "defend" their interests. But they cannot understand logically what they are fighting for, or against whom they are fighting. After all, their bosses are as poor and as downtrodden as the workers themselves ("Nokhum").

The situation is somewhat different in the country. There the old small-town Jewish life of the old country has remained more intact and obvious, changing little. True, the outward form of that life has changed, because the small merchants and shopkeepers became agricultural colonists when they arrived, forming a bond with the earth, though some more strongly than others. Internally, however, Jewish life could not have changed in such a completely Jewish milieu, and the new features are therefore much less apparent than they are in the city. The children born or raised here are gradually becoming "creolized." But they are still few in number, and do not yet exert great influence on the life of the Jewish colonies in Argentina, particularly on their inner life. In any case, the transformation is not so great that it allows itself to be perceived or observed.

José Mendelson, "Unzer svive un unzer geshtalt," in *Oyf di bregn fun plata* (On the Banks of the Plata) (Buenos Aires: *Idishe tsaytung*, 1919), pp. 6–10.

The Arrival and Welcome of Immigrants

Many organizations "solicited" immigrants right off the boat in order to hire workers and, sometimes, strikebreakers. Local conditions deteriorated in 1921, however, and the Argentinean unions declined rapidly. The Jewish Workers' Immigration Committee was a short-lived attempt to organize immigrant labor independently of employers' and philanthropic actions. The initiative did not arouse much enthusiasm, however, outside of the most left-wing Jewish organizations.

Jewish Workers' Immigration Committee

To all the labor unions of Argentina.
Comrades:

[. . .] With the United States limiting immigration, Argentina is one of the principal refuge sites for these emigrating masses.

Here one finds Israelite immigrant workers facing an abyss of demoralization and moral degeneration. What birds of prey dwell under the cloak of philanthropy, bourgeois and petit bourgeois of all stripes, trying to wield their craftiness to beat down further the already beaten wandering workers, to exploit the desperate situation of the very people arriving in a country unknown to them in search of work.

The various capitalist employers and their tools, the shop managers, exploit these desperate immigrants—who due to their critical situation settle for an insignificant salary, working unlimited hours—as a means of strikebreaking.

If the organized workers' unions were not to react, the situation would produce consequences harmful to their own interests.

Faced with this fact we saw the need to found the "Comité Israelita Obrero de Inmigración," which will serve as interpreter and intermediary between the immigrant workers and the unions, trying to avoid playing, for many of them, the sad role of "butcher" [*carnero*, strikebreaker]. [. . .]

What we ask is that they accept as brothers the professional comrades we will recommend to them, and try to inform them of work in the appropriate union, in order to avoid having these comrades fall in the net of bourgeois philanthropic institutions, which are nothing more than sites of demoralization, the results of which would bring disastrous consequences for the daily struggle of the organized proletariat.

Toward the goal of having all information necessary to be able to regulate immigration and inform the workers who must immigrate from the European countries about the outlook and conditions of work here, we beg the unions to complete the attached form and return it as soon as possible.

To be able to respond more successfully to this need, it would be beneficial to group the Israelite members within the unions, forming a commission to organize work shifts, and to serve as interpreters for the immigrant comrades, who naturally do not know Spanish.

We are confident you will address this problem appropriately and will help us resolve it, avoiding the detriment that could result, and we look forward to your moral cooperation.

Fraternal greetings.—The Secretary

"Comité Obrero Israelita de Inmigración," *La Protesta,*
May 17, 1922, p. 4.

Jewish Labor in Buenos Aires

As was often the case in other countries, the Jewish workers of Buenos Aires worked as tailors, cabinetmakers, cobblers, cap makers, and knitters in a myriad of small workshops or at home. As immigrants, they occupied the least desirable spaces in the labor market—manufacturing cheap ready-to-wear clothes and poor-quality furniture—or they stimulated what had been poorly developed industries, such as weaving. But the seasonal character of these jobs permitted them or forced them to engage in a number of different activities. Thus, many were also involved in small trade and peddling and tried to set up their own businesses. This was especially the case in the building trades.

How the Jewish Painters' Society Was Founded
by P. Miler

In 1918, when the gates of Europe opened after the world war, a great migration to the countries of the Americas got under way. The starved and long-suffering European masses, having endured all of the horror and misery of the war, streamed across the Atlantic Ocean in search of peace and bread for themselves and their families. Jews made up an important segment of this migration. Our sisters and brothers set out for South America in search of a livelihood. Others dreamed of becoming rich. Buenos Aires was the most important center of immigration.

The immigrants' lot was a sad one in their new countries. They felt forlorn and deserted, as if they had been uprooted. As a group, they concentrated in the Jewish neighborhoods of Buenos Aires. They filled the restaurants and stood around on the corners. They looked for friendship among those who were well-settled, searching for both companionship and sustenance. Some threw themselves into business as itinerant merchants and peddlers. Others looked for a trade, though they were not workers.

Of all the trades, painting most attracted the immigrants. Even as an assistant one did not earn badly at it, and very little knowledge was required. Besides, any competent person could become proficient at the trade and earn a good living. Thus, people of various classes and occupations in Europe became painters in Buenos Aires.

Despite the fact that there were already about a thousand Jewish painters in Buenos Aires, there was still no society. It seemed as if such a thing would not occur to anybody. It took a shocking catastrophe to give birth to the idea of a society. A painter fell from the third story and was killed. His family was left in great poverty without any means of support. A couple of the dead man's friends took it upon themselves to help the family.

That is when it occurred to me that the painters needed their own mutual-aid society to support the members in time of need or misfortune. I laid out my plan several times to some of my friends. Unfortunately, while many of them heard me out, they all refused to do any practical work. Once, I met with a group of painters at the Café Internacional and proposed to them that we get down to founding a painters' benevolent society for the moral and material support of the painters. I pointed out to them the example of other societies which did many good things for their members. At that point, several others joined me in agitating for the initiative.

As a result, the founding meeting took place on November 1, 1923.

> P. Miler, "Vi azoy iz gegrindet gevorn der idisher maler fareyn," in *Almanakh fun maler hilf fareyn, aroysgegebn tsum 10 yeriker yubileum* (Buenos Aires: [Jewish Painters' Society], November 1933), p. 19.

Prostitution

Buenos Aires, a city of immigrants with a relatively high proportion of men in the population, also became a principal center of the white slave trade from the end of the nineteenth century. The "Polish connection," under Jewish control, ran houses of prostitution and extended its web as

far as Central Europe. Local and international movements were undertaken to eradicate this activity of the tmeym—the unclean. On several
occasions, local workers' groups attempted to respond with their own campaigns against the presence of "the impure ones" within the community.

"Youth"

In 1908, the Socialist Zionists, headed by M. Polak, initiated a campaign in
which Po'alei Zionists, a few individualist anarchists, syndicalists, Zionists,
and nonpartisans also participated. The organization was called "Youth,"
and it assumed the task of fighting directly against the white slavers.*
Youth carried out its activities within the bounds of the Jewish community,
where the Jewish white slavers were philanthropists, altruists, and human-
itarians; supporters of religion; communal activists and leaders; patrons and
rulers of the Yiddish theater and actors; people respected by the govern-
mental authorities; and also owners of a number of votes, which they put
at the disposal of conservative electoral lists. Youth's job was to remove
prostitution from Jewish life and from the Jewish community. In addition
to oral and written propaganda, there were frequent fights on the Plazas
Lavalle and Larrea between the members of Youth and the "gangsters,"
because the impure ones, some of them well-known strong-arm men from
the old country, were always the first to arrive at the Youth meetings. They
came to fight.

Fifteen years later, in 1923, the direct fight against the "impure ones" in
the Jewish community was renewed by a special Jewish committee. The
struggle was completely independent of the labor movement, or even of
workers. But since the struggle of 1923 was morally connected to the struggle of 1908, we will note here that the relationship of the "impure ones" to
Jewish society was reduced to visits to the professional Yiddish theater, and
their influence to an indirect one on the theater repertoire. The struggle
continued until the "impure ones" were completely excluded from the Yiddish theater and no longer had any influence at all over any aspect of Jewish life. They were to disappear without a trace from Jewish communal life.

The law in effect certainly helped. It drove the white slavers from the
country in general.

P. Wald, *In gang fun tsayt* (Buenos Aires: Tall. Gráficos Julio
Kaufman, 1955), pp. 370–72.

*A campaign was being waged against white slavery in general by the Commit-
tee against White Slavery, in which the Zionist leader Sh. I. Liajovitsky was active.
In the national Chamber of Deputies, the first and only Socialist deputy, Dr. Alfredo
L. Palacios, introduced a bill to suppress the white slavers. [Footnote in original document.]

Prostitution and Our Immediate Tasks in the Struggle

Petit bourgeois elements, as well as workingmen and women, have raised their voices in the columns of *Di prese,* appealing to the proletariat to take part in the struggle against prostitution. They demand that we include this as one of our immediate tasks in the struggle, expressing the opinion "that prostitution is no less harmful to the worker than low wages or long workdays. The working class carries on a simultaneous battle for better working conditions, so why should it not also struggle against prostitution?"

These malevolent bourgeois "do-gooders" of ours mean to use various tricks to divert us from our correct path, that of the class struggle. We reject them with revulsion. [. . .]

Various petit bourgeois intellectual con artists approach the workers these days in order to draw them into struggles for their own personal interests, or in order, with ill will, to derail the Jewish proletarian from his line of struggle. At such a time, we call on you, Jewish comrades, to remember that your place of struggle is only in the ranks of the unions and revolutionary political organizations. It is never with even that part of the petit bourgeoisie that spews revolutionary phrases in order to lure you into a dead end.

Form ranks, comrades! Only together with your class will you be able to destroy the present order of robbery, provocation, and prostitution!

I. Linkovsky, "Prostitutsie un unzere baldike kamfs-oyfgabn," *Royter shtern,* April 10, 1926, p. 2.

GERMANY

The "Ghetto" of Berlin

East European Jews tended to scatter throughout Germany (much like their native coreligionists) rather than concentrate in one major city. Subject as they were to expulsion and other forms of harassment, East European Jews in Germany sought to maintain a low profile. For these and other reasons, they never established major ghettolike areas in any German city prior to World War I. Nonetheless, one section of Berlin was beginning to show signs of immigrant Jewish life, as described in the local Zionist newspaper.

We now turn from the city center to the North, where we soon encounter a completely different street scene. We see a long, narrow street, the Linienstraße, with various small, dirty alleys feeding into it. This is, after all, one of the oldest parts of the city, the area where the Jewish ghetto was once

located. Even today these alleys are typical Jewish alleys, where Jewish foreign immigrants are concentrated. If you regret not having seen any Jewish faces for some time in the bustle of the city, you will find plenty of them
here. These are recognizably Eastern European Jewish types. You can see
how long the women have gone hungry as they stroll through the streets
in comfortable house robes or congregate in front of the house doors with
their children. The men roam about with their "bundles," seeking odd jobs.

The peddler's box is their most common source of income; others trade
in eggs or herring. Only younger people can become workers, and only
those with some sort of training can hope for permanent employment in a
business.

These shy human figures make a strange impression on us if we think of
the broad streets and cheerful throngs we have just come from—where
practically every man, even the coachman and the street sweeper, is full of
self-confidence. He steps forward with a steady stride because he is "on the
job." He dares to make demands on life and his fellow men because he has
a foundation to stand on: he occupies a place in society. The timid glance of
poor Jews seems to be asking forgiveness, forgiveness for the fact that they
dare to walk on the face of God's earth. Everywhere they go, they are—out-
siders.

Why have they come here? They wouldn't be able to say. Their only
answer: is there a place where no one would ask them this same question?
One man has come completely by accident, you might say he has lost his
way here. He had another destination in mind; he was on his way to America. As chance would have it, however, the employer who was supposed to
buy his steamship ticket became ill, and he had to interrupt his journey for
a short stop in Berlin. At that time, the city made a very favorable impression on him, and he came to a firm decision: "I will never, under any circumstances, go back to Galicia. Even if I should die here, there is no point
in returning."

A second man thinks he will meet up with a distant relative who emigrated many years earlier.

A third man has come because well, after all, in Berlin there are God and
Jews, too, and they won't forsake him.

Now that he's here, what should he do? What God provides! Our Jews
are certainly not one-sided—specializing in one trade is exactly what they
haven't done. And so their main concern is to find something that will
bring in some money.

Sometimes God does provide, and they do earn something, and they get
by until they can send for their families. Of course, that goal is not always
achieved; very often there is nothing left to do but—travel on further.

Until they have their families with them, they take up residence in the kosher restaurants where they all congregate. There they can get help in bad times; there they can buy something for just a few pennies; there they can get credit as well. Naturally that means paying back ten times the amount, but when there is no other way, even this is seen as good luck.

Otherwise, the kosher restaurant is the most comfortable place to go aside from the shul; here they can spend a few pleasant hours among themselves after the worries of the day. The people who meet here come from various parts of Russia, Galicia, Hungary, or Romania, but they are all Jews and are no strangers to one another. To help and support one another is a matter of course and is recognized as a duty. For example, if one man is carrying a heavy burden and meets another, unknown Jew, the latter feels a natural, brotherly obligation to share the burden with him. "He's not my friend, but he's a Jew all the same," he says. When I ask him about a tavern, he is happy to be able to accompany me there and thereby do another good deed. *"Mitzvah goreret mitzvah"* [one good deed begets another] he says with satisfaction.

They try to observe the proper Jewish commandments, to stay true to God and to resist with Jewish endurance the temptations of life in a non-Jewish city. God often rewards them for this. For example, a peddler is offering his wares to the guests in the restaurant, patiently putting up with the taunts of the others. As evening approaches, he asks the owner for permission to recite the *Mincha* prayer. Now the guests begin to trust the pious Jew and buy more from him, and he earns two marks. "God has sent him his reward on the spot."

Since it is very difficult to observe the Sabbath here, they have founded a *shomer shabat* shul whose members all promise to obey the Sabbath laws as they have in the past. But not all of them find it possible to do so, and for this reason some of them have broken away from the strict-observance group and moved to their own location.

The fathers will keep this tradition; the children, on the other hand, probably will not. Regardless of what their parents do, the children seem determined to enjoy the benefits of advanced civilization. And that is where we see what strengths they have to offer. In every field the second generation chooses to enter, it very quickly catches up with or even surpasses the native-born population.

Die Welt (The World), June 10, 1904, pp. 2–3.

Cigarette Workers

Many immigrant Jews played a significant role in the cigarette and cigar manufacturing business in cities such as Berlin and Leipzig in the late nineteenth century. The work was attractive on a number of grounds: it required little outlay of capital to purchase the raw material; the actual labor was not too taxing and could be performed by the entire family; and, most important, workers sold their own wares, thereby serving both as laborers and as entrepreneurs.

At that time Russian-Polish Jews—who had brought with them little more than their manual skills—were trying to earn a living by making cigarettes during the day and then selling them personally in the cafés at night. The production costs were still quite low. First of all, special production rooms were not required—their sleeping rooms could double as their workshops. Thirty pfennigs' worth of cigarette papers and ninety-five pfennigs' worth of tobacco were enough for one thousand cigarettes. Especially clever workers had their names or a brand symbol printed on the papers and arranged for friends and acquaintances to ask repeatedly for this brand in cigarette shops, thereby stimulating the interest of the shop owners—a shrewd and well-thought-out advertising method. If the owner actually asked a customer where one could obtain the brand that the customer had been asking for, the latter was happy to arrange a meeting with the cigarette producer. [. . .] According to the reports of industry experts, we are safe in assuming that only immigrant Russian Jews were active in the cigarette industry at this time—and that the owners of the small, home-worker-based companies were of the same origin. Native-born entrepreneurs in the cigarette industry are to be found only in the larger factories, where cigar manufacturing was the primary business and cigarette production was only an insignificant sideline, which developed gradually as the demand for cigarettes increased. After the first hard-won successes, and despite the very modest profits to be expected from this activity, rapidly increasing numbers of Russian Jews had become adjusted to the cigarette industry. The competition among them was very intense. As we already noted, the operating capital required was very small, and the initial investment could always be earned back quickly. Cigarette production also offered physically weaker people a chance to earn money. Moreover, in this business it was possible to keep Saturday as a day of rest—a factor that was especially important to recently arrived migrants. The strongest attraction, almost a fascination for the Eastern European Jews, was the possibility of becoming economically independent in this trade. Even a wage worker had real reason to hope that he might someday become a business owner. The first group of immigrants who produced cigarettes made up a clearly recognizable entrepreneurial proletariat. The entrepreneurs themselves manufactured the products, and they themselves then developed the market for the products. [. . .] With time, the demand for cigarettes grew, and with it the industrial manufacturing of cigarettes. A few especially talented individuals had developed themselves into factory owners. They employed newly arrived immigrants as workers or even induced especially talented workers from their homeland to come here. According to a report by the senior members of the Berlin Business Council [Berliner Kaufmannschaft], there were already a considerable number of small cigarette factories in 1899. "They usually retail their product in their own shop, with the back room serving as the production area, and can apparently survive quite well using this approach." The cigarette workers, on the other hand, earned very little. The large number of workers available kept wages low. The price paid for one thousand handmade cigarettes was 1.80, 2.00, or 2.50 marks; that was the amount that could be earned in an average nine-hour workday. It was too little, even considering the very low living wage of the Russian Jewish worker. Most tried to increase their income by taking on additional home work. Assisted by their wives and children, they often continued to roll cigarettes until 2:00 A.M. A skillful worker who had several older children could produce as many as three thousand cigarettes per day in this manner. With time, the extent of home production increased. Some people began to glue together cigarette cartons as well. One carton cost about two pfennigs and could be sold for five pfennigs. With the family's help, several hundred cartons might be produced in a day. Several large packaging companies had their beginnings in these miniature factories. The few native-born workers who became involved in the cigarette business as the volume increased did not earn as much as the Russian workers. They were unwilling to take on home work after closing time. In order to produce more cigarettes during the day, however, they sometimes contracted with Jewish workers to glue the papers for them, at forty pfennigs per thousand. As we have seen, at first native-born workers were only rarely encountered. By 1899, the number of cigarette workers had already increased to eight hundred, evidence that cigarette manufacturing, which had played only a minimal role earlier, had now experienced rapid growth. It became more significant with each passing year. A 1902 account by the Berlin Chamber of Commerce [Berliner Handelskammer] states:

> In the field of cigarette manufacturing, we are happy to report that changes favorable to Berlin are on the increase. Only a decade ago, Dresden was the undisputed leader in German cigarette production, even in supplying the Berlin market. Since then, however, Berlin

manufacturers have taken over the local market and have continued to extend their sales area, aided by the good reputation their brands have won over the years. One reason for this trend, which is important for the German cigarette industry as a whole, is that the Berlin companies limited themselves to hand production from the beginning. Hardly any of them adopted the cigarette machines so prevalent in Dresden. In this way they have had considerable success in competing locally with foreign imports—primarily from Russia, Egypt, and (more recently) England.

For a long time, Russian Jewish immigrants had a kind of monopoly position as cigarette workers. For a while their numbers, their skill, their constant diligence, and their superior competitiveness were too much for the native-born workers.

> Klara Eschelbacher, "Die ostjüdische Einwanderungsbevölkerung der Stadt Berlin," *Zeitschrift für Demographie und Statistik der Juden* (1920): 22–23.

Jewish Miners in Silesia

Due to labor shortages, the Prussian government relied on imported Polish seasonal laborers to work the mines of Silesia. Polish Jews, however, were barred from such work on the grounds that they were physically and constitutionally unfit for hard labor. Nevertheless, for a brief period shortly before World War I, the government permitted an experimental program, undertaken at the initiative of German Jewish organizations that sought to aid unemployed Polish Jews. The Polish Jews recruited for this program constituted the only population of East European Jews in Germany to engage in heavy industry. By the latter part of World War I, this policy changed as the need for farm and factory workers became acute.

Jewish Miners

Several Silesian mine administrations have been hiring Jewish workers as an experiment. This has not been as unsuccessful as pessimists had feared, considering that these people come from quite different circumstances and are totally unfamiliar with mining work. They possess intelligence, an ability to pick things up easily, a serious attitude, and familiarity with the German language (since their jargon is really nothing more than an unusual dialect); all of these have helped them overcome initial difficulties. It is therefore not surprising that the mines are continuing these trials, and regrettable that untrue reports have been published, reports that tend to disturb the orderly development of the project.

The *Kattowitzer Zeitung* writes:

In order to counter such misinformation several politically independent gentlemen from Kattowitz [Katowice] and vicinity decided to conduct an investigation and form their own opinion. By interviewing people in the mines, both the workers and their employers, they got an overview of the type of work involved, the wages, and other aspects they found interesting. They discovered that the people who work in the mines, mainly underground, are generally satisfied with the work and are not afraid to take on new tasks, even very unusual ones. The wages, which amount to at least 2.80 marks per day and can reach 5 marks per day for piecework, are also considered adequate, although they understandably seem low to workers with large families to support. A few workers who have worked in foreign countries for higher wages would naturally like to get the same pay here, but they are exceptions with no effect on the general consensus. The average monthly wage is 70 to 100 marks; thanks to the thrift and family solidarity of the Jewish workers, the amount left after paying their expenses for food, insurance, dormitory lodging, etc. is regularly sent to their families at home (either directly or through the Jewish Employment Office). The shifts are worked normally, with the shift missed because of the Sabbath made up during the following night. Their rapport with the Christian miners is generally good, since the latter have been admonished by the mine officials not to insult the Jews in any way.

The employers themselves also report that the Jewish workers fulfill their duties willingly and loyally. They praise the Jewish miners for coming to work more regularly than some of the other immigrant workers, who sometimes skip two shifts per week, and for working even on their strictest fasting days. They recognize their thriftiness, which sometimes even leads them to save food. Then the employers must insist that they take more nourishment. It is generally agreed that they are more intelligent than the other foreigners, and it is especially appreciated that they try to improve their knowledge of our language by reading informative German books and newspapers. We should also note that some of these workers have English or French citizenship: with their work experience from those countries and their knowledge of the languages, they, too, can have a certain edifying influence on their fellow miners.

Considering the information above, which is reported without any embellishment, it should be clear that the experience with Jewish mine workers so far has been positive, encouraging further experiments. Unprejudiced mine administrators, even some from foreign countries, are asking the Jewish Employment Office to provide them with capable workers. The fact that one troop of thirty Lodz workers did quit their jobs on one occasion is not so surprising: such incidents are fairly common among immigrant workers and nothing new to mine officials. The cause of this particular incident was that in Lodz the workers had been misinformed about the nature of the work and the wages. A few troublemakers took advantage of this situation to incite the workers and convince them to return to Russia before they had even begun to work.

Some people harbor a fear that Jewish workers might play the role of strikebreakers in case of a work stoppage; this is absolutely impossible— first due to their small numbers, and second due to the certainty that, when the pickmen stop producing ore, all of the other jobs will also come to an end, and thus the Jews will have no work, either.

Our informants thus conclude that no one should disturb, by means of bad publicity, the efforts begun by the Jewish Employment Office and several mine administrations for unselfish reasons.

Israelitisches Familienblatt (Hamburg), September 19, 1912.

Labor Contracts for Polish Jewish Workers during World War I

The labor contracts concluded by the Deutsche Arbeiterzentrale in Warsaw with some thirty thousand Jewish workers turned out to be disadvantageous for the workers. The standard contract contained the provision that the contractual obligation "shall last for the duration of the war but not less than six months." Many of the workers thought they had committed themselves for only six months, and they were often given heavy work and work for which they had no previous experience. Wages were low, the food was poor, housing conditions were cramped, and they were subject to hostile and petty treatment. As a result, breaches of contract, substandard performance, and deliberate slowdowns were everyday occurrences.

[first page (the printed form is bilingual—German and Yiddish)]
INDUSTRY
GERMAN CENTRAL WORKERS' OFFICE
Berlin
Hafenplatz No. 4

Excerpt from the Employment Contract
of: . . . .
age: . . . . years
Home town: . . . .
. . . .
District (precinct): . . . .
. . . .
Home country: . . . .
. . . .

Passport No.: . . . .
. . . .

Stamp of the recruiting office:
Employer: . . . .
. . . .

Place of employment: . . . .
. . . .

Post office: . . . .
. . . .

Rail station: . . . .
. . . .

Border office in: . . . .
. . . .

date . . . . , 191__

[second page]
Contract duration: Duration of the war, but no longer than _____
months.
Contract may be extended by mutual agreement
Daily work hours:
    Day shift . . . . . hours
    Night shift . . . . . hours
Daily wage: . . . .
. . . .

Hourly wage: Workdays: . . . . marks; Sundays: . . . . marks
Overtime: . . . .
. . . .

Piecework wages: (minimum daily earnings at normal productivity)
    . . . . marks . . . .
. . . .
. . . .
. . . .
. . . .

Payment of wages on: . . . .
. . . .

[third page]
Travel costs from the home town to the place of employment as well as
the fee for proof of identity shall be paid by the employer.
The worker shall pay for the return trip himself.
Living quarters with heat, light, straw mattress, and wool blanket shall
be provided free of cost.
Meals shall be provided in the workplace cafeteria (breakfast, noonday
meal, and evening meal); the cost for meals shall be . . . . . marks.
Medical and accident insurance shall be like that for German workers.
The worker must pay the legally required contribution to the premiums;
this shall not exceed
    . . . . % of his wages.

Family support: money will be withheld from wages by the Support Section of the Central Workers' Office and transferred to the dependent family members entitled to
[fourth page]
support. For up to 2 dependents, 20% of wages; for 3 or 4 dependents, 25%; for 5 or more dependents 30%.
Work rules: The worker agrees to follow the work rules for the place of employment.
Main contract: All additional rights and duties shall be based on the main contract signed by the employer and the employee.

Central Zionist Archives, Z3/167.

Deposition of Two Workers

Dortmund, June 7, 1916

We work at the "Union," one of us manufacturing new projectiles and the other in the pressing plant. We heard from several Russian-Polish colleagues that they are being pressured to take up residence in the plant barracks. [. . .] It is dirty in the barracks; there are many mice there, and above all the food is bad. The dishes are poorly prepared and therefore do not taste good; and the food is also not nutritious. Yet the charge for meals is two marks per day, including lodgings. In the barracks fifteen men sleep in some rooms, twenty or even sixty in others. Anyone who wants to read or write or do anything requiring quiet and concentration will be unable to do so because of the large number of people living together. The conditions in the barracks are generally considered unpleasant; almost everyone wants a peaceful place to stay, such as we two now have, where one can be on one's own.

For these reasons, we and the other workers who have private housing do not want to return to the barracks. Furthermore, the caretaker [*Portier*] who lives in the barracks treats the residents very harshly. If someone is sick and wants to visit the doctor, the caretaker doesn't let him leave; instead, he takes him to a back room, beats him with a rubber blackjack, apparently incites his dog to attack him as well, and thus prevents him from leaving the barracks. If anyone comes home late in the evening and wants to enter the barracks *after* 10:00 P.M., he is usually beaten by the caretaker as well. For this reason it often happens that in similar situations workers, in order to avoid being beaten, simply stay away until the next morning.

We present the following cases of mistreatment of workers in the barracks:

The lathe operator Abraham Sußmann was not given any breakfast one Sunday morning when he got up a bit late; when he asked for breakfast anyway, the barracks cook beat him so badly that he was unable to work for twelve days.

The worker Hirsch Nachtigall came back from the night shift and asked the barracks caretaker if he could have his breakfast number immediately, since he was very hungry. The caretaker, however, did not want to give him the number and made him wait, as usual, until all the other workers had gathered to receive their numbers. Because of his request, Nachtigall was cursed and beaten by the caretaker.

The worker Moritz Welt experienced the same treatment in a similar situation. The caretaker cursed and beat him, set his dog at him, and flogged him with a leather whip.

The worker Moritz Käßmann is our witness that the caretaker struck another worker, who is afraid to give his name, because this worker overslept and therefore went to work late. [. . .]

Factory police officer Steffen has repeatedly taken workers who refuse to live in the barracks to the police jail; here they are threatened with further incarceration until they agree to move to the barracks. It is reported that the prison guards have beaten them until they bled. The following workers, who are now living in the barracks again, state that they were beaten: Meyer Hertz, Pinje Weintraub, and the machinist Zimmermann.

We have only one wish: our Russian-Polish colleagues should no longer be compelled by such violent means to take up residence in the barracks. Or, if living in the barracks is to be a general requirement, someone should take action to improve the conditions there. In particular we request that the workers who are again living in private quarters be allowed to remain there; likewise we express the wish (several colleagues have told us this) that those workers who were forced by the means described to move to the barracks be allowed to return to their old private lodgings. [. . .]

> Hirsch Bäckerkunst, I. Kampstraße 118
> Chaim Fromsohn, Silberstraße 32
> Jaeger, Chief City Clerk [*Oberstadt Sekretär*]

Stadtarchiv Dortmund, 5 Nr. 369.

AMSTERDAM

Classic (Unflattering) Description of the Jewish Neighborhood

After the Housing Act of 1901, Dutch cities had the power and money to start housing policies of their own. A group of socialist and trade-union representatives decided to investigate the situation in Amsterdam and appointed L. M. Hermans, who walked through the poor neighborhoods in the company of one of Holland's best socialist cartoonists. Krotten en slop-pen *(Slums and alleys) is their oft-reprinted report on the Jewish neigh-borhood. Hermans first quotes from his earlier work and then concludes that nothing has changed.*

Slums and Alleys

> Here, people do battle with vermin and often get the short end of the stick in that battle. In the summertime, when the nights are sultry, father and mother sleep lying on the window seats, because the bedbugs bite so terribly and are so numerous in the dark hole, as the bedroom is called, that there can be no question of sleep. Only the children, who are tired, tired to death from begging and peddling, are able to sleep there, despite scratching their filthy skin until it bleeds in their sleep. [1898–99]

[Nothing has changed in the last ten years:]

Everything is still the same here.

The Wide Passageway is still one of the alleys in the Jewish Lumberyards.

Two houses have been condemned; the other houses, equally uninhabit-able, have, O, unfathomable council interpretations of the civil code, not been condemned and are still inhabited.

The houses in the Wide Passageway were formerly warehouses and are of a solid construction, moreover they are very old, so old that the mortar has fallen out of all the brickwork. These houses are like dirty old men with toothless mouths. [. . .]

An old Jewish woman who is willing to see me says that she is eighty-two years old, that she was born here, that the apartment is very much to her liking and that she would not want to leave. She sings the praises of the virtues of her residence, living here is just fine, wonderful, healthy, and quiet.

While we are busy measuring the doorway outside, more Jewish women start leaning out of their windows.

They ask one another:

"Whatta they doin' here?"

We do not know how to answer.

They shout down to us that they do not have any complaints, that it is fine here, that they do not want to move, that they are content in their warehouse.

And they work themselves up to make us believe that, for they see in us members of the health commission and they are afraid that the houses will be condemned. [. . .]

I now enter a house I was in once in 1887. The same total darkness still prevails here. How is it possible that such a hole is permitted to be rented. There is absolutely no light, on the other hand it is so damp, that the wall-paper droops down in shreds. A woman, the immediate family of a knife grinder lives here, tells me that she had to place boards against the wall in the bedroom, because the bedclothes get so wet that they cannot be slept on. And this family has stayed here but one night. She will not stay here long, she believes she will become ill here and she is already planning to go out tomorrow in search of another apartment. I agree with her and inside myself I commend her fortune that she is financially well-off enough to be able to rent another room, a little more livable than this awful pit. But . . . the unfortunate ones who will have to move in after her? [. . .]

To the so-called Jewish District belong, among others, the Valkenburg, Uilenburg, and Batavierstraten.

Even in a cursory walk through these narrow, long streets it strikes us that the article in the police bylaws, whereby throwing refuse into a public street is prohibited, has been completely overlooked here.

I will gladly accept that the initial responsibility for this lies with the female residents. City sanitation wagons do come by here, as well as elsewhere, and thus the female resident can deposit her refuse at a certain hour each day. But what is to be expected of people to whom the city officials of Amsterdam have never extended a helping hand to educate them to realize that cleanliness and keeping the air clean are the primary requirements for healthful living.

> L. M. Hermans, *Krotten en sloppen. Een onderzoek naar den woningtoestand in Amsterdam, ingesteld in opdracht van den Amsterdamschen Bestuurdersbond* (Slums and Alleys: An Investigation of the Living Conditions in Amsterdam, Commissioned by the Federation of Amsterdam Administrators) (Amsterdam: S. L. Van Looy, 1901), pp. 56–64.

The Jewish "Ghetto"

Emanuel Boekman was one of the most important Social Democratic aldermen and one of the most constructive Dutch thinkers about socialist art and culture between the two wars. Coming out of a childhood of poverty himself, he loved art and saw it as a means to raise the morale of the poor. Although Boekman was mainly active in the Social Democratic Party, he never forgot his Jewish background. He became involved in the heated debate about the changes in the Jewish community, and his magnum opus was the first demographic study of the Jews in the Netherlands.

The Disappearance of the Amsterdam Ghetto
by E. Boekman, Amsterdam

When it was decided by the Amsterdam City Council in 1916 to clear out the practically uninhabitable apartments on Uilenburg and adjacent streets, a committee set up for this purpose organized an exhibit entitled "Images of the Disappearing Amsterdam Ghetto." In a certain respect that title was inaccurate, since no imposed living together of Jews ever existed in Amsterdam.

The conditions in which the first Jews came to the city, however, make it understandable that even without such pressure they would still prefer to live in proximity to one another. [. . .]

This situation continued to exist over the course of several centuries. While the term *ghetto* was not entirely applicable to this district, the name Jewish District was justified. Until the first half of the nineteenth century, the number of Jews who settled into neighborhoods that housed a predominantly Christian population was comparatively limited.

Various circumstances brought an end to this.

The very considerable increase in the number of Jews in Amsterdam necessarily required either that the boundaries of the Jewish District be significantly extended or that the Jews should start settling in other neighborhoods.

Aside from this, the economic and social isolation of the greater number of Amsterdam Jews has largely dissolved over the past decades, so that the former contrast with the rest of the population likewise diminished in significance.

It is an internationally known phenomenon that the Jewish bourgeoisie assimilates long before the greater mass of Jews and that the middle class follows the haute bourgeoisie. Confirming this observation, the more well-off Jews were the first to leave the old Jewish District. Thus over the past decades this area has not become just a district of Jews but, in particular, a district of poor Jews.

Also, changed attitudes toward the hygienic conditions which apartments must fulfill—and of which the aforementioned city council decision was a consequence—have made thousands look for better apartments than the old Jewish District could offer.

De Vrijdagavond (The Saturday Evening), 1:21 (1924), pp. 1, 2.

Secondary Areas of Settlement

In the subsequent article in De Vrijdagavond, *Boekman expanded on the fact that after leaving the ghetto, Jews moved to certain neighborhoods where, without any conscious policy, they created new Jewish nuclei. He kept asking why people behaved in this way, for as a socialist, he had assumed that Jews would integrate into non-Jewish society. But it became clear that Dutch society did not always accept the Jews, nor did the Jews want to live within a culture that they did not feel was their own.*

Old and New Jewish Quarters in Amsterdam
by E. Boekman, Amsterdam

The nucleus of the so-called Jewish quarter is much "more Jewish" than the general figures would lead one to believe. In view of the significance that the absolute number of Jews has for the total population of the neighborhood, one can say that the five first-mentioned neighborhoods are in fact completely "Jewish neighborhoods." The percentages of Jews on Valkenburgerstraat, along with Jodenbreestraat and surrounding streets, show that they are no less Jewish than they were some centuries ago. It has been established, however, that the absolute number of Jews who live in these neighborhoods has decreased significantly in the last half century. [. . .]

The neighborhoods that lie around this nucleus, such as Zandstraat, the vicinity of the Nieuwmarkt, and Rapenburg, have always been neighborhoods with a mixed population. One should therefore, in judging the figures that these neighborhoods present, also take into account that they contain a complex of streets where not many Jews ever lived. In contrast, each of these neighborhoods contained one or more streets where the percentage of Jews was probably not less than that of the truly Jewish neighborhoods.

This last point is strongly evident, for example, in the Wilhelmina Gasthuis [Wilhelmina Hospital] neighborhood, the area surrounding Swammerdamstraat. Those who are familiar with the make-up of the neighborhood know that the percentage of Jews that inhabit the Swammerdam, Blasius, and Ruysch Streets amounts to certainly no less than 90 percent of the total population of these streets. However, since the separate figures for these streets are not known, as they form merely a portion of the results for the entire quarter, the overall percentage shows but an attenuated picture of the actual situation in the heart of the neighborhood. [. . .]

The same phenomenon thus appears within neighborhoods as can be observed over the entire city: a nucleus forms around which the remaining streets and neighborhoods, respectively, cluster, with the percentage of Jews decreasing as one moves away from the nucleus.

In viewing the map, one must especially keep in mind the figures presented previously concerning the growth of the Jewish population in Amsterdam. One figure in particular might be repeated here.

In 1815 there were almost 18,000 Jews living in Amsterdam. There was enough space for them to live in the old "ghetto," and the number of Jews residing outside that neighborhood was hardly significant. In 1859 the number of Jews had risen to almost 27,000 and in 1869 to almost 30,000. The old neighborhoods could no longer accommodate these numbers, and settling in other neighborhoods was the inevitable result. It was also a time when the social distinctions within the Jewish world were becoming sharper than before. A significant portion of the Jews of better means moved into the new Plantage neighborhood.

A short while later construction started on neighborhoods like Lepelstraat, the Nieuwe Prinsengracht, Swammerdamstraat and the vicinity, which were to accommodate a portion of the Jewish lower middle class and the Jewish workers. The construction of new neighborhoods some forty to fifty years ago became necessary because of the quick growth of the population. [. . .]

It is likely that this extraordinary increase in the number of Jews in Amsterdam, which for the most part is not a result of excess births but of in-migration to the capital, is closely related to the great expectations aroused at that time as the diamond industry started to thrive, the so-called Cape Era [when the South African diamond industry was prospering, circa 1876].

De Vrijdagavond, 1:22 (1924), pp. 4, 5.

Cigar Makers

Besides diamond workers (see chapter 3), cigar makers were the other highly organized group of industrial workers in Amsterdam. Unfortunately, there are very few accounts of daily life and work, since most of the work was done in small shops. After World War I, massive industrial production replaced handmade cigars. In this transcript of an interview, Jacob, the son of a cigar maker, explains how his family tried to survive by cheating the insurance company.

"But when you were unemployed, how did you bring in any money?"

"Well, we had the little shop . . . something always came along, but . . . *ach*, it's a long story, but I'll tell you. My father was really dreadfully poor. Cigars were certainly being made. But they didn't sell well, so there was always a pretty good stock of them. That's what my father was like with money. So there was no more money, and my father needed money. We could tell that my father had a plan.

"One day we were sitting at home, and my father went out. Suddenly we heard people crying, 'Fire! Fire! Fire!' Yes, my father had . . . it's sad but true. My father had bought all that tobacco on an installment plan, and it was dampened, made wet, and then dried to prepare it before it was made into cigars. It was always lying around the heating stove. In a pretty desperate situation, my father had set it on fire—and then immediately put the blaze out. He was no arsonist. Just forced into that by the circumstances. . . ."

"He didn't really want to send the whole lot up in flames?"

"Oh, no. So, all the cigars were on the ground during the panic when they got water from the faucet and tried to quench the flames, and so on. The firemen came. I can see it before my eyes right now. They got down on the ground, smelling to see if anyone had poured gasoline around. Apparently a fire had been deliberately set more than once, but there was no gas. My father just wanted to set a very little fire, or perhaps he had been clever enough. I had no idea how he'd done it. So we got money from the insurance. You get the wholesale price, not the retail price, but he got back what he had paid in wages as well as the cost of the tobacco. So he could have more cigars made—now that he had gotten rid of his inventory. It happened a number of times. . . ."

"A number of times, that little fire?"

"A number of times. We never spoke about it. You're the only outsider who knows about it. . . . But you can write it down. It happened fifty years ago.

"And then, during a thaw one winter, he made a little cut in the lead pipe, so the cigarettes got wet. Spoiled, too, of course; and to camouflage it—I saw this—to stop the water streaming down, as if trying to prevent it, he flattened the pipe out. But the damage was already done. He did it, and that was the last time, for we kicked up a fuss at home and said that it was just too much. . . . He had to do it, had to. Had to, yes, he honestly did. So I have to say that in his own way, with his illness and all, he nevertheless looked after his family. He couldn't do it any other way."

Selma Leydesdorff, We Lived with Dignity: The Jewish Proletariat
of Amsterdam, 1900–1940, trans. Frank Heny (Detroit: Wayne
State University Press, 1994), pp. 181–82.

Jewish Shops, Jewish Peddlers, and Sunday Blue Laws

On May 1, 1932, a new law concerning shop hours set off a protest among Jewish owners of small shops. The new law forbade any sales outside the regulated hours in order to prevent competition and overexploitation of those who worked in the small shops. From now on, shops that were closed on the Sabbath could only be opened for six hours on Sunday (other shops could only be open for four hours on Sunday). It was thus impossible for the small Jewish family shop to open for enough hours on Sunday to make up for their Saturday losses. At the same time, peddling on Sunday was forbidden.

The Peddler Problem

A pushcart laden with small articles like fish, fruit, kerosene, toys, etc., pushed by a hawker, man or woman, is called peddling.

Of late, many peddlers have so-called fixed districts with a steady clientele, where they regularly sell their wares door-to-door.

They therefore do not need to shout disturbingly, but ring the doorbell and ask whether there is any business for the peddler today. This kind of peddler is therefore far less annoying than the horn-tooting bicycle-cart riders.

Lawmakers have made exceptions in the Shop Closure Law on behalf of Jewish shopkeepers, so that the Sabbath can, in fact, be considered a day of rest.

Jewish peddlers—except those in toys and small food wares—must, however, shut down their business for two days.

Street vendors belong for the most part to the proletarian class. In storm and wind, in severe cold and excessive heat, they earn a sour piece of bread. The lawmakers did think of them, but not to the advantage of those poor creatures.

We can agree that loud hawking on public thoroughfares on Sunday—particularly during the morning hours—is annoying to those who wish to rest on that day.

But what objection is there, for instance, to a kerosene peddler bringing lamp oil to his Jewish clients' homes on Sunday, without shouting while doing so. His clientele are poor people who do not have enough money at their disposal to stock up on kerosene until the coming Monday.

Why do those poor Jews, who already must live from one day to the next, be so severely punished?

Those peddlers who observe the Sabbath stand unprotected, there is no one who champions those wretches. Is the civilized multitude not interested in a poor Jewish peddler?

Would the city officials of Amsterdam still consider asking the minister, on behalf of those Sabbath-observing Jewish peddlers, who on that day—Sunday—offer their wares to the public without shouting, to give them the opportunity to earn their slice of bread, for instance from nine o'clock in the morning until two o'clock in the afternoon?

De Joodsche Middenstander (The Jewish Tradesman), no. 18,
May 16, 1932.

The Seamstress

Roosje Vos, a major leader in the trade-union movement, wrote a little-known but very political play about the life and hardships of seamstresses. Like most of the socialist theater, this play is not exclusively Jewish, but it is written by a Jewish trade unionist and describes an environment where many Jewish young women worked.

The Seamstress of the Past, Present, and Future

SECOND ACT

Characters

Dora, Jansje, Betje—Seamstresses

Mr. KAPITAAL [Capital]

A Supervisor [woman]

Several Seamstresses

A Few Members of the Board of the Seamstresses' Union

FIRST SCENE

(When the curtain goes up, six or seven seamstresses are sewing at their sewing machines. In the background, stage right, there is a small table at which a few women sit working by hand; the floor of the workshop is covered with all sorts of cloth scraps, bits of paper, patterns, etc.

Dora is sitting on the right-hand side of the stage, also at a sewing machine. As the curtain rises, all sing steadily while they continue working.)

[DORA:]

There's no joy anymore in this awful sewing,
I wish they'd come and tell me there's something else I could be doing,
All that sewing, all that sewing, it's such a misery,
From all that boring work, done in is what you'll be.
No, oh no, oh no, sewing I will not do,
No, I will not do it, 'cause I'm dying I'm so blue.

And should we get to work late, a fine we'll have to pay,

We aren't allowed to go downstairs when nature calls our way,
And if you happen to break a needle, it'll cost you money,
And all us seamstresses think, that really isn't funny.
No, oh no, oh no, a seamstress I won't stay.
No, I will not do it, 'cause I'm dying of dismay.

(While the refrain is being sung, the Supervisor appears in the doorway and suddenly all fall silent.)

SUPERVISOR (holding a nightshirt): Who was singing?

(All are silent.)

SUPERVISOR: Who was singing?

(Again silence.)

SUPERVISOR: No one, then all of you get a fine. (She pulls a notebook and pencil out of the pocket of her apron and writes.)

(The seamstresses all start muttering and a few make faces behind the woman's back. The Supervisor walks over to Dora and shows her the shirt.)

SUPERVISOR: Say, Dora, what price do you think the new model of nightshirt should pay?

DORA: Name the price yourself, ma'am, because if I name it you will think it is too high anyway.

SUPERVISOR: Well, I think that the boss will not pay more than eighty-five cents per dozen.

DORA: Eighty-five cents? So, is that what the boss wants, and what do we want? The price keeps dropping, last week we made the same kind at a guilder for twelve, they also had six pleats on the side, a yolk in front and a flat collar.

JANSJE (whispering to Dora): I think that is much too little, we cannot make them for that price.

DORA: Well then, say it, the lady is here now, and now you're not saying anything, soon she will be gone and you will all be complaining just as loudly. Better say what you have to say now.

SUPERVISOR: If you all are not satisfied with it, I will tell the boss, but I already know: he will not offer more.

(She leaves with the nightshirt.)

Roosje Vos-Stel, *De naaister van het verleden het heden en de toekomst* (The Seamstress of the Past, Present, and Future) (Amsterdam: n.p., 1900), pp. 21–22.

Chapter 2   Societies, Organizations, and Schools

Immigrants banded together for mutual aid—both "moral" and material. Particularly in an era when state welfare programs did not yet exist and when philanthropy by the native Jewish community was sometimes found wanting, immigrant workers organized their own self-help organizations which provided medical care, life insurance, free or low-cost loans, and other benefits. They also joined together to set up prayer meetings and to create burial societies as in Eastern Europe. Their organizations were places for socializing, arguing politics, or gathering to read the Yiddish press. The societies often hosted concerts, theatrical and literary evenings, and balls.

The immigrants also set up schools. As one Yiddish paper wrote, *Visn iz makht* (in knowledge is there strength); *zelbst-kultivirung* (cultural self-improvement) was stressed.[1] Local Arbeter Ring—Workmen's Circle—groups were set up from New York to Paris and organized Yiddish children's schools and other cultural activities for girls as well as boys.

The *landsmanshaftn* are perhaps the best-known immigrant organizations. They provided an important link with the past, but they were also the place where people helped each other cope materially and exchange information about the New World.[2] They too evolved over time. In England, in particular, where immigration was halted earliest, the friendly societies, which had some 40,000 members by 1911, found by the 1930s that they had to diversify their activities if they were to keep attracting the Jewish youths who were otherwise drawn to British, working-class culture.

In each country, however, the immigrant and workers' organizations took on a somewhat different character. Whereas friendly societies, mutual-aid organizations, burial societies, schools, charity organizations, and Jewish labor unions and political groups flourished in New York, London, Paris, and Buenos Aires at the turn of the century, Jack Wertheimer speaks of the "organizational impoverishment" of the Jewish immigrants in Germany.[3] Geographic dispersal heightened disunity, and there were practically no Yiddish periodicals and no Yiddish theater in Germany before World War I. The efforts of the Bundist group in Offenbach were probably the most important such organization in the Reich. In Amsterdam, while there were a certain number of Jewish workers' initiatives, especially with regard to charity, the more integrated and indigenous nature of the Jewish working class there led to the formation of social and cultural organizations different from those found from New York to Paris.

NEW YORK
Landsmanshaftn

The associations of transplanted natives of the same town in Eastern Europe constituted one of the most widespread forms of organization among Jewish immigrants in New York and elsewhere. Landsmanshaftn generally provided their members health and death benefits, along with other assistance. Several different societies often represented a single locality, reflecting political, religious, generational, or other divisions among its former residents. As late as 1938, there were some 2,000 to 3,000 such societies in New York, with a total membership close to one-half million. In their first three meetings, the founders of the Satanover Benevolent Society dealt with many issues common to most societies.

[Meeting No. 1, October 3, 1903]

A meeting of our Satanover *landslayt* [fellow countrymen] was held on Saturday evening, October 3, 1903, at 126 Ludlow Street, at the home of Shabse Fridman, chaired by Brother Zayde Tishman. The following resolutions were adopted:

1) That the society should be named for Satanov, and that the rest of the name be decided at the next meeting;

2) There were nominations, as well as elections, for officers. [. . .]

6) Income for this meeting was fourteen dollars.

[Meeting No. 2, October 11, 1903]

1) Concerning the second name of our society, Brother Gisniet proposed the name "Progressive," and Brother Tishman proposed "Satanover Benevolent Society." Brother Liptsin made a proposal that the second name be "Zion." The name "Satanover Benevolent Society" was adopted.

2) Our meetings rely on four signals, which every candidate must know. As the first signal, [. . .] the password *ken yirbu* [Hebrew: May they increase] was adopted. This is called the "admission signal." The second signal is called the "greeting signal." When a candidate enters the meeting room, he must give a greeting by putting his right hand on his left breast.

The third signal is called the "voting signal." When the president calls for a vote for or against any particular question, one must raise one's right hand. The fourth signal is called "rap of the gavel." When the president gives one rap of the gavel, he is calling the meeting to order. Everyone must then take his seat. Two raps of the gavel mean he is calling for the officers to stand. Three raps mean everyone should stand. [. . .]

8) The society adopted a decision that from now on when a candidate is proposed for membership he must be investigated by a committee, get a doctor's certificate from our society doctor, and be voted on. [. . .]

[Meeting No. 3, October 25, 1903]

1) Brother Harry Rozenblit, seconded by Brother Gisniet, moved that the following decision of the last meeting be rescinded: "that no new candidates be accepted into the society who do not come from the districts of Kamenets or Proskurov." Instead, anyone who we want is eligible for admission to our society.

2) Brother Vice-President Tsuker proposed that membership be limited to those from Russia, excluding those from other countries.

3) It was decided that any brother may propose candidates, regardless of what country they come from.

Minutes, Records of the Satanover Benevolent Society, RG 818,
box 1, YIVO Institute for Jewish Research.

By the 1920s and 1930s, many landsmanshaftn *were celebrating their anniversaries with large banquets and elaborate souvenir journals. The members often used these journals to express pride in their contributions to Jewish communal institutions, their aid to the old home town, their cemeteries, and their benefit programs.*

The tasks of the Boslover Society were thus quite modest. But the first members very quickly realized the power of unity. They understood that they and their society were called upon to be a source of assistance and support for *landslayt,* and so the society set out on a course of mutual aid. When they were sick or in need, the brothers turned to the society, and the society helped them morally and materially, with warm friendship and with money. More than one brother brought his family over with the help of the society. And it is hard to find a brother who has not at some time sought, and always received, assistance from the society.

And the Boslover Society grew in numbers and prestige, and with each year widened the scope of its activities. [. . .]

The Boslover Society is a society of Jewish workers. Jewish cries of anguish after the Russian pogroms and the World War, the needs of workers during strikes, Jewish anger at the crimes of Fascism and Hitlerism—all of these touch the heart of the Boslover Society. The great contributions made by the Boslover Society to relief in Boslov, to labor in the Land of Israel, to Jewish and workers' cultural institutions, and to charity of every sort, form one of the finest chapters in the history of our great Jewish organizations.

> Boslover Benevolent Association, 35th *Anniversary Souvenir*
> *Journal*, New York, 1935.

The Arbeter Ring (Workmen's Circle)

While some mutual-aid societies were quasi-Masonic and others religiously identified, the Arbeter Ring (along with the Zionist Jewish National Workers' Alliance and the Communist International Workers' Order) saw itself as part and parcel of the labor movement. Founded as a mutual-aid society in 1892, the Arbeter Ring was reorganized as a national fraternal order in 1900. By 1910, it had 38,866 members and peaked with 85,000 in 1925. It was closely allied with the Socialist Party until the 1930s, when it gave its support to Franklin Roosevelt's New Deal coalition. The Arbeter Ring developed a broad program of secular Jewish activities, including children's schools, lectures, publications, theater groups, choruses, and orchestras.

This old workers' benevolent society has now united with other similar societies and laid the foundation for a great countrywide federation, one that will play the same material role for the Jewish workers and their friends as do the large fraternal orders, but without the reactionary characteristics, the ceremonies and other nonsense, that make the orders intolerable to progressive workers and citizens.

THE WORKMEN'S CIRCLE CORDIALLY INVITES ALL BENEVOLENT SOCIETIES TO AFFILIATE AS BRANCHES, AND ALL WORKERS AND FRIENDS TO FORM NEW BRANCHES. [. . .]

Only the Workmen's Circle's purpose and spirit are considered immutable [*eybig giltig*].

Its *purpose* is to secure and alleviate the obligations of support of small societies through the guarantees and assistance provided by a large, strong, countrywide organization.

A small society soon goes bankrupt when it is faced with more cases of illness than is usual at one time. If it is a division of a larger federation, however, all of whose branches share in the responsibility for the benefits of each branch, all of the branches help it carry its burdensome obligations.

In a word, the federation insures the whole society, just as the society insures the individual member.

The Workmen's Circle's *spirit* is the spirit of freedom of thought and aspiration, and of workers' solidarity and loyalty to the interests of their class in its struggle against oppression and exploitation.

> "Der arbayter ring fun Nyu York," flyer, 1900, Papers of Kalmon Marmor, RG 205, folder 769, YIVO Institute for Jewish Research.

Aid to the Old Country

In the fall of 1914, Orthodox Jews launched the Central Relief Committee to aid Jewish war sufferers, followed by the wealthy uptown Jews who organized the American Jewish Relief Committee. Socialist and labor elements formed the People's Relief Committee the following year. The three organizations distributed funds in Europe through the Joint Distribution Committee, which became one of the most important American Jewish institutions engaged in overseas work.

Jewish People's Relief Committee for the Jewish War Victims
[in English and in Yiddish]

AN APPEAL FROM THE
UNITED HEBREW TRADES
TO ALL UNIONISTS IN THE COUNTRY

> A Day's Wages for the Jewish War Victims
> Union members, sisters and brothers, [. . .]
> Who will take pity on them if not we? Who can sympathize with their suffering as we workers can? At this time, when almost all of Europe is in flames, when their homes have been destroyed, when fields have been laid waste, when disease attacks their withered bodies, when the Angel of Death gallops with his sharp scythe cutting lives short right and left, when old people and young children fall like sheaves of wheat—now is the time when we organized workers should come to their aid with the massive organizations that we have built. [. . .]
> Every union man should send a day's wages to the Jewish People's Relief of America. Everyone should contribute. Union officials and shop delegates should make a start. The workers, men and women, will do the same. [. . .]

How fine it is when we are told that in Russia, the unfortunates share the small portions of bread that they sometimes receive. Let us make this relief campaign the time when we provide whole portions of bread to tens of thousands of families. [. . .]

> The United Hebrew Trades,
> Max Pine, Secretary

All funds should be sent to the People's Relief Committee, 175 East Broadway, New York.

> "An apiel fun di fereynigte idishe geverkshaften tsu ale yunyon-layt fun land," Papers of Max and Libby Grackin, RG 1163, YIVO Institute for Jewish Research.

Education

On arrival in America, the vast majority of immigrants sent their children to the free public schools as the surest road to Americanization and success. Still, many Eastern Europeans also wanted to provide at least the rudiments of Jewish knowledge to their offspring and sent their children to a local kheder, *as in the old country. In New York, these took the form of after-school classes, which all observers agreed were wholly inadequate. Writing in 1887, Rabbi Moses Weinberger was a particularly harsh critic of American conditions. He viewed the problem from the point of view of the hapless teachers themselves.*

Chadarim (religious elementary schools), where teachers (*melamdim*) give instruction in the alphabet, vowels, and Hebrew reading, are found here in abundance; such abundance, in fact, that their fees have fallen tremendously. According to reports, many teachers have now issued a handbill in which they agree to teach any Jewish child, however he may be—rich or poor, bright or dumb—for only ten cents a week, or forty cents a month. Obstinate householders won't take advantage of this bargain. They tell themselves that just as the price has fallen, so it will fall again—until teachers uncomplainingly accept fees of a mil an hour.[4] But they are wrong on two counts: (1) until this happens their sons will forget—everything they ever knew, forcing their parents to start paying all over again from the beginning; (2) what they foresee will never happen. We have already heard teachers whispering that if they do not win their battle, and cannot improve their lot, they will abandon teaching completely and return to sewing clothes, tanning leather, or making shoes—each to the job that he performed in his native land.

More advanced teachers (*morim*) with wisdom and learning are also found here in abundance, and many of them are wonderfully skilled, highly trained pedagogues. But in the absence of schools, and in the absence of any desire on the part of many of our brethren to rear their sons on "the knees" of Torah, they have trouble finding steady work. After a few years of shuffling about as if in a world of desolation, most of them give up and return shamefacedly to their homelands. The lucky ones, who successfully make their way after a great deal of grief and travail into the homes of our wealthier brethren and are handed their sons, find it impossible to use their knowledge. They must rather wrack their brains to recall what they studied in their childhood from primary teachers. For during the period when, in our native lands, they taught Jewish children Torah from beginning to end, they must teach the sagacious children here the Hebrew alphabet, from *alef* to *tov*. And during the time when the Hungarian or Polish Jewish youngster was brought to a level where he could understand the Prophets, and listen to rigorous biblical and legal studies, the American youngster is merely brought to the magnificent level of being able to stammer a few words of English-style Hebrew, to pronounce the blessing over the Torah, and to chant half the *maftir* (the weekly prophetic portion) from a text with vowels and notes on the day he turns thirteen—a day that is celebrated here as the greatest of holidays among our Jewish brethren. From that day onward a youngster considers his teacher to be an unwanted article. On the very day of the celebration—the day when his father stops assuming responsibility for his sins—an angel comes, slaps him on the mouth, and (just as happens according to legend, at birth) he forgets all the Torah that he has learned, including the blessings, the *maftir*, and, of course, the phylacteries. In their place he must learn to establish for himself a goal in life, and to become familiar with the ways of the world. The teacher is thus unnecessary. And since the parents come from Poland, and "know" that this wisdom does not require the service of a trained and learned pedagogue, they have no use for the teacher, no matter what his quality. They pay, therefore, only according to their own estimate of what his work is worth—an amount generally so small that one cannot possibly live on it. Teaching has thus become a scorned and debased profession. It does not support those engaged in it, and none will choose it save a man who, having tried his hand at all else, finally senses that his lucky star has gone black and that he is fated to see only dark days for all the rest of his life.

Jonathan D. Sarna, trans. and ed., *People Walk on Their Heads: Moses Weinberger's Jews and Judaism in New York* (New York: Holmes & Meier, 1982), pp. 51–52 (copyright ©1981 by Jonathan D. Sarna; reproduced by the permission of the publisher).

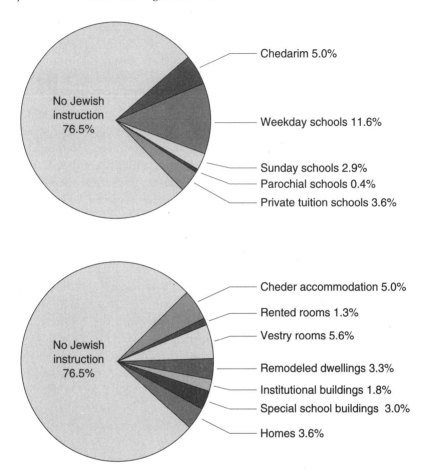

Above: types of religious instruction provided for Jewish children of New York; *below*: kinds of school accommodation provided for Jewish children. From S. Benderly, "The Present Status of Jewish Religious Education in New York City," *The Jewish Communal Register of New York City, 1917–1918* (New York: Kehillah [Jewish Community] of New York City, 1918), pp. 349–66.

Three decades after Rabbi Weinberger's lament on the state of Jewish education in America, the problem persisted. A series of studies carried out between 1908 and 1918 showed that less than one-quarter of Jewish children of school age were receiving any Jewish schooling, and much of it woefully inadequate. After 1909, the Kehillah reform movement undertook, among other things, to remake the Jewish educational system by setting up a Bureau of Education, while other groups, such as the (Labor-

Zionist) Jewish National Workers' Alliance, the Workmen's Circle, the Sholem Aleichem Folk Institute, and the (Communist-oriented) International Workers' Order, eventually opened secular schools to teach Yiddish, Hebrew, and Jewish history and culture.

By the mid-1930s the communist Yiddish schools had replaced the initial emphasis on class struggle with a more sympathetic view of Jewish traditions. The following are excerpts from one of their early children's schoolbooks.

Work, Children

> Work on, children.
> Work is good.
> He who works,
> has it good.
>
> Chairs and tables,
> houses, stands—
> are the products of
> his hands.

The Policeman

> A policeman like a bear,
> Chases after a Pioneer.
>
> Policeman doesn't think it funny,
> That Pioneers are raising money.
>
> The Pioneer quickly makes a dash,
> Red-nosed Policeman falls
>   on his fat belly with a crash.
>   Betsales Fridman, *Arbeter*
>   *shul* (New York: Farlag
>   internatyonale arbeter ordn,
>   1934), pp. 33, 110.

LONDON

Jewish Benefit Societies

In 1911, the Liberal government set about introducing a system of health insurance. Unnaturalized immigrants, however, would be ineligible for the state's weekly contribution to their insurance, and the immigrants' own contributions and those of their employers would be administered by the Post Office rather than the Jewish benefit societies. It was feared that many members would be unable to maintain weekly payments to both their benefit society and the Post Office. The largest Jewish societies responded with an unprecedented political campaign and ultimately won concessions beyond their initial hopes. Unnaturalized immigrants who had been in the country for five years became eligible for state support while Jewish orders were able to administer the scheme.

Conference of Benefit Societies

JEWISH DELEGATION TO LLOYD GEORGE

OUTLOOK FOR A MIGHTY UNION

A very important conference concerning Lloyd George's new insurance bill took place on May 17th at 10 Duke Street, the headquarters of Order Achei Ameth.

Almost all of the orders were represented at the conference: Achei Ameth, Achei Brith, Machaneh Yisrael Hagedolah, Hebrew Order of Druids, and Magen Avram. The chair was occupied by Mr. Brasch, the grand president of Achei Ameth.

Very important and serious discussions took place concerning the condition of the foreign Jews in general, and the relationship of Lloyd George's insurance bill to the Jewish benefit societies in particular.

Everyone recognized that for the friendly societies to have an influence in the state insurance scheme, they must first of all be united. This may be realized when the discussions are continued at a general conference to take place after Shvues, and to be chaired by Mr. Stuart Samuel, M.P.

The purpose of the upcoming conference will be to organize a delegation of all of the orders to go before Lloyd George at the recommendation of Mr. Stuart Samuel and present its program for protecting the members of the orders from any ill-effects of the new state insurance scheme. According to this program, the four pence that the workers contribute, and the three pence that the masters contribute as post-contributors, would be paid directly to the orders themselves. They would then use their funds to guarantee to the government that they would legally protect the workers' benefits.

It is almost certain that the delegation's demand will be accepted. The foreigner will then not feel as foreign as he would as a post-contributor.

Several other important points will be proposed to ensure that the member of an order, whether he is naturalized or not, not suffer from the new insurance bill.

Everyone must therefore strive to unite all the orders in one force. Only through unity will they obtain all privileges.

Der idisher zhurnal (The Jewish Journal), May 19, 1911.

The Achei Brith and Shield of Abraham Friendly Society

The following is but one example of a report of friendly society activity for the early 1920s. The question of amalgamation is raised, which hints at the first signs of falling membership and overall decline. Yet at the time contemporaries saw the friendly society movement as the leading community institution.

Jewish Friendly Societies

ORDER ACHEI BRITH AND SHIELD OF ABRAHAM

Annual Conference

On the second day of the annual conference held at the Monnickendam Rooms, Aldgate, a resolution was submitted by the Dr. Herzl Lodge, Manchester, in favour of the affiliation of the Order with the English Zionist Federation. After a discussion, in which the speakers expressed a desire to assist the Zionist Movement in an individual capacity rather than as a Friendly society, the voting resulted in a large majority against affiliation.

Another important debate took place upon the subject of amalgamation with the Grand Order of Israel. On this point delegates differed as to the advisability of amalgamating in the absence of any definite information regarding the solvency of both organisations. The following resolution was adopted:

That it be an instruction to the Executive to invite the Grand Order of Israel to join in an examination of the prospects of amalgamation of the two Orders and report on the conditions, if any, how an amalgamation may be effected.

It was further resolved to submit a report on the subject within six months.

A resolution that provincial delegates on the Executive should have their travelling expenses paid, was lost.

An interim report on the valuation of the Grand Lodge Funeral Fund was submitted, showing very light mortality during the period covered by the valuation 1914 to 1919. As a result of the various amendments to the General Rules of the Order providing for increased contributions to this fund and for a special system of levies, the deficiency in this fund was considerably reduced and the degree of solvency increased to 14s.7d. in the £.

The election of an Executive representative for Wales resulted in Bro. L. S. Goldstein being appointed.

The following were appointed to serve on the Board of Benevolence in addition to the Honorary Officers and Grand Trustees:—Sisters C. Abrahams and M. Buckner, Bros. J. Jacobs, M. Kissin, I. Solomons and I. Marks.

The proceedings terminated with the presentation of the Past Grand President's badge of office to Bro. J. Bader.

A dinner was held at Monnickendam Rooms on Saturday evening, in honour of Bro. L. C. Beber, the newly elected Grand President of the Order. The function was arranged jointly by the Prince of Wales Lodge, No. 23, and the Princess of Wales Lodge, No. 25. Bro. Henry Harris, J.P., who presided, referred to the pleasurable recollection of his early days in connection with the Order when it was insignificant in numbers and in financial strength. The toast of "Our Guest" was proposed by Bro. N. Isaacs, who described Bro. Beber's remarkable progress to the highest office in the Order, a position which he had reached at a younger age than any of his predecessors. Sister R. Bloom presented Bro. Beber with a silver loving cup bearing an appropriate inscription.

NORWOOD OLD BOYS' ASSOCIATION.—A general meeting was held at the Oxford and St. George's Settlement. Mr. Basil L. Q. Henriques, who presided, referred to the difficulties which the Association had to overcome in securing a meeting place with a view of carrying into effect the objects for which the Association was established. He commended the proposal to form a Lodge of the Order "Achei Brith and Shield of Abraham," as that would ensure permanency to their organisation. Mr. D. Spero urged the assembly to adopt the proposal as, in his opinion, the Jewish Friendly Society Movement was rapidly becoming the leading institution in the community. A resolution, "that it is in the best interests of the parent institution that a Lodge be formed under the auspices of the Order Achei Brith and Shield of Abraham," was carried.

Order Shield of David

STAMFORD HILL LODGES.—The male and female Lodges will give a concert and dance in the Sir Marcus Samuel Hall on Wednesday evening next. No charge will be made for admission. Residents in the district, in particular, are invited to be present. Mr. J. Goldberg is Chairman, and Mr. S. S. Fox is Secretary of the Social Committee of the combined Lodges.

Notice

Full reports of all Jewish Friendly Society matters are now given in every Thursday's "Jewish World," price 2d. Of all newsagents, or can be obtained direct of the Office, 2, Flasbury Square.

The Jewish Chronicle, January 6, 1921.

The Workers' Circle

The London Workers' Circle, originally Bundist in origin, had, by the 1920s, branches that were Po'alei Zion in orientation and others that were dominated by the Communists. The following literary account portrays the cultural activity of the circle and hints at the debate over a cultural politics for the young.

The "Circle" was tucked away near Aldgate in a turning just off Leman Street, the street of the Cooperative buildings. Like every Sunday evening, the club room was crowded. The air was thick with the steam from the urn and a bluey-grey fog of tobacco smoke. Someone had lit a cigar and its aroma came to the nostrils first, stood out arrogantly, like a rich man at a wedding. [. . .]

[. . .] Sam looked round the clubroom. He hadn't been here before, but Alec was a member. At the table back of him, he saw a quiet little man with a short grey beard, reading *Freiheit,* the Jewish Anarchist paper. One of the old guard. Quite a few of the very old members had been nihilists in Russia. Probably more than one had thrown bombs at Czars or had been sent to Siberia for their convictions. And whenever Emma Goldman was in town, she was always certain of an enthusiastic welcome at the "Circle" [. . .]

An electric bell rang shrilly in the clubroom. It was nearly eight o'clock. The concert in the hall downstairs was due to commence in a few minutes. Sam was surprised when Alec got up from the table.

"Is it really going to start on time?" he asked.

Alec laughed. Sam knew his *yiddlech* all right. If a concert was billed to commence at eight, they came at a quarter to nine, and were upset if it had started without them. But this wouldn't be a yiddishe 8 o'clock. If it was billed for eight, it would begin at eight, prompt.

They sat at the back of the hall—it could accommodate about two hundred people and was fairly full already. More people drifted inside in ones and twos. Mostly East-enders. Here and there were a few strangers. It was not their clothes which betrayed them, nor their faces, but an unconscious air of frigid aloofness. Either in search of good music or new thrills. The novelty of watching a proletarian audience lapping up Brahms and Beethoven. [. . .]

With a nod the fiddler drew down his bow and his colleagues, at exactly the same moment, fastened on the opening chord. . . Alec's head nodded to the sparkling, vivacious menueto. All round him bright eager eyes were concentrated on the stage. A miracle this audience, created from nothing by a couple of musical enthusiasts. The older "Circle" members shook their heads. "The youngsters don't want music," they said, "give them dances and light concerts," but the enthusiasts persisted. "No, let them hear good stuff and they will learn to appreciate it!" And it was so; in three years, the concerts had gathered a solid band of loyal supporters.

> Simon Blumenfeld, *Jew Boy* (London: Lawrence and Wishart, 1986), pp. 80–85.

Schools

Nettie Adler (daughter of the former Chief Rabbi Hermann Adler) sur-veyed the Jewish schools largely serving the immigrant community.

The eight Jewish "non-provided" schools provide for the religious educa-tion of some 3,800 children. They give such instruction daily during the week, and, in some cases, organise classes on Sunday mornings. About the same number of children attend classes after school hours, the schools being hired under the direction of the Jewish Religious Education Board, twice or thrice weekly. About 4,000 children attend classes attached to the synagogues, mainly in the districts outside the inner zone of Stepney.

In addition to this provision, over 3,300 children are pupils of the Tal-mud Torahs or schools for teaching the Law, at which a more intensive study of Hebrew is pursued. Although this total roll is just under 15,000, a number which would appear to leave outside religious teaching a consider-able proportion of boys and girls, it has to be remembered that there are a number of small private classes and private teachers in East London and elsewhere and that a good many parents prefer to send their children to the small class or Cheder and to the old-fashioned teacher who still imparts Hebrew translation through the medium of Yiddish. But recent years have brought about many changes. There is closer contact between all types of classes. At the Talmud Torahs at which originally Yiddish was always spo-ken, English or Hebrew is used as the medium for teaching. Girls too are admitted to these classes, following in this way the example of the Jewish Religious Education Board and the Synagogues, both of which have given great attention to the religious education of girls. Owing to the initiative of the Chief Rabbi, an increasing development of Consecration Services for girls, based on careful preparation (to some extent analogous to the Con-firmation services among Christian denominations), has taken place within the last decade. As in all denominations, there are a certain number of par-ents in the Jewish community who are apathetic in regard to the religious education of their children, but it is doubtful whether anglicisation influ-ences their attitude. The long-settled families are generally anxious that their children should receive religious instruction, though it may not be entirely on traditional lines. The constant claims which are made upon the

Central Committee for Jewish Education for help in establishing classes in the outlying suburbs, seem to prove that the more "anglicised" parent is desirous that his children should maintain contact with their faith.

Nettie Adler, "Jewish Life and Labour in East London," in *The New Survey of London Life and Labour,* vol. 6, ed. Sir Hubert Llewellyn Smith (London: P. S. King and Son, 1934), pp. 275–77.

Willy Goldman's 1940 account of his kheder *and his school can be compared to Nettie Adler's more blasé assumptions about education and Anglicization.*

We Jewish children acknowledged the superiority of the Gentile method in one field: religion. He was practically exempt. With us the Rabbi dominated one part of our lives as the school-teacher dominated the other. For four days in the week—and a good slice of Sunday—we were forced to spend the time between tea and supper cooped up in the *Kheder,* the Hebrew school. Anything less like a school you never saw. It was usually a cellar-kitchen or disused workshop where the tutor, a bearded, unkempt, smelly old man in his dotage, mumbled at you for hours on end out of a large book. You had to repeat his mumbles after him. When you mumbled wrong or took a slight rest from mumbling you received a clout across the ear. It was calculated that being mumbled at for several years would by some mysterious process turn you into an enlightened and pious Jew.

In our neighbourhood we struck it exceptionally hard with the Rabbi. He was one of the few genuine and conscientious of the breed. We considered this our misfortune. [. . .]

[. . .] We called [our rabbi] "Squinty" presumably on account of the thick, black-rimmed, enormous glasses he wore. Behind them his glare was ferocious. [. . .]

He had rented a small, disused workshop as his *Kheder.* It was in the back-yard of a crowded tenement house, and next door to the lavatory, whose door strangers often mistook for the *Kheder* door—and vice versa. We sat on wooden forms, our books resting on plain wooden desks in front of our eyes, faced by Squinty in a chair when he took the boys individually, and standing when he conducted the chanting. A cigarette never left his mouth. He puffed at it furiously through a long cigarette-holder. Sometimes we could see only his eyes gleaming at us out of a smoke screen. [. . .]

That was the kind of despotism religion was. It no doubt explains the large-scale reduction in piety amongst the new generation of adult Jews today. Religion for us is bound up with memories of stuffy cellars, perpetual beatings and a brutal curbing of our childish instincts. When you left the *Kheder* after your *Barmitzvah* at the age of thirteen it took you exactly one week to forget all you had learned. The *Kheder*, constituted as it was, proved itself to be a first-class training ground for future atheists. [. . .]

CHAPTER 3—EDUCATION

The *Kheder* was, after all, only the counterpart to school. The method of disseminating culture was identical in both: it was based on the superiority of the cane to the text-book. Each was a miniature model of an Empire out-post. [. . .]

There were more than three hundred of us in the Big Boys' section. The quota was roughly sixty to a classroom, and the number gave us confidence, if no particular academic advantage. We were all out to harass the man in front. [. . .]

The discipline was undiscerning: all were regarded as future offenders from the very first moment of entering the place. That settled one's private waverings: for the only consistent thing to do after being treated as a ruffian was to do your best to earn the title. [. . .]

There was scarcely a teacher in the school under middle age. One suspected they had spent the early part of their lives qualifying for the post as prison-warders. [. . .]

In our school, as in most strictly-controlled institutions, a great deal of bullying went on unchecked among the scholars themselves. It was impossible for a youngster to avoid being a victim of it. An older boy would bear down on you during play-time, thrust his face into yours and inquire, "Wan' a fight?" The natural retort of "Why?" wasn't accepted as a legitimate one; it would land you in a fight whether you wanted one or not. If you said yes the same consequence followed. Only by a direct no could you escape with a few short and contemptuous blows and the slur of cowardice. For many it was the more unpleasant alternative.

The playground at school therefore, was a kind of miniature jungle where the large animals hunted the small.

Willy Goldman, *East End My Cradle* (1940; London: Robson Books, 1988), pp. 23–30.

PARIS

The Warsaw Burial Society

The Jewish immigrant mutual-aid societies in Paris (registered with the French authorities) often provided medical or burial benefits for their members. These societies were organized among trade groups or according to place of origin, as in the Warsaw Burial Society whose bylaws are excerpted here. (The bylaws were printed in French and Yiddish. The two versions do not exactly correspond; the following is translated from the Yiddish.)

The Aims of the Society

Article 15. In case of death, the surviving wife (widow) or husband (widower) has the right to receive from the society 3 (three) francs a day during the 8-day period of mourning.

Article 16. When a comrade (member) dies, the entire society will be called upon by letter to accompany the funeral of the deceased to the cemetery.

Article 17. Any member who does not attend the funeral of a deceased member, or who does not accompany the body to the cemetery, will be fined from two to five francs.

Article 18. A quorum of ten men will go to worship at the home of the deceased every day, morning and evening, during the eight days of mourning.

Article 19. On the anniversary of the death of a member, the *el male rachamim* prayer will be recited for his soul in the presence of at least ten members. The president will appoint them on the condition that those members who are coming to say kaddish inform the president three days in advance.

Société de Chevré Kadischa de Varsovie, *Statuts* (Paris:
Imprimerie Zouckermann, 1895), pp. 8–11.

Immigrant Philanthropy: For Work and Lodging

Beyond self-help, the more settled immigrants sought to help others, their less fortunate brethren. The first philanthropic organization by and for immigrant Jews was founded in 1886 (Société de bienfaisance et d'humanité). In 1893, the Prévoyante israélite was created to help newcomers find work and learn French. The most important organization was the Asile israélite de Paris, founded in 1900 to provide lodging for immigrants upon arrival.

The Prudent Israelite

SOCIETY TO AID JEWS THROUGH WORK

Natives of Russia, Poland, and Romania

A certain number of Jews coming from Russia, Poland, and Romania, concerned with the lot of their compatriots and coreligionists in need and mindful not to let them fall into a state of irrevocable poverty, dependent upon charitable organizations and individuals, have resolved to form a society whose goal is to assist these persons through work.

In order to be able to accomplish this task more efficiently, the society will undertake, either on its own behalf or through the intermediary of people having relatives in their native countries, to advise against all rash movement of emigration, especially in periods of economic crisis.

Chapter I: Activity of the Society

Art. 1: The society will help Jewish workers, natives of Russia, Poland, and Romania, to earn a living through honorable work:

a) by finding them work;
b) by facilitating their acquisition of tools and necessary instruments;
c) by contributing to their technical or general education.

> La Prévoyante israélite, *Statuts* (Paris: Imprimerie D. Cemenoff, 1893).

The [Israelite] Community of Paris, however rich in charitable works, did not have the one charity that would have given a temporary hospitality to misfortunate immigrants, that would allow them to learn to orient themselves in the labyrinth of the capital. We are happy to say without false modesty that we have filled this gap. [. . .] Certainly, Paris does not lack institutions that take care of the poor. But we have wanted to practice the kind of hospitality that our fathers practiced, the kind we saw practiced in our countries of origin. We, who know the troubles of the pauper in a foreign country where he does not know the language and where he has neither friend nor acquaintance; we who have all more or less passed through this critical period, it is for us to raise the banner of hospitality and to carry it high. [. . .] We have thus wanted to come to their aid in offering them a refuge, a home where they will be considered not as beggars, but as injured brothers whose bleeding wounds command and invite respect.

> Société philanthropique de l'Asile israélite de Paris, *Rapport et exercice, 1905–1906*, pp. 14–15.

The Federation of Immigrant Societies

Various immigrant societies joined together in 1926 to create the Fédéra-tion des sociétés juives de France (FSJF), as called for in the following excerpt. The Jewish Communists later formed a rival organization, the Union des sociétés juives de France, in 1938. The FSJF was mocked by the Bundist newspaper (see the second excerpt) as the federation of the dead, because one of its principal activities was the acquisition of funeral vaults in Parisian cemeteries.

Federation

The Jew has carried his old attributes of charity and compassion with him to all the lands in which he has wandered. But along with this Jewish quality of mercy, he has also carried his old concern for offices and honors.

Every little group of Jews establishes its own little society with its own officers, honors, and distinctions.

At first, this is quite natural. The Jew who arrives in a strange land is attracted to his compatriots. The Jew from Pinsk feels more at home among Pinsker than among Keshenover. So he forms a bond with them. This, in turn, evolves into an association, union, or society, where they gather to pass the time or carry out communal obligations. [. . .]

Our national awakening of recent years has brought the most disparate parts of our people in contact with one another. Jews of every land, East and West, Tunisia and Yemen, have met up with each other. The Jews of one city, therefore, cannot and must not remain fragmented.

Let every *landsmanshaft* have its own internal organization with its president and vice-presidents. There must, however, be a point around which all of the *landsmanshaftn* and societies are united in one great social force.

A federation must be created for that purpose.

Sh. Y. Yatzkin

Parizer haynt, February 11, 1926.

The Federation of Corpses

Every Jewish family is actually a small republic, and the whole Jewish people—a federation of several million republics.

By their nature, these republics carry on a bitter competition with one another. Each is ready to drown the other in a teaspoon of water.

There are three things, however, around which they form federations:

They like to be sick together.

They pray to the Lord for a good year together.

And, they must be dead and buried together.

Lying six-feet-under together has become a historical tradition among Jews. If it were not for this, I do not know whether the Jews would still exist as a people at all. [. . .]

So the Jews of Paris have united in order to organize funerals for one another.

The Jewish societies grew on this foundation, and the societies became a federation.

A federation of lively corpses.

A great communal cemetery.

But life is stronger than death. [. . .]

The "members" do not even share a common language. One speaks a Yiddish French, another a French Yiddish. A third uses a mixture of the two.

To play cards, you do not need a society. Neither is one necessary in order to eat gefilte fish or dumplings. Every Jew can take of himself with regard to these things.

But the grave holds the members, and honor holds the president. Honor is an old Jewish weakness. In the old days, they used to have fistfights over the honor of reading a juicy Torah portion or having a seat along the eastern wall of the synagogue, for a synagogue office or for saying the prayer as the Torah scroll was taken out of the ark. Now, it is the president's chair that they buy and sell, fight over, and inform on each other for. And who knows how long this would have gone on?

Jews would have done business, played cards, and gone to the movies. They would have eaten gefilte fish and dumplings, butter cookies on Shvues and hamantashen on Purim. Their children would have gone to "ekl" [*école,* school in French] and an *ekl* [disgust in Yiddish] for their own homes would have gone in them. And everything would have been quiet and peaceful. [. . .]

So they flirted a little here and they flirted a little there. And the whole lot of communal leaders joined the federation. They joined with great fanfare. And before they knew it, the same thing had happened with them as had happened with Hindenburg in Germany. Instead of a revolution against Baron Rothschild, the people brought in their own Baron Ginzburg from Petersburg, together with a couple of monarchists and a Petersburg rabbi. In a word, it was a real Gypsy switcheroo. Instead of a baron with money, a baron without. [. . .] All the societies and all the presidents have nothing but contempt for it.

So it was all going along perfectly nicely and perfectly well, when a great historical event intervened.

A new society of communal leaders without a community arose in Paris.

Jewish social workers are actually quite used to being without a society. Jewish charity associations are, after all, a democracy with forced dictatorship. [. . .]

And now the moral of the federation for the left:

You cannot build children's homes among tombstones.

No one has yet brought corpses to life.

Democratic Jewish communal leaders in the committees have never even seen democracy face to face. They are only really leaders where there is no community, but only a few individuals.

And if the left still has any pulse at all, it should stay away from the federation.

Who does not know the old Jewish legend that when the dead call a living person up to the Torah in the synagogue after midnight, he will not live out the year.

This legend has symbolic meaning.

Der veker (The Wakening), June 11, 1932.

The Immigrant Press

Some of the immigrant societies had reading rooms where immigrants could catch up on news from Russia, Poland, England, and America. The Yiddish press appeared in Paris, as elsewhere, almost as soon as the immigrants themselves. Some 130 Yiddish periodicals (literary magazines, general interest and political newspapers) were published in France in the interwar period. The most important of these were the Zionist daily, Parizer haynt, *the Communist daily,* Naye prese, *and the Bundist* Unzer shtime. *The following excerpt comes from* Der idisher arbayter, *a pre–World War I monthly and the organ of the Jewish union sections of the French labor movement, the Confédération Générale du Travail.*

Jewish Workers of Paris!!!

All you who were driven or thrown out of your homes, or who fled on your own:

All you Jewish workers, men and women, who hope to earn your scrap of bread through labor here in a foreign land:

All you who are exploited in the Parisian workshops:

To all of you we appeal. [. . .]

When we Jewish workers arrive here in Paris, we are completely unfamiliar with the way of life and the methods of struggle of the local French proletariat.

We know that it once made great revolutions, including the great French Revolution itself. We know that it had a Commune, and that it spilled rivers of its own blood for the liberation of the working class. And at first glance, we are surprised at its current way of life.

But only at first glance.

The worker must live, struggle, and think differently, he must have an entirely different psychology, when he lives under constant political pressure, in a place where everything is forbidden, where a heavy hand lies on top of everything. Life and struggle are different in places where one is to a certain extent free.

The life and thought of the settled and cautious man of habit are different from those of one who is capable of igniting at any moment, who carries within him a fire ready to flare up, but who meanwhile enjoys the freedoms that his father and grandfather succeeded in winning.

This is in order to acquaint you with the life of the French proletariat and to explain it to you; and to acquaint the French proletariat with your life.

To acquaint you with all of its established means of struggle.

To acquaint you with the situation of the French capitalists as they and all of their political and economic institutions have accommodated themselves to all of this.

This is the task of *The Jewish Worker,* whose first issue we present to you. [. . .]

Read The Jewish Worker

Our only wish in presenting this first issue to you is that *The Jewish Worker* become a genuine guide to the Jewish worker and a shining reflection of his life.

Der idisher arbayter, first issue, October 9, 1911.

Youth Organizations

The young were one of the largest concerns of Jewish immigrants and the object of many organizations within the various societies. In 1926, a student proposed the creation of an organization of Jewish students. But, in this domain as in others, with politics came divisions. The Bundists then created their own youth movement, the SKIF (Socialistisher Kinder Yidisher Farband).

To the Jewish Students of Paris

A Letter to the Editor

The new academic year is under way along with student life. Groups, parties, circles, guilds, aid societies, etc., are all being formed. Only in one area is there deathly silence: in the Jewish student community. [. . .]

If the Jewish students were not so splintered and divided into parties, factions, *landsmanshaftn,* and language groups, and if they were only to create a common body, it would at least be able to serve as a lively protest. It would constitute a bitter cry, perhaps the bitterest cry that Jewish Paris, where the greatest number of Jewish students is concentrated, has ever heard. Maybe then, its hard-baked heart would be moved.

Such a united and inclusive body would provide a corner where comrades and friends could gather to find consolation in common worries and shared loneliness. They would then find fate easier to bear and not lose the courage to live and achieve.

Now, after a couple of years of pieced-together "student associations," we have learned to recognize the obstacles that lie in our way. We can therefore easily avoid them. The direction is evident. The most unqualified condition for our honorable and cooperative existence is now clear to us. It is a common language, Yiddish, so that the members can come to an understanding with one another. In other words, an "Association of Jewish Students from East Europe."

Parizer haynt, November 1, 1926.

SKIF Activities in Paris

SKIF made its first public appearance this school year at the anniversary banquet of the Bund. SKIF distinguished itself with its new songs, and the greeting conveyed by a member was received enthusiastically by the older comrades. The banquet expressed our attachment to our mother party— the Bund.

Three weeks ago, SKIF organized a talk, with 150 slides, by Comrade Kalmen on the international Red Falcon encampment at Ostend.

The ceremony marking the affiliation of SKIF with the Red Falcons took place at the hall of the Mutualité on Sunday, November 5th.

Comrades Pierre and Georges Manet, general secretary of the Red Falcons, greeted SKIF on its affiliation and [hailed the] cooperation of the French and Jewish worker children. After them, Comrade Kalmen explained the nature of SKIF. He pointed out our international character, and our unquenchable hatred for the Jewish bourgeoisie and world capitalism. Comrade Kalmen described our origins in the "Little Bund," and our devotion to the revolutionary party of the Jewish worker, the Bund. He ended with the assurance that the members of SKIF would prove themselves good, proud Red Falcons, precisely because they remain good and proud members of SKIF. In the name of all members of SKIF, Comrade Kalmen called out, "Long live SKIF! Long live the Red Falcons!" He conveyed our feelings of friendship [*amitié*] and comradeship to the Red Falcons, who answered with three shouts in French of *"Amitié!"* The members of SKIF, in turn, answered with our "happy" greeting in Yiddish:

"Khavershaft, khavershaft, khavershaft.
Frish, fray, shtark, tray.
Khavershaft!"
[Comradeship, comradeship, comradeship. Fresh, free, strong, true.
Comradeship!]

Der veker, November 18, 1933.

BUENOS AIRES
Landsmanshaftn

The first associations of landsmanshaftn in Buenos Aires were created on the eve of World War I: the Austro-Hungarian Society in 1913, the Polish Society in 1915, and the Bessarabian Society in 1916. As their names indicate, the first associations did not limit their membership to immigrants from the same city or region but were defined by country. In the interwar period, their numbers multiplied until there were over 120 societies by 1931.

The Hometown Societies

I.

It should be noted that a whole series of hometown societies have been formed in the course of the last few months. These include various societies of Polish Jews, Lithuanian Jews, and Bessarabian Jews, as well as of natives of Zhitomir, Podolia, and the "four provinces." Others are now still in the womb and will undoubtedly be born sooner or later so as not to shame certain parts of the Russian map.

Are these societies an unavoidable consequence of definite needs? It is very doubtful that this is the case. At best, they are a manifestation of a cultural level that is not terribly high.

Let us take a look, first of all, at how these societies came into being.

It was reported that up in North America there existed such things as "hometown associations," and that bit of news made it necessary to form such societies here as well. And so, the first society of this sort was formed, and another followed its example. This motivated others of our *paisanos,* who are just as good as anybody else (others do it, so why can't they?), to imitate the first ones, and they also founded hometown societies.

There is no evident internal impetus here, no independent consciousness. The first society was formed because of a report; the second took after the first; the third took after the first two, and so on.

Nevertheless, there is a certain point to the creation and existence of these societies. Or, rather, the communal leaders provide the hometown societies with a point. The societies have a point in that they actually organize the masses who are still too scared to join any organization that has a specific outlook and definite principles and goals. Organization in the societies must weaken this fear and serve, in many cases, as a spur to communal involvement. From this standpoint, the hometown societies are justified, but it still confirms my point that this phenomenon indicates a low level of cultural development, because a cultured public has no need for such remedies. We live here among other nationalities that have less of an interest than we Jews in settling into the new country and making it our home. Nevertheless, organizations like our hometown societies are not to be found among them.

Having established this fact, we will now see whether the hometown societies, in the form in which they were established, can attract the ordinary Jew who is afraid to join an ideological organization. Can this form of society create a critical enough mass to "socialize" the 70 or 80 percent of the Jewish collectivity that is splintered, and whose backwardness kills any sign of life in the Jewish movements, holding back the flow of modern currents? Can this sort of hometown society create a beginners' school for communal affairs, as many of their defenders maintain?

> P. Wald, "Di landslayt fareynen," *Der avangard*, no. 11 (November 1916), pp. 31–35.

Di prese

The first newspapers published in Yiddish in Buenos Aires date to the last decade of the nineteenth century, but the real growth in the daily Yiddish press came in the 1910s. Der tog appeared in 1914, followed by Di idishe tsaytung. *While the former only lasted until 1916, a conflict split apart* Di idishe tsaytung *in 1917. Part of the editorial board left and launched the daily* Di prese, *which became, along with* Di idishe tsaytung, *the main Jewish newspaper in Buenos Aires for half a century.* Di prese *was a fervent supporter of the Jewish workers' movement. In addition, more than fifty-four workers' newspapers in Yiddish were published in Buenos Aires between 1905 and 1940.*

Bosses and Workers

A strike broke out at *Di idishe tsaytung* in the second half of 1917. Bosses, no matter how progressive or "friendly," are still bosses. They exploited the idealism of the typesetters and writers (Y. Helfman and me), who worked day and night, without rest, for a miserable wage. As soon as we demanded that they introduce an eight-hour workday, or, otherwise, open the books to us, they hired strikebreakers and gave us the option of leaving our jobs.

The sympathies of the Jewish population were once again tested, and they were completely on the side of the idealistic workers and journalists. We then published five issues of a strike newspaper, *Di naye tsaytung*, which was printed at the press of Lemitshevski and Rabinovich. And, although *Di idishe tsaytung* continued to appear with the help of strikebreakers, we received a message from the bosses as we were preparing the sixth issue of *Di naye tsaytung* saying that they were giving in to all of our demands. These were signed that very evening at the printers' union, the Federación Gráfica Bonaerense. The appearance of *Di naye tsaytung* was literally a holiday in Argentina. The several issues that appeared radiated freshness, character, spirit, and combativeness, and the cessation *of Di naye tsaytung* was rightly regretted by the whole Jewish population.

The bosses surrendered, apparently, because they were afraid that *Di naye tsaytung* would become established and compete with *Di idishe tsaytung*. But, as it later turned out, they also intended to get rid of the organized workers and contributors one by one. The first one of whom they undertook to rid themselves was this writer. In order to carry this out, M. Stoliar saw to it that my situation at the newspaper was made unbearable. For example, he used to walk by my desk with an angry boss's expression clouding his face, and look over my shoulder as I wrote. He forbade the printers from taking originals directly from me, and me from entering the print shop. This last measure was designed to weaken the sense of solidarity between the editorial staff and the printers. Earlier, he used to reproach me in a friendly manner for my familiar relationship with the printers, whom I used to address familiarly and intimately as "kids." I used to address several of them with the familiar form of "you." This measure failed, of course, because the writers and the printers would just meet somewhere else and talk—no longer in the familiar language of "kids," but in the language of commitment as "comrades." And it was in this language that my comrades promised me solidarity in case I was fired. [. . .]

COOPERATIVE

After I left, *Di idishe tsaytung* instituted a very strict regime. The bosses threw their weight around and the assistant editor apparently understood well why he had been hired.

"A chill has descended on *Di idishe tsaytung*," the typesetters used to complain. "The bosses and the new assistant editor look at us like wolves."

So when Comrade Ozer Bumazhni proposed the establishment of a cooperative of printers, editors, and managers to publish a daily Yiddish newspaper, the typesetters received the suggestion enthusiastically.

The establishment of the cooperative that publishes the now ten-year-old *Prese* is described elsewhere by its initiator, Comrade Ozer Bumazhni.

It is only necessary to add that our enthusiasm and our endurance during the difficult early years of *Di prese* did not only stem from the fact that our members, particularly those who had worked at *Di idishe tsaytung*, remembered the chill there and wolfish way in which the bosses related to the workers. Mainly, they were the result of our shared sense of responsibility to the Jewish working class and the progressive Jewish public in Argentina in general. We could not leave them without a daily newspaper.

As we founded *Di prese*, we saw before our eyes the tremendous sympathy exhibited to us during the strike at *Di idishe tsaytung*, and the enthusiasm with which people received the five issues of *Di naye tsaytung*. This sympathy and enthusiasm on the part of the broad Jewish laboring masses still accompany us and are demonstrated at every opportunity.

P. Katz, "Tsen yor *Di prese*," *Di prese, yubiley numer, 1918–1928* (Buenos Aires: n.p., 1928), pp. 3–4.

The Communist Party's View of Community Organization

Renewed immigration after 1920 caused a rapid growth of the Jewish community of Buenos Aires. Among the new arrivals were those who had participated in revolutions in Central Europe. Jewish workers' institutions (political, labor, cultural, educational, sports) abounded. The Jewish section of the Argentinean Communist Party, the Idsektzie, created in 1921, grew. The report that follows gives us a glimpse into the Communist view of this world.

The Communist Party

ORGANIZATIONAL REPORT TO THE SECOND CITY
PARTY CONFERENCE

Among the laboring population there are many different institutions. But they are of ordinary scope, partly because most of them have only recently been founded, while the bourgeois institutions have already been active for decades, especially in the city. We will mention a few: The Right Po'alei Zion have neither their own newspaper nor any influence, and their leaders work with the Zionists. The Left Po'alei Zion maintain two rickety schools, but do not have any influence in the provinces (while the Right Po'alei Zion do). About a year and a half ago, the Bund was established here, but it devotes itself exclusively to collecting money for the Polish Bund. It opposes the Socialist Party because the latter is mostly supported by the local Right Po'alei Zion. It has no influence at all. There is also a writers' union of petit bourgeois nature that strives without success to influence the working masses.

The daily newspapers also constitute active institutions with influence and initiative. The daily *Di prese* has something of a predominance in the colony. It is petit bourgeois in nature, with sympathy for Soviet Russia. Its owners are former workers who belonged to left-wing organizations. But the newspaper is purely commercial. It has pretensions to being a "workers' cooperative," despite the fact that it is not one. This is an institution that profits only those who manage it.

In the cultural sphere, the workers have the following organizations: the worker's library in Villa Crespo, with nearly 150 members, led by party members, already in existence for fourteen years; the worker's library named for A. Vayter in Paternal with close to 100 members, eight years in existence. It is led by Communists and red syndicalists; the I. L. Peretz Library, which was under Zionist influence until a year ago, and is now led by nonpartisan workers.

The Central Workers' Library has been in existence for twenty years, but is now in a state of financial bankruptcy thanks to the negligent management of elements that have been excluded from the Party; the Free Library led by the Left Po'alei Zion and some anarchists, with little influence. Several other libraries have just been founded in Belgrano, Floresta, and Villa Alsina by nonpartisan workers of the recent immigration. They are very weak. There is also a dramatic-musical organization called *Frayhayt* [Freedom]. The expelled elements, recognizing the poor condition of the central library, claim to be merging the two institutions in order to save both from collapse.

In the course of the last four years, the following workers' schools have been founded: the first worker school in Villa Crespo has 650 members, three teachers, and special evening courses for older children and adult workers. Altogether, up to 250 students and auditors attend classes at the school. The Communists have an absolute influence there. Both the directors and the teachers are Communists or sympathizers. The second workers' school, in Paternal, counts up to about 100 students and visitors. The management of the school is in the hands of Party members and sympathizers. The first school has been in existence for four years, the second for two and a half. When the saboteur elements in the Jewish Section were expelled from the Party, they took it upon themselves to create new institutions in order to gain leadership. These are the following: the first school in Villa Crespo, organized three months ago with the aim of competing with the already existing school and wrecking it; the third worker school in the center of town, organized four months ago. They have about seventy members, are in quite a bad condition, and do not have even the slightest influence. They also had a fourth school in Floresta, but it closed because of its bad economic condition. It never had more than about fifty children. The last three named schools made up the Workers' School Council, which the schools under our influence left. This institution is now in a very shaky condition, about to disappear.

In the area of relief are the following institutions: the "Procor" (Proletarian Relief Committee for the Jewish Immigrant Colonists in Russia), composed of delegates from sixteen proletarian institutions. The executive committee of Procor is composed mostly of Communists. There are branches in almost all of the provinces and colonies where there are Jews. There is also a branch in Rio de Janeiro, with sections in a number of cities in that republic. Concerning the work of this institution, it is sufficient to note that in the course of its one and a half years of existence, it has sent twelve thousand pesos to Russia. In addition, there is the Polish committee of MOPR,[5] in which our comrades are active. Some time ago there was a Committee to Aid Political Prisoners in Poland with eighty members led by the elements that have been excluded from the Party. Recently, the majority of members decided to join MOPR, so the Committee is on the verge of dissolution.

In the area of trade unions, the following organizations exist: the tailors' union, with five hundred members, under the leadership and influence of the Communists; the hatmakers' union, sixty members under the leadership of the elements excluded from the Party, recently on the verge of dissolution due to their negligent leadership; the Jewish bakers' union, with eighty members, led by independent and nonpartisan elements; and the most recently formed union, that of the parquet workers, with seventy workers, under the leadership of Communists and sympathizers. These four unions are affiliated with the USA [Unión Sindical Argentine]. There are also language sections in the unions, including a Yiddish committee in the furniture workers' union, influencing an estimated eight hundred to one thousand members, under the leadership of Party members, sympathizers, and red syndicalists. It carries on various cultural activities, maintaining a Yiddish library with an educational and class character and a special children's section, and publishing a Yiddish periodical with a circulation of one thousand copies. The Yiddish sections of the metal, shoe, and textile workers' unions have either been dissolved or are half disorganized.

These are the institutions that are generally considered active among the workers of the local Jewish colony, and more or less the activity that each pursues. It remains only to say that Communist work needs to be broadened much more in order to have significant success.

Komunistishe partey, "Organizatsions barikht tsu der tsveyter
shtotisher partey-konferents," *Royter shtern*,
August 21, 1926, p. 3.

Secular Schools

The first proposals for Jewish secular education were raised during the Jewish Culture Congress convened in 1915 by various workers' groups. The resolutions led to different attempts to create schools or night classes. In addition to the anarchists' efforts described in the next extract, the Left Po'alei Zion created the Folks-Shuln and the Borojov-Shuln, and the Communists set up their Arbeter-Shuln, referred to in the previous text.

On the History of Jewish Secular Pedagogy in Argentina

The program of the "Workers' Federation," founded in 1909, included the establishment of rationalist schools. The cultural conference held at La Plata in 1915 adopted a similar resolution. In practice, however, this was hard to carry out. There were still few Socialist families in Jewish Argentina. Luis Mas once said at that time that the initiative to build schools would never be realized because "workers do not have children." This statement struck us as funny at the time, but the truth is that Mas's words contained an element of truth despite their imprecision.

It was the Jewish Rationalist Society, founded September 13, 1916, that approached the matter in a practical, rather than theoretical, way. It began with a Sunday school, which was founded at the beginning of 1917. The teachers were A. Botvinik, Sojolov, and Y. Goroditzky. The goal of the society, however, was not a supplemental school, but a well-established rationalistic day school in Yiddish. It was a very ambitious aim, and the society sought the support of all progressive Jewish parties. It also sought to further prepare the soil for this undertaking among the Jewish masses. The Rationalist Society carried on a lively campaign for years. Five propaganda pamphlets were published,* which in itself was quite an accomplishment in Jewish Buenos Aires at the time. These were distributed in editions of between two and three thousand copies. Dozens of conferences were organized in various locations. The goal was to build a school on about a hectare of land in the vicinity of Villa Urquiza, so that the parents would be able to put their children on the tram, and the school personnel would be waiting for them when they got off. One must remember that at that time there

---

*By Jean Grave, Federico Urales, Elslander, Anmitsh, and Sébastien Faure. [Footnote in original document.]

were no such things as school buses. Such a project required some time to realize. In the meantime, interest in the work had to be maintained. From this necessity arose the initiative at the beginning of 1918 to create a kind of temporary modern school. In order not to detract from the goal of a firmly established rational school, the teachers Y. Goroditzky and A. Botvinik accepted responsibility for the temporary school. At that time, the bitter and barren fanaticism later introduced by the Bolsheviks was unknown. We were not all saints then either, thank God. But narrow-minded, exclusive partisanship had not yet reached such absurd levels. The initiative was therefore received very warmly. An example of this was the editorial that appeared in *Di prese* on May 23, 1918, under the headline, "For Jewish Children." We reprint it here:

> And speaking about our life here as Jews, we cannot overlook a homegrown national Jewish project being carried out by the Jewish Rationalist Society. So that the readers know what we are talking about, we print the announcement as it was sent to us by the society. We will leave commentary for another occasion.
>
> Daily Yiddish classes for children of both sexes will begin in June of this year at the offices of the Jewish Rationalist Society, Lavalle 2346, under the direction of the teachers, Y. Gorodisky and A. Botvinik. The curriculum is as follows: 1. a) Yiddish conversation, reading, and writing; b) Yiddish grammar and literature; c) Jewish history; d) Spoken Hebrew for older children; 2. Spanish instruction. The Jewish courses will aim to instill in the children a feeling of affection for the Yiddish language, and to enable them to express themselves freely in the same.
>
> "Tsu der geshikhte fun idish-veltlekhn shulvezn in Argentine,"
> *Dos fraye vort,* no. 39, May 1941, p. 4.

Organizing against Anti-Semitism in the 1930s

After the coup d'etat of 1930 and the coming to power of the Nazis, anti-Semitic propaganda began to spread in Argentina. There were attacks, boycotts against Jewish businesses, and graffiti on walls. The community responded by organizing itself. In March 1933, one meeting in Buenos Aires brought together 30,000 people. Two main groups took the initiative: the Committee against the Persecutions of Jews in Germany, supported by community institutions and dominated by Zionist groups; and the People's Committee against Anti-Semitism, organized by the Communists. The first gave birth to the DAIA (Delegación de Asociaciones Israelitas Argentina, the present central organization of the Jewish community in Argentina); the second led to the creation of the Argentinean League against Racism and Anti-Semitism. The following resolutions were drawn up at the first congress of the league.

Resolution on the Report of Activities of the People's Committee

The national convention of the People's Committee, meeting in Buenos Aires on May 11–14, 1934, having heard the report of the completed work of the People's Committee, resolves:

1. That in the course of its existence up to the time of the congress, the People's Committee has oriented itself toward and worked in the direction of anti-fascist struggle, explaining to the Jewish popular masses the true reasons for fascism and anti-Semitism.

2. The People's Committee has exposed the treachery of the Zionist Persecutions Committee, which has betrayed the vital interests of the Jewish masses in Germany, who stand together with the German masses in a bloody struggle against the Hitlerite beasts.

The congress approves the report and expresses its fullest recognition to the central committee for its untiring work in spreading the word in both speech and print.

3. The Jewish popular masses in Argentina, in their struggle against fascism and anti-Semitism, strive to join with the popular masses of other nationalities to carry on a common struggle against fascism and anti-Semitism, and for their right to live and create in this country.

4. The congress maintains that an orientation toward emigration to Palestine, where the Jewish masses suffer the same consequences as in all Fascist countries, creates false illusions among the Jewish popular masses, and dulls their sense of the necessity for struggle against fascism and anti-Semitism.

5. In order to reinforce our work, it is necessary to work together with the entire population. The congress calls on the Jewish working masses, peasants, ordinary people, professionals, and intellectuals to join the organization and to transform it into a mighty weapon against fascism and anti-Semitism.

Folks organizatsie kegn antisemitizm, *Fir yor kamf kegn antisemitizm* (Buenos Aires: Alerta, December 1937), ch. 2.

GERMANY

Landsmanshaftn and Clubs in Berlin

Even in Germany, where they did not concentrate in immigrant quarters, Jewish immigrants from Eastern Europe managed to form self-help societies, which were usually connected to an immigrant synagogue.

The Eastern European Jewish Organizations

Over the years, the Eastern European Jews who have become permanent residents have come into close contact with the native Jewish middle class. All of the mutual-aid societies, trade associations, B'nai B'rith lodges, and Masonic lodges include Eastern European Jewish members. Nevertheless, a group of exclusively Eastern European Jewish organizations has also developed and maintained itself. It is based mainly on religious and charity principles. In the *chevras* [societies], the religious principle is the only basis for the solidarity of the members. The task they set themselves is "the performance of religious services on weekdays, on Saturdays, and on all Jewish holidays in their own prayer rooms." On Eastern European Jewish streets there are a large number of these "rooms" [*Stuben*]. The services held by the different *chevras* show some variation, since Hasidic influences play a greater or lesser role in some of them. The members of these religious groups are mainly Galicians, but there are sometimes individual members from other areas. These *chevras* do not actually engage in club social activities, which are therefore all the more intense in the mutual-aid societies. Each individual group has its brotherhood and its lodges. In these clubs, Galicians, Russians, and Romanians are separate from one another, although the divisions are not strict. The Russian lodge, for example, also has members from Galicia. But it is stated in the bylaws that, for example, the president, the treasurer, and six board members of the Romanian club must be Romanian. Political biases are strictly forbidden in these organizations, and they do not differ in their principles. The purpose of each and every one of them is "to provide members with free medical care and medication, to visit sick members, to pay the last respects to members who have died, to speak the morning and evening prayers in the house of mourning during the seven days of grieving, and to aid and counsel members and nonmembers from their homeland in cases where statutes prevent other organizations from helping." The philanthropic functions of the clubs are directed by four medical supervisors [*Krankenväter*] and two trustees who inform the club officers when help is needed. Members who have belonged to the club for at least two years receive support in emergency situations. A "permanent fund" is set up for this purpose, and a quarter of all club income normally goes to this fund.

Along with the philanthropic functions, the lodges cultivate intensively the sense of community of their members. The families of the lodge brothers also become friends and meet regularly. The lodge officers take part officially in all the family celebrations within the lodge circle and are thought of as belonging to the family.

The Eastern European Jewish organizations are naturally quite small in Berlin. Probably no lodge has more than three hundred members. But club life is so intense that these small country-specific groups can maintain their Eastern European Jewish character among the numerous Jewish organizations.

In this connection we should also mention the Jewish People's Home [*Volksheim*] on Dragonerstraße, even though it was not founded by Eastern European Jews. A large majority of the people who frequent the home, especially recently, are immigrants from the East. "Based on the settlement-house system, the Jewish People's Home performs social service work in the health and economic sectors; in addition, it has set itself the task of uniting the children and young people who live in the streets surrounding the home (mainly populated by Eastern European Jewish families) in community organizations such as kindergartens, youth groups, and clubs. In this way, and with appropriate leadership, the home hopes to have a cultural influence on coming generations."

> Klara Eschelbacher, "Die ostjüdische Einwanderungsbevölkerung der Stadt Berlin," *Zeitschrift für Demographie und Statistik der Juden*, no. 1–3 (1923), pp. 17–18.

Welfare and Transmigration

In early 1918, a number of Jewish societies set up the Eastern Jewish Workers' Welfare Office, the Arbeiterfürsorgeamt der jüdischen Organisationen Deutschlands, which came to play an important role in the transmigration of newcomers. The demand for foreign labor led to the establishment of a Duisburg offshoot of the Berlin office, in October 1919, and then similar centers in Cologne and Bochum in 1920. The foremost tasks, wrote Heinrich Glaser, head of the Duisburg Jüdisches Arbeiterfürsorgeamt, were to "get the masses of refugees [. . .] off the street" and "take them abroad," while "finding work for those not yet fit to emigrate." The center urged the appropriate consulates to issue passports to the Jewish workers in order to reduce the number of those who were stateless.

Foreigners in Germany

The Workers' Welfare Office writes us:

> A very interesting news story, clearly government-inspired, appeared in most German newspapers a few days ago. The story claimed that some 250,000 to 300,000 Russian emigrants are presently living in Germany, nearly all having crossed the border illegally as refugees. Although such large numbers of Russian refugees are clearly unwelcome in Germany,

the report continues, practical considerations make it impossible to deport them at this time.

This story is especially interesting in light of more precise data obtained by the "Workers' Welfare Office of the Jewish Organizations of Germany," indicating that about 55,000 to 60,000 Eastern European Jewish refugees are still in Germany at this time. This figure includes everyone who arrived in Germany between August 1, 1914 (i.e., the outbreak of the war), and January 1, 1922, in particular those who were brought to Germany during the war as workers, at the instigation of the military high command. One should take into account the fact that the total number of Jewish refugees was significantly higher. Through the hard work of the Workers' Welfare Office, the lead agency for the larger German-Jewish organizations, it was possible to help about 50,000 of the Jewish refugees to go on to countries accepting immigrants.

Thus the anti-Semitic propaganda claiming that Eastern European Jews are flooding Germany has no basis in fact. It is clear that Eastern European Jewish immigrants make up only a small percentage of the overall foreign immigration, especially if one considers that the above-mentioned figure of 250,000 to 300,000 Russian refugees includes neither the numerous refugees from other Eastern European countries presently residing in Germany nor the foreigners from other regions. The figure of 55,000 Eastern European Jewish immigrants, on the other hand, includes people coming from Polish, Galician, and Hungarian regions.

Jüdische Rundschau, no. 3, January 10, 1922.

The Jewish Employment Office in Duisburg

The following report by Werner Fraustädter (1894–1962) describes the work of the Jüdisches Arbeitsamt in Duisburg. A German Jew, Fraustädter was director of this Jewish Employment Office in 1919–20. From 1923 on, he became editor-in-chief of various Po'alei Zion weekly newspapers: Jüdische Arbeiterstimme, Unzere bavegung (in Yiddish), and Der neue Weg; from 1927 to 1933, he was director of legal services at the Jewish Workers' Welfare Office in Berlin.

It is only with a certain hesitation that we can speak of the growth and increasing importance of the Duisburg Employment Office, for this growth reminds us of the mass migration of the Jewish people; of the immanent economic collapse of Polish Jewry; and of the unrelenting political, social, and national pressure which bears down upon the majority of our people. On the other hand, it is also a sign of the growing trust that Jewish workers have for the Duisburg Jewish Employment Office.

The Duisburg Employment Office has many tasks, but its main purpose is to find positions for Jewish workers in Rhineland-Westphalian industry. Because of the increasing numbers of Jewish workers coming through Germany, the office's previous practice of "opportunistic" job placement has become impractical and has been abandoned in favor of a systematic approach: open positions are found by sending advertisements to companies seeking workers and by cooperating closely with the public employment services. This method also helps distribute the Jewish workers evenly over the entire industrial region—now more than ever the crowding of masses of Jewish workers into one location is to be avoided. The attitude of the employment services toward us has been, with a few exceptions, friendly, since the Jewish Employment Office is often able to help when there is a temporary shortage of workers.

Inseparably linked to the employment service is a comprehensive welfare system. This resembles old Jewish philanthropy on the surface but actually serves as a replacement for unemployment insurance payments, to which Jewish workers are not entitled. It is an inadequate replacement, since our resources are not sufficient to protect the Jewish people from all the terrible effects of poverty. Homeless and penniless after suffering terrible hardships, these people have but a single goal: to get work and earn at least enough to survive. The Jewish Employment Office gives unemployed persons small amounts to cover minimal living costs, travel to the place of employment, and passport photographs, always with the understanding that the money must be repaid later. In Duisburg the Employment Office has taken upon itself all of the burdens imposed by the transmigration of Eastern European Jews, including medical care for the sick and the cost of hospital treatment. It has thus taken over many of the responsibilities that should actually be borne by the Jewish religious community. The Employment Office has encountered serious difficulties in its efforts to find housing for workers in transit. [. . .]

One source of problems for Jewish workers is that their identity papers are not in order. In cooperation with the local police, the Duisburg Employment Office now issues temporary identity certificates to workers who can present proof of acceptance by an employer. The police have made these certificates the prerequisite for issuing official identification papers. The Employment Office is thus offering a very important form of assistance to people desiring to work, and more and more are taking advantage of it, including some non-Jewish foreigners, especially Germans with Polish citizenship. The authorities do not deport people from Rhineland-Westphalia without first checking with the Employment Office—another effective way it helps hard-working, deserving Eastern European Jews.

The Duisburg Employment Office is maintained through contributions from Jewish communities in Rhineland-Westphalia; unfortunately these contributions have been very limited. This shows that neither Western European Jews nor the Eastern European Jews who have grown rich in Germany as yet understand what an important and beneficial institution of Jewish life the Employment Office has become.

Jüdischer Bote vom Rhein (Bonn), no. 43, March 26, 1920.

The Yiddish Press

The leading organization of the Eastern European Jewish workers' cultural movement in Germany was the social-democratic Zionist workers' party Po'alei Zion. Between 1921 and 1923, besides the German-language Jüdische Arbeiterstimme *(1921–22), the Po'alei Zion published a Yiddish literary-political weekly newspaper named* Unzere bavegung.

To the Jewish Workers in Germany

We consider it our duty to call the attention of all foreign Jewish workers in German to two extraordinarily important laws which were adopted by the administration and are already in effect. We are talking about the law that the [Prussian] state labor ministry has published concerning the employment of foreign workers in Germany, as well as the law concerning identification cards [*legitimatsies* in Yiddish; i.e., work permits, *Arbeiter-Legitimationskarte*] for foreign workers in Prussia, which has been published by the Prussian interior ministry. These laws are of decisive importance for all foreign workers. Anyone who does not take them into consideration must expect most severe consequences. [. . .]

According to the two orders, foreign workers are divided into two groups. Different regulations apply to each group. We will consider them in order. Find out which group you belong to, and pay attention to the regulations that apply to it.

I

The first group consists of all those who arrived in Germany before January 1, 1919, and have worked as wage-workers (except commercial and office workers). The same regulations—which we will delineate below—also concern agricultural workers who arrived in Germany before January 1, 1913, and have worked in agriculture. [. . .]

IIA

All foreign workers who began to work in German industry only after January 1, 1919, belong to the second group. All agricultural workers who began to work in Germany after January 1, 1913, also belong to this group. THE MAJORITY OF FOREIGN JEWISH WORKERS WHO ARE NOW IN GERMANY BELONG TO THIS GROUP, because one must take into account that this group also includes those who worked in German industry before January 1, 1919, or German agriculture before January 1, 1913, but in the meantime left Germany and only later returned. The only thing that matters is the last time one came to Germany. If it was after January 1, 1919, one comes under the following regulations as an industrial worker. If one is a farm worker and arrived after January 1, 1913, these regulations are also applicable. [. . .]

IIB

Acquiring permission to employ you is the employer's matter. As someone who belongs to the second group, you must also personally acquire AN IDENTIFICATION CARD. Without this identification card, you will later have no opportunity to remain in Germany or find work. You or your employer may request this identification card from the local police. CONCERNING THE FEE WHICH, ACCORDING TO THE LAW, MUST BE BORNE BY THE EMPLOYER, GO TO THE EMPLOYMENT BUREAU for help and advice. THE CARD COSTS 2,000 MARKS. At that time, one must show last year's worker identification card, a valid passport, or personal documentation. For those workers who did not receive the previous year's worker identification card, the cost is 5,000 marks instead of 2,000.

Certain exceptions are foreseeable, particularly for so-called workers of GERMAN HERITAGE. Therefore, any of you who ATTENDED A GERMAN SCHOOL, or who come from a GERMAN-SPEAKING AREA, especially in the former Austria, should report immediately to one of the employment bureaus, so that they may help you.

One must request an identification card from the local police by FEBRUARY 15. Otherwise it will be more expensive and both the worker and the employer will meet with great difficulties. [. . .]

III

All those foreign workers who are just now starting a job in Germany—regardless of whether they have just entered the country or had different employment earlier—must report to an employment bureau, because only on the basis of designation as exceptions can they receive an identification card, and thereby the right to work for companies with permission to hire foreigners. To the extent that you belong to this group, report immediately to an employment bureau.

In general, we can only advise all workers to inform themselves precisely concerning the two new ordinances at an employment bureau, in order to avoid the danger of great damage due to misunderstanding and lateness. Moreover, when you receive an identity card, change your position, or want to work in a new occupation, and the designations are not completely clear, report immediately to an employment bureau. If you cannot report in person, do so in writing.

We ask all Jewish workers who read these regulations to inform their acquaintances and friends about them. We emphasize once again that it is in your own interest to adhere to the regulations. If any foreign Jewish worker loses his job because of these regulations; if anyone is thrown out because he does not have a worker's identification card; or if anyone has other difficulties because of this new law, he should report to an employment bureau for advice and assistance. You may be certain that we will try to help you to the best of our ability.

> Worker Employment Bureau of the Jewish
> Organizations in Germany

> *Unzere bavegung*, no. 1/2, January 25, 1923.

AMSTERDAM

The Joodsche Invalide (Jewish Invalids' Hospital)

In the following letter, published in the moderate Zionist newspaper Nieuw Israelitisch Weekblad, *Meyer de Hond, the rabbi of the poor, defended the importance of a separate institution for elderly and invalid Jews. His argument was part of a polemic with those who doubted the need for a special Jewish home and who argued that there was already a poor-house where Jews too could go. The Joodsche Invalide ultimately became a model institution of social and medical aid, but de Hond quit its board shortly after it was set up, criticizing, as he often did, the practical outcome of his ideas.*

Now, your beginning.

"It is a praiseworthy Jewish principle not to judge anybody before he has been heard."

I am not criticizing you for not being well-acquainted with this Jewish proverb. You probably mean the following: ". . . Do not judge your (Jewish) neighbor until you have been in his situation."

I *am* in the situation of my *Jewish* neighbor, yes, even in yours. We—because my "I" has little to do with it—we are the Welfare Board, directors of the Jewish poor, the sick, the elderly, the mentally and physically hand-icapped, inside and *outside* institutions, albeit on a *small scale.* Yes, no matter how inadequately this goes on, we are practicing practical psychology and psychiatry in the large Amsterdam Jewish community.

Furthermore, we even share in your function as *cook;* we tally and calculate what beans and peas cost. *Jewish* soup with *Jewish* soup bones, or without, or soup bones without soup, or no soup at all, or no bones at all (which of course simplifies the bill); yes, honest to God, doctor, we are *now* for the first time truly feeling what an overwhelming task rests on your shoulders, for *one* person—as you are—who makes the effort to perform his task according to duty and conscience, nearly to succumb to it.

Medical Superintendent of the Hospital and of the Mental Hospital, director of the OL hospital [well-known early twentieth-century hospital located in a neighborhood where many Jews lived], First Chef of a kitchen offering a varied [kosher] menu and then, too, your private psychiatric practice, no, no. We do not need to hear *you* out first to know that *what you do* is duteous, and I do accept that our demand might be a little extreme: on top of *all of this* and *all of that* to expect *Jewish* feelings and *Jewish* thinking of you. I refer hereby to my motto.

But still, even *you* do something *Jewish.* You write expressly about "De Joodsche Invalide" [the Jewish invalid]: an ambition I admire very greatly, *because I am fully acquainted with the needs of these poor devils.*

Please understand, you sympathize officially with our cause, you as representative of the Welfare Board, among whom there are members to be found who, albeit off the record, have made their *strong antipathy* known. (Why?) Fine. Fine, a *Jewish* handshake for that, doctor!!! I suspect that you are writing here on your *own behalf,* for according to your superiors *en bloc* you should *not* have expressed this frank sympathy.

Now, to move ahead: You criticize me for speaking "unfavorably" of the food that is offered by the kitchen of the institution and letting these "unfavorable" words ["]be reprinted in January 1912."

I will permit myself to tie on another sentence from your response:

"One cannot judge tastes. What is pleasant to one is found to be unpalatable by others."

In the institutions in your charge the food is good, fine, but now for the "other side." It cannot be expected that you would stand over the cauldron to see what gets passed out here, much less someone from the Welfare Board. So you do not know if sometimes the "bottom of the pot" or *burned* kugel gets passed out here and that it is the *only* meal, even on the Sabbath afternoon or holiday. Note well: the *only meal.* Now I am going to be a little finicky. From the nature of the stuff I do not like the "bottom of the pot" (you, either, who would?), nor hard, cold kugel (I will simply translate baked matter). And as for the cooling down of the food, you are not to be blamed, or that there is sometimes a layer of congealed fat over the brown beans because they are frozen before they are "dished up," I do not blame you (see motto). If *I* have real soup first and meat after, I will sometimes tuck into burned-to-the-bottom kugel, myself.

But, doctor, if it is your only meal, on holidays also (Yom Tov in Jewish speech), the last meal before *fasting for twenty-four hours* and in addition if you are in that situation, in which you get caught if you are so stupid as to be poor and starving, not dead, now, what and how? You are a physician and psychiatrist, do you think this is good for the body and soul of "wretches"?

Dishware you say is provided by *you*.

What do you mean? Certainly the cauldron in which your "single course" is brought over here? Because the "Invalid" provided plates, etc. after one of the supervisors (a Christian) had declared, and we had seen, that the plates that were there were so shabby ["]that he would not have served his dog on one." This is written in the brochure and has not been contested by you, either.

Now I ask you: if you get bread twice a day (did I mention that there isn't any natural butter on it?) and once a day *a single course* that in "running its course" does indeed get cold and stiff and is often unpalatable and hard, cold kugel is harder than warm kugel, particularly when toothless folks of eighty and ninety have to flim-flam cram this down on their Sabbath. Now then, I cannot speak "flavorably" of the menu, even if I do not do it "unfavorably" right away. But, see my motto. [. . .]

[. . .] You claim that 15, to wit (fifteen) individuals were indicated by the inspector to be invalids for whom the city would henceforth no longer pay ninety cents a day, but *half* of that, room and board, etc. included. But no one managed to maintain those *fifteen* people on their own, they were brought like old rags and bones to the dump and among them were very proper wretches whose only crime had been that they remained proper their entire lives. To the "other side" was your typical answer when you had "cleaning up" to do. But did you know, doctor, that those old rags and bones were picked up because there is still value in them? And we did that because we were so backward as to express our sympathy with Jewish "wretches" not just "formally" in words. We discovered still some quality of life, Jewish quality of life, in frayed simple folk. And when we could permit ourselves, we wondered naughtily (say, doctor, is that indicative of psychological deviance?) if we can *do that with three-cent* little men, what wouldn't three-guilder men be capable of? But who is ever interested in the "other side"? [. . .]

Yes, Doctor, in your institutions a great satisfaction prevails regarding your food. And outside on the "other side"? Well, if YOU were to ask them: "Say, men and women, do you have any complaints about the food?" then you would be psychologist enough to understand that those demoralized old folks would answer you with "no."

Nieuw Israelitisch Weekblad (New Israelite Weekly),
January 26, 1912.

The Joodsche Invalide became well known in non-Jewish circles through its use of media in fundraising. Even the prime minister devoted a radio speech to the hospital.

Disabled Workers and. . . "The Jewish Invalid"!

Two questions immediately loom in your mind. You see in the first instance an apparent contradiction between the words *worker* and *invalid*. But promptly the next question already comes up, whereby the emphasis falls on the word *disabled:* are there not, in De Joodsche Invalide, many disabled to be found whose ability to work until now has been limited due to their disability?

See, when you answer this second question correctly, then it is necessarily clear to you what De Joodsche Invalide is and what it has brought about in the relatively short time of its existence. And to describe, summarily, who "the Jewish invalid" is, we will quote the words from a number of years ago by Mr. P. H. Ritter, Jr., written in the *Utrechtsche Dagblad* [Utrecht Daily]. He gave this definition:

Who is "the Jewish invalid"?—That is the snapped, broken, socially downcast Jewish person, who cannot work anymore on account of an incurable physical ailment, who has no money and no strength and no roof, because not a single hospital offers him the possibility of care. Is that not true? Hospitals are for those who want to become healthy . . . or for those who will die, but someone who is maimed by Nature or struck by paralysis, who has to stumble on with an incurable ailment—he wanders through the world and finds no home.

Yes, in fact, he does find a home. There is the other "Jewish Invalid,"—this is an association that reaches out its hand to the disconsolate, that has erected a building in Amsterdam to take them in—to take in, first of all, the absolutely destitute invalids. . . [. . .]

A graphic presentation clearly shows the visitors to the exhibit in the "Stand," which was kindly placed at our disposal by the Conference Board, how these patients slowly but surely showed improvement. And a chart hanging nearby speaks a clear language. How many applications have not come in over the past seven years! Each plea more tragic than the next, including pleas for speedy, foremost speedy, admission. After the first House a second, yes a third, came into being. But this was all only a preparation for the inauguration of the first large Central Institution for Jewish Invalids, not only in the Netherlands, but also in many countries in the world where Jews live, the very first.

But despite this, despite the increasing capacity for admissions which, thanks to large sacrifices by many who offered their support, could be achieved, the number of those who, as their last, yes perhaps their primary hope for happiness in life, wished to become residents of the large building on the Nieuwe Achtergracht 98, has kept growing. [. . .]

We can divide those who have found admission to the Central Institution for Jewish Invalids into three categories. There are those who have been deprived of the light of day. There are those who are physically maimed. And there are also adults who are retarded.

Disabled workers!

There lies, sequestered in a sickbed, one who for years cared for others in this country and abroad. But for fifteen years already her body refuses her any and all service.

There is a female chief editor of one of the largest fashion magazines in Amsterdam, who has become needful of total care due to Paralysis Agitans.

There is one Dutch-Jewish woman of sixty-eight, formerly residing in America. But because the light faded from her eyes, she had to leave the land of promise.

There is one given care who served the French Opera for fifty years as a soloist, but, unfortunately felled by a stroke, had to be admitted into The Jewish Invalid.

But there is also a boy of nineteen who can barely talk because he became totally paralyzed by the age of eleven.

And finally, not to continue with this dreary list, there is a young man of twenty-five, whose parents found a long-awaited place of rest in America following years of misery endured in Eastern Europe, who will never be able to share the house there with his parents, his arm and leg being partially paralyzed. For America does not admit invalids!

De Joodsche Invalide (The Jewish Invalid), brochure, circa 1928, pp. 5–10.

Jewish Religious Schools Questionnaire

In March 1895, there were 2,123 pupils enrolled at the Jewish schools in Amsterdam. The schools were free, since most of the students could not pay. The following is an excerpt of the annual report for that year.

Report on the State of Dutch-Israelite Religious Schooling in Amsterdam for the Year 1895

Question No. 1: How large is the Israelite population?
a. number of families? b. number of souls?
Answer: Circa 51,000 souls in the community; circa 10,000 families
Question No. 2: How large is the number of those who receive public assistance or who are incapacitated?
a. families? b. souls?
Answer: Permanently on public assistance: 6,300; Temporarily Id. [on public assistance] 5,900. [. . .]
Question No. 6: Is instruction given on the Sabbath also, or are lectures given to the advanced students?
Answer: From 11–12 o'clock
Question No. 7: Is repeat instruction given to former students? If yes, on which days and at which hours?
Answer: No
Question No. 8: How old must children be to be admitted? And to which age are they kept at school?
Answer: 6 years; 14 years
Question No. 9: What are the days on which and hours at which social studies instruction is given at the public schools?
Answer: On each weekday from 8:30–11:30 and from 1:30–4 o'clock. Morning only Wednesday. Two highest sections 2 times per week from 5–7 o'clock.
Question No. 10: Do *all* students go to the public schools?
Answer: Yes
Question No. 11: Are children from the religious school also excluded on grounds of nonpayment by their parents of their church tax?
Answer: At the Poor Schools there are no children whose parents pay church tax. [. . .]
Question No. 24: What is done to encourage faithful school attendance?
Answer: Clothing is offered to the children

Question No. 25: Is there also an annual prize presentation? If yes, what is the manner of reward for the diligent and faithfully attending?
Answer: Following completion of the annual home economics exam, prizes consisting of books and baked goods are awarded to those children.
Amsterdam Municipal Archives.

Train 828 (The 8:28 Train) for Poor Children

The famous Train 828, set up for sick children, was part of a Socialist-sponsored municipal initiative. A debate ensued over providing kosher food and with regard to the special needs of Jewish children versus the idea of a mixed facility. In 1925, a strictly kosher house was opened in Den Dolder to replace the train.

You are no doubt familiar with The 8:28 Train, a foundation that has made it its goal to send frail, pretubercular children, who must exchange city air for fresh outdoor air, to its holiday camp lodge. Among these children there have also been Jewish ones; an independent institution sending out Jewish children, in particular, did not yet exist. Of course, the rabbinate stood up for Jewish interests and attempted to have The 8:28 Train offer kosher food and the possibility of observing Jewish ceremonies. This was approved, although in practice not much came to pass.

Complaints were heard from various sides about the ritual etc., with the result that some prominent people from among the Jewish orthodoxy started to gain an interest in the matter. Initially they did not want to set up a new, independent, Jewish association, but wanted instead to reach an agreement with The 8:28 Train which would guarantee that the Jewish children would receive kosher food and would be able to observe their religious ceremonies properly and without hindrance.

As a result of this, the Chief Rabbi had a meeting with the daily staff of The 8:28 Train. It turned out, however, that this 8:28 Train was not an express train. No progress could be detected. They were strung along and in the end cooperation was refused. The 8:28 Train did promise to bear the responsibility for kosher food, although no additional favors were to be expected.

The staff of The 8:28 Train did not, however, enjoy rabbinical confidence, so that the Chief Rabbi was unable to guarantee the kashrut. Many parents, who were keen on their children not circulating anywhere but in a religious

Jewish setting, were put in a grave predicament by this. But, as good Jews, they did not stand by with idle hands, but rather laid them on the plow.

In February 1925 a temporary board was set up to organize an independent Jewish association which would take upon itself the task of sending out frail, pretubercular Jewish children, who would be cared for and looked after in accordance with the laws of our religion. This association was founded in the meeting of March 15, 1925, whereby the Chief Rabbi, the Honorable A. S. Onderwijzer, was named honorary chairman and Rabbi L. Sarlouis was named chairman.

Already on April 19, the Jewish Forest Camp—the name given to the association—was started with its sympathetic work of sending out eight children; this number rose on April 26 to forty. Every six weeks forty poor children are sent out.

This is fine Jewish community social work, a job that indeed fully deserves our respect. And that this work attempts to provide a solution for an urgent need is proven by the number of applications. At the moment, there are two hundred children waiting to be sent to the camp lodge in Den Dolder.

Is it not a pity that this large number of waiting little pallid faces must be disappointed? *Pas d'argent, pas de Suisses!* [No money, no mercenaries!]

Di Vrijdagavond, January 8, 1926.

The Jewish Library

In the mid-1930s, two journalists, Joseph Gompers and Fré Cohen (who was also a designer), wrote a report about Jewish life in Amsterdam. They described charity institutions, libraries, children's nurseries, and all that they saw and considered to be Jewish.

Wandering through Little Jerusalem
by Joseph Gompers and Fré Cohen

XIV. THE JEWISH LIBRARY

The Jewish Library is certainly the youngest of the large number of Jewish cultural institutions that Amsterdam has. It should therefore not come as any surprise that this young institution found its home in the heart of modern Amsterdam, in the Amsterdam-South district, namely on Coöperatiehof, the quiet square in the beautiful working-class neighborhood with which the name of the late Mayor Tellegen will forever be connected.

Undoubtedly there are important cultural centers of Jewish-Amsterdam that have longer-standing rights to being reviewed in this series of articles. They will not be forgotten, but they must surrender their rights of seniority this time to the young Jewish Library, because it has proven in the short time of its existence to provide for a great need.

The Jewish Library was founded in January 1933. [. . .]

The Association of Public Reading Rooms accepted these stipulations, and it was decided to house the Jewish Library in the Public Reading Room in Coöperatiehof. The decision to bring the collection there proved from the outset to have been a good one. From the very beginning this new Jewish library enjoyed great interest. Thanks to the excellent leadership of Miss Strooban, librarian of this reading room, visitors receive exactly the reading material that interests them. The library is regularly visited by unemployed Jews who, with the aid of modern textbooks, familiarize themselves with modern Hebrew. In addition, members of various Jewish youth organizations make grateful use of this library.

Mister J. M. Hillesum, the former curator of the Bibliotheca Rosenthaliana, holds office hours a few hours per week in the reading room, and he has already supported many in word and deed in order to show them the right path for their studies. The Jewish Library also makes grateful use of the counsel of Misters L. Hirschel, curator of the Bibliotheca Rosenthaliana, and J. S. da Silva Rosa, librarian of the Port. Israel. Ets Haim Seminary, who have been giving their advice regularly ever since the beginning. [. . .]

Those who remember the extraordinarily successful exhibit "The Illustrated Jewish Book," held under the auspices of the foundation in 1934 in the Stedelijk Museum in Amsterdam, will know how important the work of the Jewish Library is.

Although the number of consultations may be estimated at 2,500 per year and borrowings run into the thousands, the Jewish Library wishes in no way to be in competition with the previously existing public Jewish libraries. Those who wish to study Judaism strictly scientifically should turn to the Bibliotheca Rosenthaliana and the Ets Haim Library. But those who wish to refresh their knowledge of Judaica or who wish to form an opinion regarding Jewish problems and the Jewish way of life, will find sufficient material in the reading room on Coöperatiehof, which can be a stimulus to dig deeper into the rich soil of Jewish learning.

One should not forget that countless non-Jews also harbor a great interest at the moment in everything concerning the Jewish people and Judaism. Especially at the present, now that in certain printed media, from a specific quarter, attempts are made on a regular basis to turn popular sentiment against the Jews, it is of the greatest importance that, as a defense against the anti-Semitism no longer dormant in our country, sufficient facts are at the disposal of all who want to form their own opinion about Jews and things Jewish.

> Joseph Gompers and Fré Cohen, "Zwerftochten door Klein-Jeruzalem" (Wandering through Little Jerusalem) (Amsterdam: *Nieuw Israelietisch Weekblad*, 1935–36).

NOTES

1. *Der idisher arbayter* (Paris), July 4, 1914.
2. See especially Daniel Soyer, *Jewish Immigrant Associations and American Identity in New York, 1880–1939* (Cambridge, Mass.: Harvard University Press, 1997).
3. Jack Wertheimer, *Unwelcome Strangers: East European Jews in Imperial Germany* (New York: Oxford University Press, 1987), p. 119.
4. A *mil*, or *mill*, is one-thousandth of one dollar, or one-tenth of one cent.
5. International organization to aid revolutionaries, or "Red Aid."

Chapter 3   Politics and Ideology

Politics, as defined in its broadest sense—reaction to political events; grassroots strikes and sit-ins; and the founding of political organizations—played an important role in the Jewish workers' communities. From spontaneous strikes and boycotts to organized demonstrations, the Jewish workers protested their living and working conditions, very often against Jewish bosses.

The Jewish labor movement had several competing agendas in each city: those activists more interested in economic or political matters, those who argued for a specifically Jewish movement (particularly the cultural autonomy advocated by the Bundists), and those who felt the priority was to "walk hand in hand" with their local (non-Jewish) comrades. The Jewish labor movement was thus constructed both against a generic capitalism and against often identifiable Jewish factory and shop owners. It was also conceived of as a means of carving out a space within, or sometimes parallel to, the often circumspect native labor movement. The Jewish workers, along with other immigrants, also helped internationalize those national labor movements.

A Jewish left appeared in every country, in varying strength and with varying tendencies. One characteristic was true everywhere: the Jewish left was decidedly, and animatedly, divided within. There were anarchists and Socialists, Bundists and Communists, Zionists and assimilationists, not to mention diverse factions within each of these groups. The occasional anarchists of the deed drew attention to the specter of Jewish revolutionaries, while anarchists of the word theorized radical social change more quietly. Mensheviks kept up their debates with Bolsheviks as many diasporic disputes continued dialogues engaged before emigration from Russia. Zionists disagreed, divided between those who would settle for a Jewish homeland anywhere and those who would settle for nothing but Palestine. Even within labor Zionist circles, there were substantial divisions, particularly after 1905.

The Jewish left was also divided over language. Aaron Liebermann chose to agitate in Hebrew, and the first Jewish Socialist group, which he set up in London in 1876, was called the Agudat ha-Sozialistim ha-Ivrim, the Hebrew

Socialist Union. There were others who continued to publish in exile in Russian, and those—by far the more numerous—who chose Yiddish in order to "go to the masses." Still other activists used the language of the new land.

The Jewish labor movement changed over time and changed in relation to the country in which it was located. For many years the precocious English movement was more anarchist than socialist (and led by a non-Jewish German, Rudolf Rocker, who learned Yiddish for the cause). The Jews in New York voted Socialist before World War I, helping send Meyer London to Congress in 1914. But by the 1920s, they became increasingly committed to the Democratic Party. In 1940 and 1944, the Jews voted overwhelmingly (over 90 percent) for the Democratic ticket headed by Franklin D. Roosevelt. Many Jews were Bundists in France or Social Democrats in Amsterdam. In the interwar period, however, they were often attracted to the Communist Party everywhere it took hold. The Jews helped found the Communist Party in Argentina. Some of them joined the Party or became fellow travelers in the United States. There were pitched ideological battles between Bundists and Communists in Paris, and between Zionists and Communists in London. The Depression and the rise of fascism helped radicalize the Jewish workers all over Europe.

NEW YORK

Grassroots Protests

Politics often begin at home. Jewish immigrant women in New York led a kosher meat boycott (in 1902), two rent strikes (in 1904 and 1908), and two food riots to protest the rising cost of living (in 1907 and 1917). When the price of kosher meat rose from twelve to eighteen cents a pound in 1902, women of the Lower East Side, soon joined by others from the Jewish neighborhoods of Harlem and the Bronx, led mass meetings, door-to-door canvassing, and appeals at synagogues. A Ladies' Anti-Beef Trust Association coordinated the strike, although a rival, male-dominated organization usurped leadership after the boycott was well under way. The boycott received strong communal support from both orthodox and radical circles.

Bravo, Bravo Jewish Women

PIECES OF MEAT ALL OVER THE STREETS
Thousands and Thousands of Housewives Make a Revolution against the Meat-Racket—The Quarter Has Not Witnessed Such Scenes Since It Became Jewish—Clashes at Hundreds of Butcher Shops—Police Wagons Packed with Arrested Women—Butchers Forced to Close Stores

KEROSENE POURED ON MEAT

In all the 25 or 30 years since the Jewish quarter of New York began to be settled by Russian, Polish, Galician, Hungarian, and Romanian Jews, it has not witnessed such scenes as are taking place now. On dozens of streets, thousands of women clashed with butchers and their customers. Almost every housewife in every tenement throughout the Jewish quarter swore, with tears in her eyes and curses on her lips for the inflation in meat prices, not to buy meat. The women agitated for their ban and demanded that it be observed. In many places, butchers met the brave working-class women with blows. Fights arose. Meat was torn up, thrown in the ash cans, and doused with kerosene. In many places, horses trod on piles of discarded meat. It began on Monroe Street, near Pike. But within a half an hour, the fire spread from tenement to tenement, from block to block, and from street to street. By ten o'clock the entire Jewish quarter, from Cherry Street to Houston, and from the Grand Street Ferry to the Bowery, was aflame with courageous striking housewives.

Every sidewalk was packed with them. They stood in the hundreds, gesturing with their hands, shouting, bewailing their poverty, and cursing the racket against the poor people. Dozens of them were left bloodied in fights. Police wagons flew by continually, loaded with arrested women.

By ten o'clock, they had arrested 70 people, most of them women. They were treated very leniently by the courts. Several were released, and the rest were fined three dollars each.

The courageous women will hold a great mass meeting this evening at New Irving Hall, 218 Broome Street. [. . .]

MORE SCENES

At one location stands a butcher in a white apron. A woman walks by and shouts venomously: "Just look at him. Look at the thief in his apron!" And all the women began to shout and whistle. [. . .]

A SICK PERSON MAY EAT NON-KOSHER MEAT—SO SAYS ONE PIOUS JEWISH WOMAN

A woman bought a pound of meat from butcher Louis Glozman, 23 Essex Street. When she tried to leave, a crowd of women fell on her. "I have a sick husband. He must eat meat." "A sick person may eat non-kosher meat," responded an elderly woman in a wig.

Others said, "In the old country we made do with herring and bread. So now we can make do without meat."

THE POLICE

At first all of the policemen treated the women very sympathetically, and even protected them. Later, however, they became much more strict. One could see many members of the trusts at the station houses. [. . .]

SCENES IN COURT

"But we want to strike against the trusts. We are poor people."

"What do you know about trusts? It is none of your business."

"Whose business is it? Our pockets our empty. They are sucking our blood for nothing but bones."

"But it should make no difference to you what your neighbor eats, or whether or not she wants to pay high prices for meat," says the judge.

"It would not make any difference to me what she wanted to do, except that we have to suffer because of it."

"Three dollars!" said the judge. "Next."

Rebecca Ablovits of 420 Cherry Street was brought before the judge.

"Why did you riot?"

"Your honor," answered the woman, "We know our pain. We women see how skinny our children are, and how our husbands no longer have the strength to work, because others want to get rich from their toil. If all women followed us, they would not be able to drain the money we have earned with our blood in exchange for nothing but bones."

"But you must not riot in the street."

"We are not rioting. But if we sit at home and cry, no one will see. We must do something to help ourselves, after all."

"Three dollars!"

Annie Rozen of 419 Cherry Street said more or less the same thing.

Most characteristic was the women's attitude. They were not scared. They were self-confident that they were doing what needed to be done.

"Bravo, bravo idishe vayber," *Forverts* (Jewish Daily Forward),
May 15, 1902.

The "Great Revolt"

The period from 1909 to 1914 witnessed the "Great Revolt," a strike wave that rocked the Jewish immigrant community. Strikes by shirtwaist (blouse) makers in 1909–10, cloak makers in 1910, furriers in 1912, men's tailors in 1913, and others finally established the unions as powers to be reckoned with in the garment industry and other Jewish trades. The opening salvo was fired by the makers of ladies' shirtwaists in a strike that became known as the "Uprising of the 20,000." The hard-fought, some-

times violent, strike was eventually won by the strikers, most of them young, unmarried Jewish and Italian women. At the beginning of the strike, Clara Lemlich, a young Jewish worker and union activist, delivered an impromptu speech which galvanized the audience and became legendary.

Clara Lemlich, who was badly beaten up by thugs during the strike in the shop of Louis Leiserson, interrupted Jacob Panken just as he started to speak, saying: "I want to say a few words." Cries came from all parts of the hall, "Get up on the platform!" Willing hands lifted the frail little girl with flashing black eyes to the stage. And she said simply: "I have listened to all the speakers. I would not have further patience for talk, as I am one of those who feels and suffers from the things pictured. I move that we go on a general strike!"

As the tremulous voice of the girl died away, the audience rose en masse and cheered her to the echo. A grim sea of faces, with high purpose and resolve, they shouted and cheered the deliberation of war for living conditions hoarsely.

When Chairman Feigenbaum put Miss Lemlich's motion to a vote there was a resounding roar of ayes throughout the hall, and once again the vast crowd broke into roars of applause. The demonstration lasted several minutes.

> "30,000 Waist Makers Declare Big Strike," *The Call*, November 23, 1909 (the Socialist daily was overly optimistic in its count).

For five minutes, perhaps, the tumult continued; then the chairman, B. Feigenbaum, made himself heard and asked for a seconder of the resolution. Again the big audience leaped to its feet, everyone seconding. Carried off his feet by the emotional outburst, the chairman cried: "Do you mean faith? Will you take the old Jewish oath?" And up came two thousand hands, with the prayer: "If I turn traitor to the cause I now pledge, may this hand wither from the arm I now raise."

> Louis Levine, *The Women's Garment Workers* (New York: B. W. Huebsch, 1924), p. 154.

Socialism

Politics in the Lower East Side ran the gamut from anarchism to the Democratic Party in the period under study, but the overriding image of Jewish workers' political activity is bound up with the socialist left. Yiddish-speaking and (predominantly Jewish) Russian-speaking socialists organized branches of the Socialist Labor Party (SLP) in the late 1880s.

After the SLP split in the late 1890s, the Socialist Party of America became the premier party of American socialism. It ran the flamboyant Joseph Barondess for Congress in 1904 and Morris Hillquit in 1906 and 1908, and regularly garnered between 21 and 26 percent of the vote. Hillquit, born in Riga in 1870, became a major figure in the Socialist Party on a national level. In this "letter of acceptance" for his 1906 nomination, Hillquit speaks eloquently of the social needs of the Lower East Side, but, as a cosmopolitan socialist of the old school, he was generally uninterested in specifically Jewish concerns.

Our district covers a territory of only one square mile. But in this little piece of earth there is a population of over 200,000 souls. The population of this district leads a very sad life. They have little pleasure, little sunshine. The men are melancholy and worn out by worry and toil. The women are ragged, gloomy and depressed. The children are pale, sickly, and stunted. Everywhere, you see worn out, hungry, badly clothed men, women and children. [. . .]

The majority of citizens and residents of our district is composed of Russian immigrants. As loyal as they are to their new fatherland, they still love the country where they were born. They watch in great suspense the heroic struggle that is going on now in Russia against the despotic regime. They give their last pennies for their heroic compatriots, who are thrown into jail, sent into exile in Siberia, or murdered on the gallows. Their blood runs cold when they hear of how their fathers, mothers, brothers, and sisters are slaughtered by the thousands on orders from the murderous Russian officials. They hate and condemn the blood-thirsty oppressors of their old fatherland, the criminal inciters of the bloody pogroms. [. . .]

The representatives in Congress of the 9th congressional district have until now all been professional politicians, chosen by irresponsible political bosses. They have not at all understood the interests and the needs of the populace, or taken an interest in them. They were completely foreign to their lives, needs, and ideals.

Neither a Democrat nor a Republican can be the proper representative of the 9th congressional district. The district can only truly be represented in Congress by a convinced and outspoken Socialist. And, if elected, I will speak, act, and vote in Congress as such. And as such, I ask for the votes and support of all workers and all progressive, freedom-loving citizens of the district.

"Letter of acceptance of Morris Hillquit," 1906, United States
Territorial Collection, RG 117, YIVO Institute for Jewish Research.

Hillquit was unsuccessful, but the Jewish Socialists in America achieved their greatest victory in 1914 with the election of Meyer London to Congress, where he served three terms. Principal legal counsel for many of the garment unions in their recent epic battle, London was well known on the Lower East Side. Moreover, unlike Hillquit, London was an outspoken advocate of unrestricted immigration. London's election ushered in the short golden age of the Socialist Party in New York: for the next several years the party was able to elect several candidates from Jewish districts to the state assembly and the city board of aldermen.

Meyer London Goes to Congress!

By two o'clock there was no doubt that London had been elected. We conveyed this happy news in an extra edition. (The *Forward* published five "extras" yesterday.)

More than 10,000 people were then gathered outside the Forward Building. The crowd began to sing and dance for joy. People who did not even know each other hugged and kissed, their hearts united at that moment. One celebration, one ideal, united these strangers. Many had tears in their eyes—tears of joy.

STATEMENT BY CONGRESSMAN MEYER LONDON

I believe that we have good reason to celebrate the results of our struggle on the Lower East Side. The truth is that we have all sinned a little from a Socialist standpoint by concentrating our main energies on one candidate.

From the standpoint of Socialist propaganda, however, the Congress of the United States is the greatest platform from which to make the Socialist message heard.

Informed by his credo of social justice, the Socialist's concept of legislation is very different from the general concept.

Advancing his philosophy and doctrine on the floor of the Congress, the Socialist must force the lawmakers and all thinking elements in America to delve into the serious problems that touch the very foundations of the life of the people.

I still have much to say. But I am terribly exhausted. I will make a more detailed statement in a day or two.

Forverts (Jewish Daily Forward), November 4, 1914.

Communism

The Russian Revolution and the Soviet Union exercised a powerful attraction to many Jewish workers. Even moderate socialists such as Forward *editor Abraham Cahan and Socialist leader Morris Hillquit at first took a cautiously positive approach to the Bolshevik regime. The American Communist movement found a reservoir of potential support in the garment trades, where rank and file discontent over union leadership led to Communist control of the Dressmakers' Local 22 by 1923 and of the union's New York Joint Board two years later. The Communists' attempt to form a rival Needle Trades Workers' Industrial Union in 1929, however, lasted only several years before most of its members rejoined the International Ladies' Garment Workers' Union.*

Why Every Militant Needle Worker Should Be a Member of the Workers (Communist) Party

The needle workers have been the backbone of the revolutionary movement of New York City for many years. The Socialist Party has lost its working class and revolutionary character and has become nothing more or less than a party of petty bourgeois, professionals, labor bureaucrats and lawyers. It has renounced the class struggle. Its leaders, Sigman, Schlesinger, Beckerman and Hillquit have committed the most dastardly crimes against the working class, and have been exposed as the most treacherous betrayers of the labor movement. It is against the treachery and class collaboration policy of the socialist traitors that the new union is fighting its hardest battle. The needle workers know better than anyone what their policies have led to. It is these socialist officials who are mainly responsible for the reappearance of the sweatshop conditions, piecework, loss of job control and the revival on a much more aggravated form of the worst conditions known in the industry.

> "Why Every Militant Needle Worker Should Be a Member of the
> Workers (Communist) Party," leaflet, circa 1929,
> United States Territorial Collection, RG 117, YIVO Institute for
> Jewish Research.

The Hitler-Stalin Pact of August 1939 put American Communists, and Jewish Communists in particular, in a very uncomfortable position. The Jewish community felt betrayed and outraged. Faithful Jewish Communists were forced to put on the best face they could, arguing that the pact was actually a blow against Hitler. (Of course, after June 1941, when Germany invaded the USSR, the Communists became staunch advocates of the war effort.)

Is the Treaty Good for the Jews?

SEVERAL FACTS ABOUT THE SOVIET-GERMAN
NONAGGRESSION TREATY

Is it good for the Jews that the Fascist alliance has been shattered? Is it good for the Jews that Hitler has been weakened thanks to the treaty, as reported in the *New York Times* in two important dispatches, one from Paris and one from Warsaw, Saturday, August 26th? [. . .]

An agricultural exhibition is now taking place in Moscow. In this exhibition there is a Biro-Bidjan pavilion, where the work of the colonies (*kolvirtn*) in the Jewish autonomous region are on display. In this pavilion, Stalin's words are etched in golden letters: "Anti-Semitism is cannibalism."

This is Stalin's position on anti-Semitism. This is the position of the entire Soviet government on anti-Semitism.

Anti-Semites are swept away. Coughlinism is not possible in the Soviet Union. Jews fill the highest positions. A Jewish autonomous region is being built. Yiddish literature is flowering. [. . .]

In the interests of the Jewish popular masses, in the interests of the struggle against fascism and anti-Semitism—do not be fooled by the incitement and hysterics. LISTEN TO WHAT THE SOVIET SIDE HAS TO SAY. LISTEN TO WHAT THE COMMUNISTS ARE SAYING. DO NOT DEPEND ON WHAT OTHERS SAY IS THE SOVIET OR COMMUNIST POSITION. CHECK THE FACTS YOURSELVES! FIND OUT THE TRUTH! [. . .]

> New York Committee of the National Council of Jewish
> Communists

> "Iz der opmakh gut far yidn?" leaflet, 1939, United States
> Territorial Collection, RG 117, YIVO Institute for Jewish Research.

Zionism

Despite the existence of Hovevei Zion circles in the 1880s and 1890s and the founding of the Federation of American Zionists in 1898, Zionism in the United States remained a relatively weak movement before World War I, attacked by both upper-class assimilationists and immigrant Socialists. A turning point for American Zionism came when future Supreme Court Justice Louis Brandeis assumed leadership of the Zionist organization in 1914 and played a central role in identifying Zionism with American values. The Zionists had already grappled with the question of reconciling the movement with American patriotism.

A Cable to the Congress

PUBLIC SCHOOL GIRLS AND FLAGS OF ZION

The concert and mass meeting organized yesterday by the United Zionists at Cooper Union in honor of the 6th Zionist Congress in Basel was a great success.

The Great Hall of Cooper Union was crowded with ladies and gentlemen who came with one heart and mind—to send their blessings to the "Men of the Great Assembly" in Basel, and to wish them success in their great mission as representatives of the whole Jewish people, scattered and dispersed throughout the world. As representatives, they are charged with doing something important to take the Jews out of those countries where they are left powerless under the heavy yoke of exile and bring them to Mount Moriah, the place where God appeared to them for the first time and took them as his beloved people.

The great concert and mass meeting of the United Zionists of Greater New York was opened with a short speech by the president, Mr. J. Deitch, who introduced Dr. Moses Mintz as chairman of the evening.

Dr. Mintz explained the purpose of the gathering in a very successful speech on the theme, "Patriotism and Zionism." He argued that Jews can be the best American patriots and at the same time be devoted Zionists. After his speech, he read a copy of the cable that was later sent by the gathering to the Congress. After he read the cable there was such thunderous applause that it was impossible to quiet the audience for a quarter of an hour.

The members of the Flowers of Zion society then sang in chorus the Jewish national anthem, "Guardian of Israel."

The Flowers of Zion consist of pretty young girls who have finished public school and who are Americans in the street and Jews at home. They were a beautiful sight, these charming Jewish young women standing with the flags of Zion in their hands and singing the Jewish national anthem to the melody of "The Star Spangled Banner." Their singing elicited great applause from the audience.

"A keybl tsum kongres," [*Yidishes tageblat* ?], August 23, 1903,
United States Territorial Collection, RG 117, YIVO Institute for
Jewish Research.

Labor Zionism

Labor Zionism represented an attempt to synthesize the currents of international socialism and Jewish nationalism. The first Po'alei Zion group in

*America was founded by seven immigrant Jews in New York in March
1903. Over the years, the Labor Zionists participated in general Zionist
activities such as the Jewish National Fund (JNF) but also conducted independent campaigns for their own Palestine Workers' Fund. Their appeals
for the JNF were couched in terms of both class and national loyalty.*

The Jewish National Fund and the Jewish Working Masses

When it founded the Jewish National Fund (JNF) in 1901, the world Zionist movement laid the cornerstone for one of the most important bases for
securing the Land of Israel for the Jewish people. The fund serves as the
instrument for acquiring open land in the Land of Israel as property of the
Jewish people.

The basic principles of the JNF have appealed to the broad popular
masses, who form a large segment of the Jewish people. These masses long
for the Land of Israel and hope to see it rebuilt as a national home on the
basis of labor and social justice.

As of 1936, the Jewish National Fund has brought under its jurisdiction
more that 356,000 dunams [16,014 acres] of land. It has never received significant support from so-called Jewish big-money. It has always aimed its
fundraising efforts at the poor popular masses. They cannot contribute
large sums, but they can infuse their contributions with spirit, content, and
heartfelt devotion. [. . .]

The activities of the Jewish National Fund have so far been permeated
by the true ideals of socialism and the aspirations of the progressive laboring masses. [. . .] The fact that land bought by the JNF can never again be
sold to anyone, but remains the permanent property of the people, as well
as the fact that he who works the land also owns it [. . .]—the basic foundations and firm laws of working one's own land to avoid exploitation—
have made the fund the most important national and social instrument of
the Jewish people.

> L. S., "Der idisher natsional-fond un di idishe arbayter masen," in
> "Shtime fun idish-natsionaln arbeter farband," special section in
> *Der tog,* February 2, 1936.

Support for Roosevelt's New Deal

*By the 1920s, the Democratic Party became the dominant party among
New York's Jews, and their support for it reached a peak during the New
Deal when Franklin Roosevelt claimed over 90 percent of the Jewish vote.
Even most Jewish Socialists supported the president, as evidenced by this*

editorial from the Jewish Daily Forward. *Some New York Socialists and labor leaders formed the American Labor Party so that they could campaign for Roosevelt without entering the "bourgeois" parties.*

Be Prepared! Tomorrow Is the Big Day!

Workers! American citizens!

Tomorrow is finally the day. They call it Election Day. But make no mistake: It will not only be a day of elections, but a historic day of great and terrible warfare. True, there will be a festive air in the streets. Peace will reign in the cities. Nevertheless, this day will be counted among those that "shook the world." [. . .]

The magnates of America, the money bags, the aristocracy, the upper layers of our country, entered this campaign with a hatred and determination unprecedented in the history of America. Their hatred for Roosevelt burns so deeply that it has become a kind of social disease among them. That is what serious observers have said. Future generations will be amazed, say these observers. Scholars and psychologists will study it as a strange, rare form of hysteria, which attacked our "upper crust" in the days of Roosevelt. [. . .]

The love of the people set out to challenge this hatred. Roosevelt betrayed the upper classes in favor of the lower, in favor of the downtrodden and demeaned, the forgotten and exploited, in favor of humanity. And the people came to love him as only the people can.

And tomorrow the battle will be fought to the finish, the battle between the hatred of the moneyed class and the love of the people. Who will win? Who is stronger in America: the moneyed magnates or the people? [. . .]

The magnates in America are determined to make it their day of joy. They have mobilized millions in gold. They have conjured up the worst passions and awakened the lowest instincts. Fascism, Nazism, anti-Semitism, hatred of immigrants, lies, tricks, slanders, revilement of the finest and best. They have brought all of these to the struggle. And if they are successful, it will be the biggest blow to democracy since Hitler came to power!

This should not happen! This must not happen! This will not happen! Roosevelt must be reelected!

Every worker's vote must go to Roosevelt and only to Roosevelt. Every single vote. [. . .]

For years thousands of Jewish workers voted for the Socialist or Communist candidates out of principle. But this time, tomorrow, that principle must give way to a greater principle—together with all of the workers of America to reelect Roosevelt.

Forverts (Jewish Daily Forward), November 2, 1936.

Organizing against Nazism—Jewish Labor Committee

The Jewish Labor Committee (JLC) came into being in 1934 as a response to the rise of anti-Semitism and fascism in Europe. The JLC aided Jewish socialist and labor movements abroad and participated in a boycott of German goods. It also educated the American labor movement to the dangers of bigotry and anti-Semitism and enlisted its aid.

On Boycott Work

The boycott against the Hitler regime [. . .] has proven to be an effective tool in the struggle against the medieval conduct of Hitlerism, which spreads hate, national antagonism, war, and the suppression of national, political and economic freedoms.

The poor, almost catastrophic, condition of German finance and trade is a result of the boycott movement. Even the official leaders of German economic and financial life have admitted this.

Our slogan in daily life must be: Boycott German goods, German trade, and any contact with Germany! [. . .]

ON THE OLYMPIC GAMES

Taking into account that the main idea behind the international Olympic games is the creation of good will among peoples, as well as the highest level of sportsmanship, this convention states, as strongly as possible, its opinion that the current Hitler Germany has by its brutality and repression of national, religious, and racial groups, as well as by its crushing of all labor institutions and strongholds, and by its robbing the German masses of their political freedoms, demonstrated that the principle of sportsmanship is nonexistent under the Hitler regime. [. . .]

The convention resolves to devote all possible resources to agitation in order to demonstrate to the American sports world and general public opinion the importance of not participating in the Olympic games in Berlin, in accordance with the best principles of honorable American sportsmanship and democracy. [. . .]

A successful campaign in this area would be the biggest slap that the civilized world could give in the face of the Hitler gang.

> Resolutions of second convention of the Jewish Labor Committee,
> October 17, 1935, United States Territorial Collection, RG 117,
> YIVO Institute for Jewish Research.

LONDON

Strikes

After a successful strike in 1889, Jewish tailors in the East End of London held another mass strike in 1906 (as they would again in 1912) with the hope of abolishing "sweating." The strike came at the end of a successful period of organizing among Jewish workers by the English trade union, the Amalgamated Society of Tailors. But the strike also revealed divisions between the majority of the immigrants and the cautious approach of the English union.

The Tailors' Strike in the East End

[. . .]We therefore decided to call a large members' meeting and see what we could do.

Before the gathering even took place, the members passed a resolution to strike for better conditions. When the day of the meeting arrived (last Sunday) the enthusiasm of the tailor workers was immediately evident. By about 6:30, the Vunderland [Wonderland] Hall was already packed with our members. Everyone was waiting for the resolution. That everyone had come firmly decided was made clear when a certain speaker took the floor to express his opinion about the strike. Proudly, very proudly, he pronounced the words that he was against the strike. But this provoked a tremendous commotion. People shouted from all sides: "Get off the platform!" And the poor speaker had to get off.

It took several minutes to quiet the gathering, and the meeting proceeded in order, except when the officers of the executive committee took the floor. Generally, they did not come out openly against the strike, apparently because they were afraid of the same verdict. They only wanted to point out that the strike was not legal. But shouts of protest came from all sides.

On the other hand, it became very quiet when it was announced that the resolution would be read. It went as follows:

> This meeting of tailoring workers declares itself firmly determined not to return to work as long as the following demands are not met:

1) The shop should be recognized as a union shop;
2) Every shop must have a shop chairman, recognized by the master;
3) Piecework must be abolished and day work instituted;
4) The workday should be from 8 to 8, with an hour for dinner and half an hour for tea time;
5) Work should be distributed equally among the workers;
6) The master must give a week's notice and sufficient reason to the committee;
7) Humane treatment in the workshops.

When the chairman called out, "Who is in favor?" everyone enthusiastically raised his hand, shouting, "Long live the strike! Down with the sweating system! Long live the struggle!" Singing the Marseillaise, the inspired workers left the hall.

Der arbayter fraynd, June 15, 1906.

The politicization of Jewish immigrants, in London as elsewhere, often began on the shop floor. Simon Blumenfeld depicted an interwar strike over a new managerial speed-up plan called the Bedaux system.

And then, one Monday morning, the manager was waiting for them with a pile of blue cards. He explained the system. It was quite simple. Each operation became a unit. So much time was allowed for each unit, and there was a fixed price to be paid per unit, calculated from the old rates of wages. [. . .]

. . . MINUTES ALLOWED FOR TEA. WAITING FOR WORK. MINS. MINS. MINS. TOTAL. ANY OTHER REASON FOR STOPPAGE OF WORK. MINS. MINS. MINS. TOTAL DELAY . . . ODD JOBS—SPECIALS. MINS. MINS. . . . ALTERATIONS ON ACCOUNT OF WRONG WORK. GIVE NAME. (Phew! That was a hot one. If it meant anything, it meant spying on the others, sneaking, toadying to the manager!) MINS. MINS. MINS. TOTAL TIME ON ALTERATIONS. TOTAL TEA—DELAYS—ODD JOBS—ALTERATIONS. CLOCKED ON TIMECARD. MINUTES ON BONUS. UNITS EARNED. BONUS UNITS. VALUE PER HUNDRED. BONUS IN PENCE . . . CALCULATED BY . . . INSPECTED BY . . .

Columns, and columns, and columns. Yes, simple enough, if you'd been to Oxford or Cambridge, but not so easy if you'd spent all your life in workshops. STANDARD/MINS. AND UNITS + 60/MINS. ON BONUS . . .

[. . .] A presser held up his card in the air.

"They've made a mistake with mine. They've left no space for mother's maiden name, or fingerprints!"

The laughter rolled round the workshop. [. . .]

"And what shall I do with the card?" asked the presser.

"I told you what. Fill it up. You won't get paid otherwise!"

Very deliberately, Marks tore his card into little pieces, and with his strong fingers he forced open the manager's hand, and dropped the bits into his open palm.

"There! There's your card!" he said. "You know what you can do with it!"

The manager went livid. He brushed the pieces on to the floor. [. . .] Marks must go!

"All right then," shouted the voluble little presser, "if Marks goes, we all go!" [. . .]

[Alec jumped on a table.] He picked his hands above his head, and tore the blue card, and scattered the pieces in the air, and in a moment, the workroom was filled with fluttering blue flakes.

"Out! Out! All out against Bedaux!"

Simon Blumenfeld, *Jew Boy* (London: Lawrence and Wishart, 1986), pp. 216–21.

Difficult Relations with the English Labor Movement

In 1892, 1893, and 1895 the Trade Union Congress in Britain passed resolutions opposing immigration. Following the last of these a number of Jewish trade unions commissioned Joseph Finn, the secretary of the Mantle Makers' Union, to write a defense of the Jewish workers.

A Voice from the Aliens

ABOUT THE ANTI-ALIEN RESOLUTION OF THE CARDIFF TRADE UNION CONGRESS

We, the Jewish workers, have been spoken of as a blighting blister upon the English trades and workers, as men to whose hearts it is impossible to appeal, and were it not for us, the condition of the native worker would be much improved. He would have plenty of work, good wages, and what not. Well, let us look into facts [. . . .]

It is alledged [sic] that we are cutting down the wages of the English worker, and no proof is given in support of such an allegation. We on the other hand claim that English workers are reducing our wages and we will prove our claim.

That the ready-made clothing trade, the second class—made to order—tailoring trade, the mantle, waterproof clothing, cap, slipper, and cheap shoe trades have been created by the Jewish workers in this country—no one who knows anything about it will deny. Mr. Booth in his book "Life and Labour of the People," declares "That the ready-made clothing trade is not an invasion on the employment of the English tailor, but an industrial discovery." [. . .]

Not only are we engaged in trades which we have introduced, but we have to a very great extent provided work for the English workers. According to the report mentioned above, the Jewish workers that are employed in the boot and shoe trade are less than 1–1/2 per cent. of the total number of workers employed in that trade. The export of boots and shoes from the United Kingdom from the year 1873 till 1893 increased about 25 per cent. Taking into consideration that the Jewish products are mostly exported, and that their influx into the boot and shoe trade took place during that period, is it not reasonable to assume that the great increase in trade is to some extent due to them? [. . .]

When you, our English fellow workers, cry out so loud against our competition, while you fail to prove that it exists at all, when you call us a blighting blister, then what ought we to say to our English sister-slaves who are actually taking the bread out of our mouths by working for half the price, and are driving us out of the workshops which we have built up? Can they deny that they are making a mantle for a shilling, for which we have received two shillings? We feel their throat-cutting competition in every trade which we have created, and which they have stepped into. Those who investigate the subject readily admit it. Thus we read in the report of the Board of Trade the following statements:—"At present the Jews need only fear the competition with the English female labour." Again:—"In the machining department, where foreign men compete with English women, the latter are gaining ground on the former."

In view of the foregoing facts, we ask the impartial reader: Who is competing with whom, who is displacing whom—the Jew the English, or the English the Jew?

> Independent Tailors, Machinists, and Pressers'
> Union et al.
>
> Joseph Finn, *A Voice from the Aliens* (London: n.p., n.d.
> [circa 1896]), pp. 1, 3–6, 8.

Internal Dissension

Jewish trade unions were notoriously unstable; workers came together to fight strikes but only a minority of them continued the work of organization. Trade-union weakness was underpinned by the seasonality of the immigrant trades and the threat of unemployment.

From 1893 to 1895 I was secretary to the Mantle Makers' Union, and during that time I acquired some knowledge about the trade. I came in contact with most of the workmen, their masters, and some City firms. The number of workmen in this trade at that time was about 1,500; from 600 to 700 were organised; now the number of workmen in the trade is about double, but the number of organised about the same. The reason of the weakness of the organisation is partly due to the lack of efficient leaders and organisers—this holds good for all Jewish organisations—and partly to the intimacy between Jewish masters and men. The masters of to-day have been workers yesterday, and even strong and devout members of the Union, and many workmen of to-day will be masters to-morrow. Some, after having been masters and failed to succeed, become workmen again. This state of affairs will last so long as the trade will be in a transitory period, and until it will develop to the factory system proper, like the ready-made clothing trade developed in Leeds. A third reason for the weakness of the organisation is the antagonistic interests of the workmen themselves. The machiners and pressers are working by piece, the basters by week, the under presser is employed by the presser, and the plain machiner by the principal machiner. We have here five different working men, each one having a natural grudge against the other. The machiner works by piece, hence it is for his interest to hurry up. In order to keep pace with him the baster must hurry also, although it is not for his interest to do so, as he is working by the day. The presser has a grudge against the baster because the latter gives him the coat to press in a state not to his liking; for instance, the edges are not straight enough, the shape is not well worked out; the baster leaves those finishing touches to the presser, to which the latter objects, as he is working by the piece, and, therefore, objects to all labour which he considers not his duty to do. The plain machiners and under pressers have complaints against the chief machiners and head pressers. It therefore follows that when people are working under such conditions natural unity is impossible; they can be united artificially, so to say, when proper organisers and good speakers take them in hand, but these are at present lacking. I entered into these details to show how shallow are the reasonings of some people who, seeing that at times the Jewish Unions are weak, blame the character of the men for it. These philosophers did not take the trouble to study the matter in detail; they do not even know the secret, that some English Unions are strong, not because the English working man is of a more fraternal disposition, but because the trades they are engaged in have developed to the factory system proper, namely, large numbers of workmen are working under one roof, they are all working under one system—by the day or hour; they, therefore, have all one interest in common.

> Testimony of Mr. J. Finn, April 30, 1903, *Royal Commission on Alien Immigration*, pp. 732–33.

Socialists and Freethinkers: The Unemployed and Sweaters' Victims' Parade

The early Jewish socialists were in many cases freethinkers as well. They ascribed the poverty of the Jewish masses not only to capitalism but to ignorance, largely due to religion and the influence of the rabbis. To discredit the Chief Rabbi, Jewish socialists asked him to preach a sermon on the evils of "sweating" and unemployment. Correctly anticipating a refusal, they also organized a parade through the East End to the Great Synagogue. Philip Krantz and Benjamin Feigenbaum, two of the organizers, later became prominent figures in the Jewish socialist movement in New York.

The Synagogue Parade

THE MAGNIFICENT DEMONSTRATION OF THE
JEWISH UNEMPLOYED

That which even the committee of unemployed did not anticipate has happened! Two to three thousand (as even the English capitalist newspapers report) Jewish workers answered our call and came freely and openly before the entire world to call attention to their poverty and the inhumane exploitation of which they are the victims under the present robbery economy! [. . .]

The speaker explained to the crowd the purpose of such a procession and reported that a letter had arrived on Friday evening from the synagogue board inviting us to come to the synagogue, without music, to hear a sermon, not by Dr. Adler, but by a certain Meisels. "This, however, is not what we want. What can a ritual bath-house beggar tell us about the labor question? Has he ever held a hammer or a plane in his hand? (Thunderous bravo!) We will go to the synagogue and ask if Dr. Adler wants to speak to us. And when they answer 'no,' we will not go in, but march to Mile End waste [a waste ground where people often assembled], where we will hold a meeting and pass a resolution." Then he encouraged the crowd and instructed it to remain peaceful and calm. Stormy applause was the response. After Feigenbaum, the English comrade, Mowbray, spoke in the same vein.

Courage and emotion ruled the impatient waiting crowd. They waited just a little longer in order to arrive at the synagogue at just the right time.

At a quarter past one, the black banner, the banner of poverty and hunger appeared on the street. On one side, in large white letters, it read [in English],

JEWISH UNEMPLOYED AND SWEATERS' VICTIMS.

WORK AND BREAD

And on the other side, in Yiddish,

EVERYONE MUST WORK.

NO ONE SHOULD HAVE TO WORK TOO MUCH.

The band gave the first signal to march, and under the powerful tones of the Marseillaise, the populous procession moved from Berner Street onto Commercial Road. Marching in perfect order, step by step, peacefully and honorably to Duke Street. On the way we were greeted in many places with bravos. In other places, gangs of the rudest and most ignorant sort (mostly Jews of Dutch origin) stood by and exhibited their vulgarity with contemptuous shouts.

It was festive to see the army of Jewish workers, conscious of its righteousness and determined to fight courageously, marching like soldiers in the best of order to the strains of the Marseillaise!

We found Duke Street packed with people waiting to see the Jewish Sabbath Revolution (?) that was about to take place. Our best old friends, the loyal dogs of our bloodsuckers, the keepers of "order," in a word, the police, stood in great numbers, headed by the police chief of the city, Commander Frazier, and other inspectors, ready to protect the sacred residence of the almighty god! They ordered us to "Halt!" saying that the synagogue was already full. Nevertheless, they allowed in a delegation consisting of Lyons, Krantz, Gallop, and Feigenbaum.

But the great synagogue, which was, in fact, unusually heavily attended by sweaters and moochers, was not nearly as full as the police and sextons had claimed. At least three hundred people could have gone in.

But, DESPITE THE INVITATION OF THE SYNAGOGUE SECRETARY, they did not want to allow anyone to enter the synagogue except the four delegates, who naturally refused this "great honor." They simply asked whether or not Dr. Adler would give the sermon as demanded. When the sextons in their clown costumes shared the highly important news that a Meisels would babble, the delegates wanted to leave immediately. The sextons, however, held them up, saying that one of the trustees who was to arrive shortly would be able to give them more and better information. None of these great sweaters wanted to say anything. In the meantime, a kind of yellow sheep jumped up and shouted angrily several times in English, "This is a disgrace to the Jewish community!" Then he started to curse in the refined manner of Petticoat Lane. In response, Krantz said loudly, "It is a disgrace to be a sweater and an idler," and Lewis Lyons said, "Is it not a great disgrace that people who are willing to work are starving to death?" And the delegates immediately left the synagogue of the sweaters under the almighty protection of a couple hundred policemen.

The whole crowd stood calmly waiting for the delegates. To the great consternation of all the sweaters, the black flag waved proudly at their head, very close to the entrance to the synagogue. Just then, the sun, an infrequent guest in London during the winter, began to shine and its pale rays bathed the narrow, dirty little street, which was flooded with people. Above their heads stood the flag of mourning, like a beacon by the sea. No one who was there will ever forget this magnificent and moving scene.

Krantz was the first to leave the synagogue courtyard, squeezing past the line of policemen and shouting, "To Mile End waste!" The whole crowd swelled like a wave in the ocean. The band began to play just then, but was immediately silenced by Herbert Burrows and others in order to keep their word that there would be no music near the synagogue. The German drummer, ignorant of such foolish rabbinical laws, poor thing, got a little excited and again began to drum energetically. A trumpeter in the band played the Marseillaise, heedless of the committee, which soon had to give in. In this way the poor sweaters and idlers in the synagogue were forced to hear the "godless" music.

Der arbayter fraynd, March 22–29, 1889.

Anarchism

The Berner Street Club became a focus of political and union activity, but the socialists and anarchists often appeared to fight each other as much as the capitalist society they denounced. By the first decade of the century, however, the anarchists (and their newspaper, Der arbayter fraynd*) had become the leading political force among Jewish workers in London.*

To the Comrades!

After a two-year interruption, the *Arbayter fraynd* reappears today for the first time to continue its old struggle against the spiritual and material slavery of our time. As always, its most important task is still to awaken the rebellious instincts of the Jewish working masses and to spread the exalted ideas of light and freedom, anarchy and independence, in the hearts of those who suffer oppression. [. . .]

In the last few years, a powerful revolutionary workers' movement has developed on the continent under the direct influence of anarchist ideas and aspirations. The general strike in Barcelona, the greatest event in the modern history of the revolutionary workers' movement, inspired new courage and hope in hearts everywhere. The tremendous distribution of propaganda for the general strike in Spain, France, Holland, and Italy represents a new epoch in the revolutionary socialist movement. This propaganda eliminates the spirit of skepticism and pessimism which spells the death of any energetic movement and the end of any idealistic enthusiasm. This propaganda is also developing the desire for struggle and the sense of solidarity among the proletarian masses.

This propaganda gives the movement a more practical character and a more positive basis. It demonstrates to us the great significance of the revolutionary economic struggle as a means of liberation from the yoke of wage slavery and as a period of preparation for the future revolution. It acquaints us with the effectiveness of organizations of revolutionary socialist struggle, through which the workers' initiative finds a powerful expression. The *Arbayter fraynd* will place particular weight on all practical details of this movement and will devote all its energy to developing similar tendencies and aspirations within the Jewish working class. It will acquaint its readers with the method of the so-called idealistic strike used by our Spanish comrades to bring about general social improvements and certain political rights through direct economic struggle of the masses, without parliamentary intervention.

Der arbayter fraynd (The Worker's Friend), March 20, 1903.

Zionism

Although international Zionist leaders could attract large audiences from among the Jewish workers in London, Zionist organization remained weak. However, the anti-Semitic tendencies of some British socialist leaders led some Jewish workers to turn toward Jewish nationalism.

Zionism and the Workers

Now the ban has been broken and this idea, which is taking the world by storm, has found its way into the very midst of the platforms of the labor movement. [. . .]

At Christ Church Hall, where the larger labor meetings are held weekly, two Saturday evenings in a row were devoted to Zionist debates. One was over the lecture by Mr. Shire, "Can a Socialist Be a Zionist?" As many already know, Mr. Shire has become an ardent Zionist recently, and he by no means wants to keep his newly found knowledge hidden within his breast. Rather, he wants to display his conviction openly to his brother workers, to those to whom he preached socialism for many years. He called them to a public meeting, standing before them and baring his heart. "God sees the wounds that bleed deep within my heart. I do not change my opinions frivolously now. I am and remain a socialist. But I have been driven and forced to be a Jew, and do not want to stop being a Jew. I have a Jewish heart and I must feel Jewish sorrows. You are also Jews. How can you not recognize where you stand in the world? Look around with your eyes open, and you will see what I see. You will also know what you have to do. People without ideas remain in one position. People with understanding can change their ideas in response to events and developments. The times are leading Jewish socialists back to their people. Zionism is our national movement, and Jewish workers belong to the Jewish people and to the Zionist movement."

Shire now talks to his comrades in more or less this way. But however easy his words are to understand, and however enthusiastically he proclaims his new viewpoint, he meets with stubborn resistance among his former comrades and students. So it looks like the debate will not come to an end. The first gathering was only like a sudden clap of thunder, startling everyone in Christ Church Hall. The next week, they prepared for a formal attack against the socialist "traitor."

Mr. Shire, however, once again bared his heart by explaining why he had become a Zionist. "There is a Jewish question in every country in which we live. And it is blindness not to see that. The Jewish question is a product of exile, because Jews do not have their own country as other nations do. Some time in the future, the solution of the Jewish question may come through total assimilation, or through religious equality in a socialist society. That is how others think the Jewish question will be resolved. But I believe that after having survived so long, after such a historic past in the Land of Israel and, later, in exile, the Jewish people will by no means mix completely with the gentiles. Only individual Jews, particularly the capitalists, can assimilate, not the entire people. The working class will usually live apart from the gentile world. As far as future socialist society is concerned, I am convinced that religions will also continue to exist then. And if we Jews hold on to our religion, they will continue to hate us. History teaches us that in the Middle Ages we were hated only for our religion. Now, religious hatred is also mixed in with the economic hatred for us. This religious hatred will always remain, even in the future socialist society. And if Jews cannot live and believe in their own way, socialism has no value for us."

It is unfortunate, he says, that the Jewish socialists do not know socialism. They have only had a small taste of it. The gentile socialists are nationalists. Why should the Jewish socialists not be nationalists? Jaurès is a fiery

French patriot. Liebknecht is an ardent lover of the German fatherland. Hyndman is an English patriot. Why should he, Shire, not be a Jewish patriot and Zionist?

The Social Democratic Federation in England is quite nationalistic. Like all the other [word illegible] whistlers, justice calls for a strong navy to defend the English fatherland. The socialists do not want the smaller nations to be absorbed by the larger ones. Socialists here demand home rule for Ireland. The great Stepniak himself went to wage war for the independence of Montenegro. Why should Jewish socialists not struggle for the independence of the Jewish people? If Hyndman can demand a navy, why should we not want a Jewish state?

Der yidisher ekspres, March 30, 1900.

The Zionist movement in England had a crucial role to play while England was the dominant power in Palestine (1917–47). Yet the English Zionist Federation suffered a serious decline in the early 1920s, and when the movement revived in the early 1930s, its social bases were now predominantly middle-class and suburban.

The East End of London

Zionism and the East End—the juxtaposition of the two evokes a flood of memories. It was to the East End that Herzl directed his first public appeal, and the Beth Zion in Fulbourne Street, Whitechapel, often visited by Nordau, Weizmann, and Sokolow in the early days, may truly be regarded as the cradle of English Zionism. But now, a generation later, there has occurred what may be described as a western orientation of Zionism. The central body of English Zionism and even the blue box of the Jewish National Fund, the original symbol of working class Zionism are now governed from Bloomsbury whence the official gaze is directed rather to Hampstead and Golders Green than to Aldgate pump. Nevertheless, the real essence of English Zionism is still to be found in the East End. The idealism of the Jewish masses must be used to counteract, if not to Zionise, the Jewish middle classes in other parts of London who, as a general rule, tend to be Anglo-English rather than Anglo-Jewish and who, in some cases, are only liberal at the expense of religious observance and unutterably conservative in every other respect.

[. . .] [Let the English Zionists] not forget the East End, but for which they would have been generals of a non-existent army. If they want to be re-inspired with that throb of pride in Jewish achievement which comes from the heart rather than from the pocket, they should render account, more often than they do at present, to their real constituents, the Jewish tailors, cobblers and mantle makers in the side streets of the East End.

The problem of East End Jewry is a mighty and complex one, with many phases. Despite all the charges that can be leveled against the East End, its sordidness and incoherence, there is a specific Jewishness in the East End, even if it is only the Jewishness that comes from segregation, contiguity and weight of numbers. It can be harnessed to great and noble ends.

(From a correspondent)*The Zionist Review*, 1:12 (January 1935): 167–68.

Communism

Communism became an important force in the immigrant community in the interwar community. In the following excerpt from his proletarian novel, Simon Blumenfeld portrays a protest march against Nazism in 1933, from the point of view of the Jewish Communists. Although Communism was still seen as a liability for Jews at that time, by 1936 the Communist Party became warmly regarded by many Jews as their champion against fascism at home and abroad.

In the street there was an undercurrent of excitement. It was Thursday. The walls were placarded with posters. MEET AT STEPNEY GREEN. The Jews were going to march to Hyde Park.

[. . .] Even the shopkeepers had shut up as a protest. [. . .] Throwing away trade worth tens, perhaps hundreds of thousands of pounds to march to Hyde Park because other Jews were being ill-treated in Germany. [. . .]

[At Stepney Green] the banner bearers formed up first, immediately behind them, the ex-service men. Marshals went over them suspiciously. Any man who looked like a Communist was challenged. If he admitted his crime, he was cast from the ranks. This was a Jewish March—they didn't want any bloody Communists. But the Communists were Jews too—they insisted on marching. They formed their own contingents and marched behind the main body. [. . .]

Alec marched along with the last contingent, with the reds. Pariahs! Double outcasts! Jews and Communists. The rich said "Damn Jews! They're all Communists, reds—revolutionaries!" and the ignorant befuddled poor said, "Bloody Jews! They're all rich—they're all millionaires." So between the two—smacked in the face and kicked in the backside at the same time.

But all that bigotry would crumble away when workers ruled the land. Jews wouldn't be lumped together as financiers and bolsheviks. Nor would they be pointed out like tame zoological specimens by tolerantly superior Anglo-Saxons, "See here—these are our Jews. They've got black hair, dark skins and long noses, but they're quite harmless. They're different, but they can't help it." Under the rule of the proletariat Jews would have the same rights as other workers. In Russia, anti-Semitism was a crime. [. . .]

> Then raise the scarlet standard high;
> Within its shade, we'll live and die. . .

A scandalized marshal came up. "Don't sing that," he begged. "They'll think we're all communists. We don't mind you marching with us so long as you're quiet."

They pushed the marshal aside contemptuously. They knew what THEY were marching for. Always consistent; their aim was the brotherhood of man. The rich Jews would soon find a compromise with Fascism. So long as their profits were safe, they didn't mind who was in the saddle, but when their fat bellies were hurt, they squeaked, they marched, they shouted; in a year, two years, they'd raise some other red herring. Last time, the Arabs were the villains; now the Germans. But this contingent wasn't being fooled. Their quarrel was not with the German workers or the Arab workers. Their enemies were the bosses, whatever their religion, whatever their language. So they marched along steadily, lifting up their voices, singing more lustily than before:

> Though cowards flinch and traitors sneer
> We'll keep the red flag flying here!
> Simon Blumenfeld, *Jew Boy* (London: Lawrence and Wishart,
> 1986), pp. 40–50.

In the following interview conducted by Anne Kershen, Mick Mindel, a leading official in the United Ladies' Tailors' Trades Union, recalls the work of Sarah Wesker. Wesker was a key figure in the Communist Party in the East End between the wars, a doughty anti-Fascist and a charismatic union organizer who was crucial for bringing women into union life.

We had first class tailoresses, most of whom were Jewish. They generally gave up work when they married. We pushed women all the way through, onto factory committees, onto union committees, onto becoming shop stewards. Of course, during the war years this became a necessity. They replaced the men. But after the war the women played a dominant part on all the Union committees.

Q: What was Sarah Wesker's role in the Union?

A: A great deal. Sarah and I were neighbours in the East End and both lived in the Rothschild Buildings but I didn't really meet her until the early 1930s when I joined the Communist party and she was very active in the Stepney branch of the Communist party. When I became active in the Union, Sarah was one of the few that we worked with because she was a very prominent member of the party. We had the extraordinary situation that it was the Communist party membership that was for the amalgamation and the Labour party membership who were on the Executive of the Union who opposed the amalgamation. So we had a political issue.

In 1937 I said now look, because there was hostility to it we must have a woman union official. I said Sarah Wesker's going to be the one because the membership, particularly on the manufacturing side, has grown to such an extent that we needed a woman to appeal to women, because within the tradition of the Union as such one wanted a new approach, a new style, a new propaganda to welcome the women into the industry. We were no longer thinking only in terms of the men. I was making speeches all the time, "Women are our natural allies, they work in the workshops, we've got to protect them." When I began to argue for half a crown an hour for the basic rate, which was well ahead of the wages of the trade boards, which was 1s 4d an hour for finishers, and felling hands should get 1s 6d an hour, I met with opposition from the men, they thought it was too high a wage to ask for girls. That is how deep-rooted it was but one has to take it in its historical background.

Sarah and I became very much involved in the work of the Union. She had two qualifications: one was that she was a first-rate speaker. Secondly, she could not only understand Yiddish but she could speak it. It was still a Yiddish membership right up until 1936/37. Our balance sheets were published half in English, half in Yiddish. Members' meetings were conducted in Yiddish. She had been a trouser machinist. She became active in 1926 when she led the girls out on strike for a farthing extra for a pair of trousers. She had a history and then she became active in the breakaway Union—The United Clothing Workers' Union. But in spite of all that Sarah then became an official.

Anne J. Kershen, ed., *Off the Peg* (London: London Museum of
Jewish Life, 1988), pp. 64–67.

PARIS

The Dreyfus Affair and the Jewish Workers

The Dreyfus Affair rocked French society in 1898 after the publication of Emile Zola's J'Accuse! For those Jewish immigrants who had emigrated to

France with images of the French Revolution and the emancipation of the Jews in mind, the Affair shook their belief in republican liberty, equality, and fraternity. Their disappointment was all the keener vis-à-vis the French socialists, who were initially divided on whether or not to defend a bourgeois army captain.

Anti-Semitism, the Socialist Party, and the Jewish Proletariat

We note that your attitude toward anti-Semitism is not frank enough, indignant enough, or energetic enough as it has been in other similar cases, where a principle of progress and humanity is in question, or when an old barbarous act is perpetuated against the weak. We state this fact with pain, for we consider you to be the true perpetuators of those who made the Declaration of the Rights of Man, of those who made the French Revolution, whose strong hand has reached even us, who remain at the bottom of the ladder of oppressed peoples, bringing us a bit of air and hope. [. . .]

For a long time, France has held the respect of the world, of all those who suffered, of all the weak and oppressed, and of all those who walked toward light, of all the brave, of all the militants for progress and for great humanitarian causes. For some time, you know, France has tended to abdicate this admirable role. But the eyes that have been turned in one direction for a century and a half cannot turn away so fast; they continue to follow the same direction, mechanically, for some time, even when the object that had attracted them has disappeared.

It is you, French Socialists, who represent the new doctrines of equality and of liberty, to make these traditions live again!

It is you who should defend us against the hatreds of race and religion.

It is for you to come to our aid in order to work together for the dejudaization and dechristianization of all people.

It is for you to come to our aid, in order that we can plant among the Jewish masses the seeds of the future.

> For the Group of Socialist Jewish Workers in Paris,
> KARPEL and DINNER

> Groupe des ouvriers juifs socialistes de Paris, *Le Prolétariat juif: Lettre des ouvriers juifs de Paris au Parti socialiste français* (Paris: Imprimerie typographique J. Allemane, 1898), pp. 17, 20–21.

World War I

With the end of the Dreyfus Affair, most Jews in France hailed the republic's ultimate defense of the Jews against anti-Semitism. Thus while some immigrant radicals pursued a pacifist line in the years leading up to World War I, an estimated nine thousand immigrants (some of whom had left Russia to avoid military service) expressed their gratitude toward France by volunteering when war broke out.

Against War

So, what do you say to our patriots,
The devil take them?
They really want war,
May they break their necks and that is all.
And, truly, I ask you,
Are the capitalists not rich enough?
Do we have to make them even richer,
And stuff their fat bellies even more?
I swear to you, truly and in all honesty,
That the capitalists are looking for war.
You see, once upon a time, in the old days,
A war meant something else.
That is, in the name of faith,
One land would loot another.
But, nowadays,
We have been liberated from faith.
Now war, which is everywhere,
Is for the sake of cursed capital.
But for the poor people,
I cannot make sense of it.
They try to persuade them,
Just like my great-grandfather.
They explain to them and declare
That they should shed their blood for their country.
Is Morocco really their country?
Is it not a disgrace even to say so?
Yes, they took it by force from the Moroccans,
And still they go on boasting.
But the German also wanted a taste
Of just this tasty cake.
And just like one of the family,
He crawled into the very middle.
And that is why a war will break out,
And one land will stab the other to death.
And that is why the patriots
Are seething and simmering everywhere.
They want to drive out the German,
And remain the sole owners there.

And when they are completely victorious,
The gold and the mines will belong to them.
Yes, it will all belong to the capitalist,
But we will lose our lives for nothing.
But, no, we do not have to listen.
We should obstruct the war.
We will get nothing out of it,
We will only be buried there.
The capitalists, they will benefit,
So we have to shoot one another.
No, we will no longer hear
The cries and the tears
Of the unfortunate victims,
Who leave behind young widows.
Should we lose our lives,
While the bourgeoisie continues to call the shots?
No, we should struggle against them,
And give the capitalists a severe beating.
I tell you, no, a thousand times no.
We should not go to war.
Love live the social!
Down with capital!

A Cap Maker

Der idisher arbayter, October 9, 1911.

Jewish Comrades

THE GROUP OF RUSSIAN-ROMANIAN JEWISH VOLUNTEERS OF THE
18TH ARRONDISSEMENT
FRANCE, LAND OF LIBERTY, OF EQUALITY, OF FRATERNITY
France, the first of all nations to have conferred upon us Jews the Rights of
Man and of Citizen, this dear country where we and our families find
refuge, protection, and happiness.

Currently France is in a state of war. What can we do to prove to our second fatherland our love and our attachment?

Can we, while the French people rise as one man to defend the fatherland, stand with our arms crossed? No! For if we are not yet French in law, we are in heart and soul, and our most sacred duty is to place ourselves at the disposition of this beautiful and noble nation in order to participate in her defense.

Comrades, it is the moment to pay our tribute of recognition to the country that hosts us.

All of one heart, hand in hand, in the service of France.
Long live France!!

Poster placarded in the 18th arrondissement, published in *Les
Archives Israélites,* August 27, 1914.

Of these 9,000 men who have presented themselves, 4,000 have been recognized as fit for service and enlisted on August 21, 1914, by the military
office.

"You had to have seen the anxiety that reigned among the volunteers,
all at odds with that observed among the men who only show up to military service against their will!" wrote Mr. Poinsot in his brochure "Foreign
Volunteers Enrolled in the Service of France." Here people feared refusal,
kept quiet about small defects, or hid a little-apparent physical deformity.
One man with a hernia took off his bandage and one myopic left off his
pince-nez; a skinny man stuck out his chest to appear "large around the
middle" and a bronchitis sufferer made an effort not to cough. The volunteers arched their backs, straightened up, proudly raised their heads and
pretended to be "tough."

There were men of all ages: boys of eighteen years, still beardless, and
forty-year-old fathers. Men of all religions and all political parties. Persons
earning a comfortable living, and miserable wretches leaving a nest of children deprived of the essentials.

"My comrade Fishman (tailor, thirty years old, Israelite) fallen on the
field of honor, enlisted because he could not stand the shame of remaining
inactive while the French people spilled their blood on the field of battle,"
wrote one volunteer to us. [. . .]

Although the official numbers are not yet known, there is every reason
to assert that of the 4,000 Russians enlisted at the beginning of the war,
there now remain at most barely 1,500. The others fell during the attacks
at Carency on May 9, 1915, in Champagne on September 25, 1915, in
Argonne, around Verdun and in the Somme.

Their unknown tombs lie shoulder to shoulder with those of French soldiers.

Volontaires russes au front français, *France et Russie* (Société de
secours aux Russes combattant sous les drapeaux français) (Paris:
Imprimerie D. Mendel, n.d.), pp. 6, 8.

Revolutionaries

The "Groupe des ouvriers juifs socialistes de Paris," which signed the let-
ter to the French socialists during the Dreyfus Affair, left no other trace in

the archives. It was but one of the more or less formal groupings of Jewish immigrant radicals in Paris before the war. The police department had their eye on them all, however, and described the Russian colony of revolutionaries as follows.

Only religious questions seem to divide them: Throughout the world, the Russian Orthodox and the Jews have the reputation of practicing their respective faiths with a superstitious devotion which would suppose fierce antipathies between them.

Yet this isn't the case, in Paris at least.

Almost all the Orthodox are indifferent to religious matters. [. . .]

Similarly, the Polish Catholics have no priests of their language.

The Jews are more religious or at least they appear to be; but it is increasingly evident that if some of them have true faith, many others practice more than they believe, and most often only practice in order to aspire to the generous help granted by their rich Parisian Jewish coreligionists.

At the last Yom Kippur, the Russian Jews organized a banquet followed by a ball, an unthinkable event for practicing Jews. This celebration, similar to our old "Saint Friday" banquets, brought together more than four hundred participants! We must add that almost all of them are supporters of anarchy.

Religious difference therefore does not separate Russian revolutionaries. [. . .]

In their meetings, Jews and Slavs intermingle and are friends; while chatting, they share their hatreds; the Israelites can only be distinguished in that they are more uncompromising, more explicitly violent. . .

"Les Réfugiés révolutionnaires russes à Paris," report, circa 1907, pp. 4–5, 25–26, Archives nationales, Paris, F⁷12894.

Bundists and Communists

The General Jewish Workers' Union in Lithuania, Poland, and Russia was founded in 1897 to organize the Jewish proletariat in the East. The "Bund" was allied with the Mensheviks and eventually came into conflict with Lenin and the Bolsheviks over the "national question." These differences were carried over into emigration, where dissension within the immigrant left became apparent. In the interwar period, Bundists and Communists went at each other in the press and sometimes with fisticuffs, paralleling the Socialist-Communist split in France after 1920.

Our Youth

Youth today plays a significant role in public life. All parties, tendencies, and organizations make every effort to attract young people.

Our duty is self-evident—to remove the youth from both bourgeois and Communist influence. To that end, *Der veker* will from now on give periodic reports, illuminated from our socialist standpoint, on the life of the young.

FOUNDING OF WORKER YOUTH FEDERATION

Young Jewish workers in Paris are spiritually neglected and abandoned.

There is not a single youth organization that truly defends their interests or engages in a broad range of cultural and political educational activities.

Today there are two kinds of organizations: bourgeois and Communist.

The bourgeois youth federations, of which there are many, engage in either assimilationist or Zionist activities.

Their entire cultural program consists of denying their own identities, cultivating dreams of the Land of Israel, and dabbling in "Judaism," as if the world would not survive without the "eternal Jewish race." Most of their effort goes into organizing dances. The young people are drawn into this muck, and are distracted from the important social problems that should and must interest young workers in this day and age.

The Jewish Communist youth group carries on the same criminal activity among the young as the Party does in the adult working class.

By contrast, we must unfortunately state that today there does not exist in Paris the sort of federation of young Jewish workers that would organize the youth honestly and correctly, and bring it into a truly cultured and socialist environment.

Despite the economic crisis through which we are living, which has greatly affected the young Jewish worker, a group of young people has taken the initiative to form such a youth federation.

Der veker, October 15, 1932.

The Communists became the most active political militants of the Jewish immigration of the interwar period. In the following article, they settled their score against their former members who had joined La Jeunesse juive (a pro-Zionist organization) and Morgnshtern (a Bundist organization).

Red Sports

WHO ARE THE "LEADERS" OF "LA JEUNESSE JUIVE"
AND "MORGNSHTERN"?
They were both members of "YASK" [Jewish Workers' Sports Club]. One's name is Tshapazhnik and the other's is Banet.

Tshapazhnik came to us right at the founding of our club. He went along with us in almost all questions, spouting revolutionary phrases. In a word, he did everything to win our trust. We entrusted him with responsibilities. He served as treasurer. But he was quietly looking for an opportunity to split our organization. And he found such a moment. In the first months of 1930, when two of the leading members of YASK had to leave Paris, Tshapazhnik found the appropriate moment to leave our camp and run to "La Jeunesse juive" to make a career. In the process, he did not forget to take with him the treasury of YASK, consisting of several hundred francs gathered from the hard-earned centimes of the worker-athletes. He also took the financial ledger and some documents. This renegade and thief is now the honored "president" of "La Jeunesse juive."

The story of the second "hero," Banet, is shorter. He joined YASK as a former member of "Morgnshtern" in Poland. Believing in his honorable intentions, we let him too play an active role. But when Banet saw that he was not going to be made head instructor of the gymnastics section, he began an ugly campaign of sabotage, to such an extent that he was disciplined for it. It was at that point that he revealed his true cowardly face. He did not want to recognize his faults. He laughed contemptuously at the decision. And, most important, he took advantage of the moment to create a counter-revolutionary Bundist sports group at the bosses' Medem Club.

Tshapazhnik and Banet—two renegades. Both were spit out of the ranks of revolutionary sport, the first for robbery and embezzlement, the second for sabotage and breach of discipline.

Let the young workers who are members of La Jeunesse juive and Morgnshtern know who their leaders are, their president and their secretary, respectively. Let them contemplate this and turn away from such "leaders."

Yunge gvardie, April 2, 1932.

The Popular Front

Jewish workers were enthusiastic over the Popular Front of 1936, and during the World's Fair in Paris in 1937, the Communist newspaper Naye prese *published an almanac, a veritable tourist guide to Paris, in which it described glowingly "The Popular Front in Power."*

What the Popular Front Has Given the Jewish Masses

The overwhelming majority of the Jewish population in this country received the defeat of fascism and the victory of democracy with enthusiasm. In the first place, the defeat of fascism meant to us Jews a death-blow to anti-Semitism, race hatred, and xenophobic agitation. The victory of democracy opened up the great possibility of providing legal status to immigrants, of easing their naturalization, and improving their economic condition.

And, in fact, barely several months after the advent of the Popular Front government, the Jewish deputy from the Communist parliamentary faction, Georges Lévy, introduced in parliament a bill to give legal status to foreigners in France. In the meantime, as a result of the activity of the Joint Committee for Legal Status, a number of administrative ordinances have improved to a certain extent the legal situation of foreigners. Jewish workers have benefited from all of the social reforms to the same extent as their French comrades. They have joined the unions of the CGT [Confédération Générale du Travail] in great numbers, participating together with their French brothers in all demonstrations and campaigns of the Popular Front.

Naye prese, Almanakh, 1937.

Darkening Horizons

Léon Blum's government did not effect any long-lasting measures in favor of immigrants, however, and after its fall, xenophobic propaganda continued apace.

The Jewish Artisan in France: His Needs and the Struggle for His Rights

M. Melman

The artisans' organizations with which we are familiar from the past in the old country are very old and varied in character. For the most part these movements consist of people who grew up in that class. They are essentially extremely conservative, bound to generations of artisanal tradition, and running their organizations according to the old traditional ways. In recent years, these organizations have had a difficult and bitter struggle for survival. They are far from answering the needs of their members.

The picture is not very different here in France. In the country with the most classic petit bourgeoisie, the artisan plays a very important and honored role in production. His organizations, in existence for decades, are far from representing a movement that can express the needs and defend the interests of the great class of artisans in the French population. This well-known fact can serve as an illustration: Recently, large industry has been growing and becoming stronger in this country. As a result, the bases of many branches of artisanal production are becoming narrower. Large strata of artisans and small producers are faced with the dilemma: to go under or to fight for new ways and means of survival, of which there are many available in this country. This should be the task of the French artisans' movement. The French artisans' movement, however, sees the immigrant artisan as the guilty party in the crisis, and has waged an unjustified struggle to have him ousted from the country. The immigrant artisan has, for the most part, actually built and developed a number of branches of industry in this country (such as raincoats, hats, fancy leather goods, clothing, etc.).

Very different is the Jewish artisan or home worker who has settled in this country in the last two decades. This is a new sort of artisan, on whom artisanry or home work has for the most part been thrust, especially the changing conditions in the country. The majority of them are recruited from the ranks of the workers, and some of them have many years of public activity behind them.

Sensing the imminent onset of hard times, the young immigrant artisanal and home worker element began to organize hurriedly. [. . .]

After a serious and to-the-point discussion at a conference of all trade unions in December 1936, the Central Artisans' Alliance was formed and a leadership elected.

The establishment of a central leadership for the new artisans' movement made a tremendous impression on the Jewish community. It forced the organized Jewish community to take an interest in the particular difficult situation of the Jewish artisan and home worker.

A coordinating committee of all groupings in the Jewish community was created to help the newly established central artisan's alliance defend the Jewish artisan against danger. The committee includes the Federation [Fédération des sociétés juives de France], which these days usually avoids any unity campaigns. It was clear to the Central Alliance that in order to really soften the impact of the decree, it was necessary to interest the French artisans' movement in the special needs of the Jewish artisans, who will be hit hard and mercilessly if the decree takes effect. "L'Artisan français," which by all appearances was the initiator of the law, remained deaf to the various delegations and many appeals. The *artisanat* has recently intensified its campaign against foreign artisans, affecting the Jews most strongly. [. . .]

Of great significance was the united bloc in the elections to the Chambre des métiers [Chamber of (artisanal) trades], which plays an official role in the country. The chairman of the Central Artisans' Alliance, Comrade Nodelman, was among the candidates. The question of coming to an understanding with the French *artisanat* is far from settled, and is always on the alliance's agenda.

Hantverker vort, June 1, 1938, p. 4.

BUENOS AIRES
The Tailors' Union

The first Jewish workers' unions in Buenos Aires were founded between 1906 and 1910, but their real growth began in 1917–18. The Jewish clothing workers' organization became the main trade union organized along ethnic lines in Buenos Aires when it broke with the Argentine general union over the issue of subcontracting, about which the general union had done nothing.

A Little History, and More . . .

Next month will be the 24th anniversary since a small group of tailors and pressers founded the Tailor Workers' Trade Union. [. . .]

THE SUBJECTIVE FACTORS

At that time there was a commonly held belief about the wage workers [employed by the home tailors and workshop artisans], that they were a bunch of boys and girls, or gentile girls, who worked in order to . . . pass the time. Or something similar. Anyone who knew the trade somewhat, and who had a sense of himself as a worker, soon became "independent." That is, he bought a machine and ran to a store for a bundle. This was considered reaching a higher level, the first step on the ladder of "working one's way up." In the best of cases, a young man worked for someone else until it was time for him to get married. This seemed so natural that no one could even understand how it could be different. Not only the employers and bourgeois society in general thought this way. The workers, and especially the leaders, were completely under the influence of this concept. Of course, with this kind of thinking, no one paid much attention to the wage workers. [. . .]

The real producers were considered to be the home tailors and contractors, who were directly exploited by the stores, and whose side the organization had to take.

A strange situation therefore arose. The organization argued that any improvements had to be demanded directly from the stores by the home tailors and contractors. These were the ones who had to be organized in the first place, and theirs were the problems and needs that had to be resolved first. The wage workers would also benefit from this. Their point of departure was this: What demands can be made of the "poor bundle-carrier" (poor thing)? Furthermore, the home tailors and contractors were never a very militant element. Always absorbed by thoughts of working their way up, they could not keep the organization in mind. It was much easier to drive a whole room full of boys and girls, or gentile girls, to work more, while paying less. Not clearly understanding these conditions and bound by various "special interests," the organization, or, better put, the leaders, tried to accommodate themselves. The union was thus transformed into a bureaucracy from which the workers kept their distance.

These were the positive and negative factors of that time, which we can only now correctly comprehend and evaluate.

And it so happened that special circumstances brought several tailors' union activists from New York to Buenos Aires, among whom was the well-known

MAX HELLER

We do not like cults of personality. It just so happened, however, that this person embodied all of the necessary elements to be able to make use of all of the positive factors and oppose all of the negative factors. With the help of a small group of workers, he laid the cornerstone for the Tailor Workers' Trade Union. Only now, after so many years, can we correctly comprehend how tremendous this achievement was.

In order to do this one needed clear vision and logical consistency. Max Heller had these things.

Free of any prejudice and endowed with great seriousness, he saw only one thing: the needs and problems of the workers, for which solutions must be found. As a "stranger" he was not bound to any "higher interests." Although he was then a member of the organization "Avangard," he believed that the interests of the wage workers stood above all else. He had to wage his most bitter struggle against those merciful souls who never stopped pleading, "What demands can be made of the 'poor bundle-carriers' (poor things)?"

He answered with a simple and logical argument:

For whom do we work? Who pays our wages? The home tailor. The contractor. It follows that they are our exploiters, so we have to demand improvements from them! They can't meet our demands? Let them demand improvements from the stores. Not only will we not interfere with their struggle, but, on the contrary, we will help them to the best of our ability. We are not helping anyone with our pity. The home tailors will not fight against the stores until they are forced to do so, because they are not a militant element. We wage workers are the only ones who can force them to fight for their own interests, and the interests of all of us.

Dos fraye vort," no. 39, May 1941, pp. 10–11.

The Woodworkers' Union

Unlike the garment workers' union, the furniture workers' union avoided a split thanks to the creation of a Jewish section within the general union in 1916. Nevertheless, conflicts still arose periodically due to political tensions, and spiteful comments were made against the "Russians." The tone became angrier during the 1920s, when the union leadership denounced the autonomy of the Jewish section, by that time under the influence of the Communists.

To All Furniture Workers

BE PREPARED FOR THE NEXT MEMBERSHIP MEETING!
It is no secret to anyone that the Jewish Committee of the furniture workers' union is under the influence of the red fraction. This is enough reason for the leaders to look constantly for all kinds of ways to kill the activities of the Jewish Committee. The last membership meeting determined precisely the rights appropriate to the Jewish Committee. But since this decision takes away from the "Amsterdamer"* the possibility of sneaking through their maneuvers, they are trying to abolish the Jewish Committee altogether. Although the question is not on the agenda, they will force it on the meeting in order to annul the previous decision and subject the Jewish Committee to the orders and political maneuvers of the Amsterdam reformists.

For years the Jewish Committee has carried out an important mission of propaganda and organization among the Jewish workers. The Jewish Committee has always had the right to carry out propaganda work among the Jewish workers, to publish its own newspaper, to hold conferences and events, etc. When the Amsterdamer saw that they could not turn the Jewish Committee into their own political tool, because it was always headed by comrades from the red fraction, they tried by any means to destroy the committee altogether. That is why the disgraceful war against the "Cossacks" was waged.

"Tsu ale mebl arbeter [sic]," *Royter shtern,* July 10, 1926, p. 5.

*"Amsterdamer" were adherents of the so-called Second-and-a-Half International of left-wing socialists and syndicalists.

The Bund of Buenos Aires

The first center of Jewish workers in Buenos Aires was the Russian Library, founded in 1906. Shortly after its creation, however, the Social-Democratic group split into two factions: the assimilationists, or "Iskrovzes," and the Bundists, or "Avangardists" (from the name of their newspaper, Der avangard*). The first group dissolved itself into the Argentine Socialist Party, while the second continued its independent but intermittent activities for the next decade.*

Jews and Socialism

There is today no disagreement in the world of scientific socialism that the proletariat is the bearer of the socialist ideal, the builder of the future order. Still, the correct definition of the term *proletariat* is a matter for discussion. [. . .]

According to the scientific outlook, there should be a very small percentage of adherents of socialism among us Jews, for the simple reason that we have a proportionately small industrial proletariat. And yet it would certainly not be wrong to say that we can compare with the largest nations in the production of adherents and sympathizers of socialism.

If there is a general rule that the proletariat is the bearer of socialism, then the Jewish people are an exception. The great majority of our people sympathize with socialism!

True, we cannot prove statistically, as the Germans can, that such and such a number voted for the Socialists. If, however, other evidence besides ballots may be given, evidence of spirit and blood may be felt on the Jewish streets.

Why are we an exception to the scientific rule?

There are two basic reasons. First, socialism is a national characteristic of ours. It is in our blood, just as music is in the blood of the Italian.

If anyone feels like saying that it was simply a coincidence that our prophets quite abstractly, yet with great revolutionary ardor, preached in favor of the finest and best human order; if anyone wants to argue that it is a coincidence that Marx and Lasalle, the fathers of scientific socialism in Europe [were Jews], together with a great number of adherents and fighters from the Jewish intelligentsia everywhere in the world where masses of Jews live—to this one can only answer that all national characteristics that are ascribed to the North Americans, English, French, and Italians are also coincidental, and that in truth they are not characteristics on which it is worth dwelling.

Second, in order to be inclined toward socialism, one must be, if not a proletarian, then a child of an oppressed people.

It is a great question who suffers more from the capitalist order—the Yankee proletarian or the Jewish poor of all descriptions.

It is as clear as day that as long as the system of murder and robbery continues to exist the military system will also exist, since it has to support the order. War is therefore inevitable, and war rests on our people with all the heaviness of lead and cannons.

That is why we Jews so welcome socialism, which strives to abolish the system of blood and fire.

If socialism is elsewhere purely proletarian, with us it is, and will remain, national, because no other nation so needs an order that does away with hatred between peoples as we Jews do. And no one needs peace and quiet like the Jews.

L. Mas, "Yuden un sotsializm," *Der avangard*, no. 1, January 1916, pp. 12–14.

Anarchism

The Jewish anarchists of Buenos Aires also took part in the creation of the Russian Library. From the beginning, they recognized the importance of editorial activities as well as union organizing. They published a Yiddish column in the celebrated Spanish-language anarchist daily of Buenos Aires, La Protesta, *and they were also in contact with the English* Arbayter fraynd *group.*

In 1908, there were already three Jewish unions: those of the tailors, bakers, and cap makers. There were already three parties in the Jewish community that spoke to the Jewish worker and ordinary persons through their publications. Anarchists, Bundists, and Po'alei Zionists issued occasional publications and newspapers. With the exception of the Bundist organ, *Der avangard,* they had very little staying power. None of the leaders of the Jewish parties and anarchist groups, and none of the writers in the publications, had an academic education. They were all workers. It would have seemed that these more advanced workers, who spoke and wrote on behalf of the masses, should have set an example for the laboring masses and been the first to join trade unions. However, this was not the case. Precisely the more conscious workers in the parties looked down on the labor unions "where they wage a struggle over a penny," as they used to say in the party circles. There was, even then, simply a lack of understanding of the value of the labor union as a reserve of forces for greater demands than a penny. The Yiddish speakers and writers of the parties floated, as Zhitlovsky put it, "in the zephyrs of heavenly abstraction." They made great sacrifices for abstractions. The real was neglected. [. . .]

[. . .] Just as among the socialists there were different currents that interpreted socialism differently on the way to its realization (these currents included Mensheviks, Bolsheviks, Socialist Revolutionaries, and Maximalists), so there were various currents among the anarchists. There were adherents of Bakunin's "collectivism" and Kropotkin's "communism," out of which grew anarcho-syndicalism with a theoretical basis provided by the Spanish anarchist, Anselmo Lorenzo. There were also individualist anarchists. The latter did not even go near the labor unions. They used the same argument as the Jewish party members—the labor unions struggled over pennies . . .

In 1917, the Jewish anarchists published a monthly organ, *Broyt un frayhayt* [Bread and Freedom]. In contrast to earlier anarchist publications, which were devoted to theoretical issues, *Broyt un frayhayt* was completely devoted to the organization of the workers. The anarchists called on the workers not to let themselves be exploited. They spoke to them in a simple language, which they understood. Hundreds of workers grouped themselves around *Broyt un frayhayt*. Even Bundists used to sell the publication.

> H. Brusilovsky, "Der onteyl fun idishe arbeter in di argentinishe arbayter organizatsies," *Yoyvelbukh lekoved "Di idishe tsaytung" tsum 25tn yubileum* (Buenos Aires: *Di idishe tsaytung*, 1940), pp. 563–80.

Relations with the Argentine Socialist Party

Despite the presence of Jewish members within the Argentine Socialist Party (the SP), its relations with Jewish leftists remained conflictual. The Bundists and the Socialist Zionists opposed the assimilationist positions of the SP. The latter demanded direct membership to the party and, after 1910, barely tolerated the national sections. Certain Bundists maintained a dual membership, however, and defended the Argentine SP within the Jewish community.

The *Idishe tsaytung* and *La Vanguardia*

It is worth noting the commentary in the *Idishe tsaytung* [Yiddish newspaper] on the unfortunate and ignorant remark made in an item in *La Van-*

guardia [socialist paper], where it says: "The 46 *bolicheros* [small-time bosses], Russian Jews who left the rule of the czar, fleeing from pogroms and persecution, have become oppressors here in this country." This is unfortunate in the sense that it singles out the Jewish bosses, without qualifying the non-Jewish bosses in the same way. It is ignorant in the sense that it lumps all "Russian Jews" together as having left the czar's rule and fled the pogroms.

The *Idishe tsaytung*'s commentary, however, loses any justification because of the way it seized on the remark, clumsily exaggerated its significance, and blamed it on the entire tendency represented by the newspaper and the Socialist Party. Especially noteworthy is the attack, couched completely in street language, in the editorial by K-z on June 29th. There is always a danger of stumbling in such cases. The faults of the accuser often outweigh the faults of the accused. The *Idishe tsaytung* accused the entire party of hypocrisy, anti-Semitism, "thuggery," and everything else.

The position of the Socialist Party in regard to the Jews is neither antagonistic nor friendly. It is the same for all other nationalities. It is a principled position for assimilation, one that can be criticized, discussed, and changed. If a hostile mention of Jews makes its way into *La Vanguardia*, it must be ascribed to the individual who says or writes it. Who knows whether he has not derived all of his knowledge about us from the well-known textbooks? Of course, the greatest blame lies with the Jewish members of the party who keep quiet about such cases. [. . .]

In an article on July 14th about the carpenters' strike movement, *La Vanguardia* writes, among other things:

> The Jewish workers, united in the solidarity of the trade union, set a fine example of working-class consciousness, fighting enthusiastically for the triumph of the strike.

As is apparent, the same *La Vanguardia* writes very sympathetically about Jews. It is therefore nonsense to say that its position is antithetical to the Jews. [. . .]

As a Jewish socialist organization, we are in direct opposition to the assimilationist outlook now dominant in the party. This is, after all, one of the motives justifying our independence. It would be unreasonable, however, to make a mountain out of a mole hill and ascribe such things to the party. This could only be done with the purpose of creating an atmosphere of hostility toward it.

"*Di Idishe tsaytung* un *La Vanguardia*," *Der avangard*, no. 7,
July 1916, pp. 38–40.

The Tragic Week of January 1919

During the general strike of January 1919, Buenos Aires was paralyzed for one week in a context of political crisis and generalized fear. "Patriotic brigades" attacked the Jewish neighborhoods and accused the Russian Jews of being Soviet agents. Pedro Wald, a Bundist leader, was arrested for a supposed Maximalist plot.

I heard it said that they were burning the Jewish neighborhood, and I directed my steps toward it. I walked through Junín, Uriburu, and Azcuénaga Streets, without finding any patent sign of disturbance, save the presence in doorways and corners of groups of expectant men, women, and children. It was upon arriving at Viamonte, near the College of Medicine, that I came to witness what could be called the first pogrom in Argentina. In the middle of the street there were burning pyres of books and old furniture, in which one could recognize chairs, tables, and other household goods, in a reddish blaze amid the faces of a gesticulating and trembling crowd. I made my way through and could see that a few meters away there was fighting inside and outside of the buildings. I inquired and learned that it concerned a Jewish businessman who was accused of creating Communist propaganda. It seemed to me, however, that the cruel punishment had been extended to other Hebrew homes. The noise of furniture and drawers being thrown violently into the street was mixed with shouts of "Death to the Jews! Death to the Maximalists!" From time to time old bearded men and disheveled women passed by me. I will never forget the pale face and entreating look of one of them being pulled along by a pair of youngsters, nor that of a sobbing boy clutching to an old dark frock coat, already torn to shreds, worn by another of those poor devils.

Juan A. Carulla, *Al Filo del Medio Siglo* (Paraná: Ed. Llanura,
1951), p. 159.

Details of a Maximalist Plot

THE POLICE ARREST THE PRESIDENT OF THE CENTRAL "SOVIET."
HUNDREDS OF AGITATORS AND SUSPECT PERSONS ROUNDED UP
BY THE AUTHORITIES . . .

The police, aware of the Maximalist plot, and ramifications in Montevideo, initiated measures to clarify the matter as much as possible and arrest those involved.

Numerous security measures were taken in the Russian neighborhoods since reports indicated that unionized elements of this nationality were the leaders in the recent days' disturbances. [. . .]

Among those arrested included Russian subjects, the presumed authors of a "Soviet Republic" that was to be established after taking by force all of the government buildings. The man designated to be president, Pedro Wald, a thirty-year-old Russian, was working as a carpenter.

La Razón, January 13, 1919, 3rd edition.

Socialist Zionism

The first Socialist Zionist group (created in 1906) later gave birth to the local Po'alei Zion. Their principal leader (deported following the strikes of 1909–10) was denounced by the Jewish Colonization Association for wanting to organize workers in the Jewish agricultural colonies. Four years after the Russian Revolution, the organization split over whether or not to join the Communist International. In the interwar period, the Po'alei Zion remained active in wide-ranging Yiddish secular school activities and came to cooperate with the mainstream Zionist Federation.

In response to the attempt to create an undemocratic supposedly representative Jewish body, the so-called Committee of the Jewish Collectivity, the Po'alei Zion Party initiated a strong movement throughout the country for an Argentinean Jewish Congress. This campaign had broad repercussions in all Jewish population centers in the country. [. . .]

The Po'alei Zion participated actively in the campaigns of the Jewish National Fund (JNF), especially after an agreement was reached with the Zionist Federation concerning joint interparty management of the JNF. Po'alei Zion members were the initiators of and played an active role in the "JNF Harvests."

Because the management of the Jewish Foundation Fund was for many years under the exclusive control of the Zionist Federation, the Po'alei Zion Party remained passive regarding collections for the Foundation Fund. The question of how to relate to the Foundation Fund prompted certain disagreements in the Po'alei Zion Party.

In the last several years, the situation has changed radically. The Po'alei Zion gained appropriate representation among the directors of the Jewish Foundation Fund. It now participates actively in both the direct and the cooperative campaigns for the fund.

The United Po'alei Zion–Tseire Zion participated actively in relief work for German Jews. The grand protest action against the persecution of German Jews (April 1933) was carried out at the initiative of the party. This in turn prompted the creation of a united committee against the persecution of German Jews. Later, the party struggled to democratize the committee, which later led to the creation of the DAIA [Delegación de Asociaciones Israelitas Argentina].

The party took a very prominent role in the committee for the million-peso campaign and the organization of the relief congress in 1939, which initiated the relief campaign for Polish Jewry.

The unified party received the greatest number of votes in the elections to the World Jewish Congress.

M. Regalsky, "Politishe shtremungen un parteyen, in'm argentiner idishn yishev," *Yoyvelbukh lekoved "Di idishe tsaytung" tsum 25tn yubileum* (Buenos Aires: *Di idishe tsaytung*, 1940), pp. 553–55.

The Communists and the Politics of Culture

After the Russian Revolution, the Idsektsie in Argentina was formed out of a Bundist faction along with, subsequently, other political activists (former anarchists, Po'alei Zionists). Its stormy history followed that of the Argentine Communist Party. Two factions split off from the group in the 1920s, and the section finally disbanded in the 1930s. The Communists' attitude toward cultural politics shifted as well over the years. In the following article from the 1920s, they defended Yiddish as a language of expression of the oppressed and exploited social classes and as a tool for the revolutionary struggle in the cultural realm. (By the 1930s, their view on Yiddishism had changed: see chapter 4.)

As a language, Yiddish is a product of the poor toiling masses. Born and raised among servant girls and poor workers, it was later adopted and dressed up in flowery words by the Jewish intelligentsia (*maskilim*), who wanted to serve (or do a favor for) the poor workers (out of pity).

The masses have had to withstand many difficulties for the sake of the Yiddish language. From its earliest development to this day, they have had to clear many stones from its path.

And however much the bourgeoisie, through its assimilationist and national chauvinist elements, has tried to smother the language (as the hated language of the masses), they have not been successful. The language grew over the heads of its enemies, and later developed and ripened in spite of its opponents.

The conscious revolutionary workers recognized that they had to exploit and utilize all the resources that could bring them closer to their goal. In addition to struggling on the economic, political, and social fronts, they also had to struggle on the cultural front to free themselves from bourgeois misleaders who pretended to be concerned for the interests of the workers, but were really only thinking of themselves.

The Communist Party, as the revolutionary vanguard, considers it necessary to broaden its field of cultural work. In those places where the Communists are in power, languages are created for backward peoples, and already existing languages and dialects are reformed by study. The Jewish Communists, for their part, have accepted the responsibility for making the Yiddish language easier and more accessible for the Jewish workers. They are therefore instituting a "new orthography."

In fact, the Jewish Communists are everywhere the first to introduce the new orthography. Here in Argentina, as well, *Royter shtern* was the first newspaper to appear with the new orthography from its first issue.

The first issues have therefore flashed [across the scene] and elicited joy. Friends of the Yiddish language have been inspired by the accomplishment.

Only a few have not been able to forgive the Jewish sections for being the first to introduce reforms, and have therefore become opponents of the new orthography.

The annoyance is still greater when we see how a segment of the "labor press" does not want to institute the orthographic reforms, even though it spouts revolutionary phrases, saying that it fights to make things easier for the working class in every way. They often even fight against the reforms out of spite.

In this way, all of the anarchist and socialist Yiddishist adherents of the old, decrepit, deformed conservative orthography have struck a pose which simply makes them ridiculous.

M. Tishler, "Yidish un di yidishe arbayter," *Royter shtern*, no. 72,
May 15, 1926, p. 2.

GERMANY

Worker Solidarity: Relations between German and Immigrant Factory Workers

In many Western lands, native workers often opposed Jewish immigration on the grounds that employers would exploit the newcomers to drive down wages or that the immigrants were potential strikebreakers. In Germany, such fears were exacerbated by cultural prejudices against the immigrants both as Poles and as Jews. Occasionally, groups transcended their biases and forged alliances with the newcomers.

The Immigrant Question in Offenbach

On Monday evening there was a meeting in the Drei Könige restaurant for Jewish workers in the leather goods and luggage industries. The president of the association, Mr. Weinschild, spoke on the topic: "The danger of deportation—what is the position of our Russian-Jewish fellow-workers on this issue?"

The speaker gave a brief general overview of the development of the industry and his organization. At present, he claimed, certain Russian-Jewish immigrants have undermined the solid basis of the industry, lowered the prestige of the field, and led consumers to question the quality of material and workmanship. Many of the people who came here, he continued, presented themselves as Russian revolutionaries and received a lot of support, but then they became terrible exploiters, real scourges of the industry and of their compatriots. [. . .]

[. . .] Instead of "diving in" and working hand in hand with their German colleagues to improve their miserable situation, [the Russian-Jewish families] have isolated themselves. They live in the most disreputable buildings, work for "peanuts," and allow themselves to be abused and exploited. A number of them arrived on the brink of starvation: we gave them shelter, money, and food; we did all that was humanly possible to help them—they withdrew from the union, stirred up trouble, and completely ignored the contract provisions. Because they pay no taxes and live and work crowded together in veritable "caves," they have become a threat to the health of the population of Offenbach. The speaker alluded to recent city hall debates and demanded equal rights for the foreigners, but also *equal responsibilities.* He who will fight at our side is welcome, but a healthy sense of self-respect demands that we show the others the door. They are the worst agitators for anti-Semitism: they turn the motto "Workers of the world, unite!" into an empty phrase by establishing Russian rooming houses, shops, schools, temples, and so on—Russian conditions, in effect. The speaker concluded: "Become workers and raise yourselves to the cultural level of the German workers! Become class-conscious and fight with us—otherwise we will see to it that your stay in free Hesse comes to an end." (Applause and dissent.)

In the following discussion, a *split among the Russian colleagues* became apparent. The older people, who have become informed and adjusted to German conditions, portrayed the misery of their Russian brothers in the most vivid and dramatic terms and criticized their exploitation (the word is really much too mild) and disgrace at the hands of their fellow Jews and fellow Russians. Others, however, heaped insults on the

German party and labor movement in general and on the leather-workers' union and this local organization in particular. The leaders of the organization recalled that German colleagues gave the Russian-Jewish immigrants all the financial and moral support they could. The union treasurers and officers are having difficulties with these people: as soon as they join, they demand support, but their dues are very hard to collect. There is a lot of fluctuation in the membership, and only a few remain loyal to the organization, get used to an orderly way of doing business, and pay their dues regularly. Despite all this, the Offenbach labor movement will remain ready to come to the assistance of its Russian brothers, to educate them and inform them. All of the German speakers appealed to the sense of duty and solidarity of the Russians, asking them to lend a hand themselves to pull their fellow sufferers out of the quagmire. Then the Germans might be able to make common cause with them against the official deportation proceedings which may be beginning soon.

Offenbacher Abendblatt, January 5, 1909, supplement, p. 1.

A Bundist Group in Offenbach

The following statutes, typical of others drawn up by Bundists abroad, show how they continued to militate for revolution in Russia while providing aid and companionship for members in exile.

Statutes

§1

The association shall bear the name "General Jewish Workers' Confederation [*Arbeiterbund*], Offenbach Section."

Membership in the association is open to anyone who agrees to follow its principles.

§2

The goal of the association is:

1. To lend both material and moral assistance to the Russian labor movement in general and the Jewish Workers' Confederation in particular. Individual workers, however, shall receive no support.

2. To try to recruit workers from Russia, Lithuania, and Poland living in Offenbach for the local trade organizations.

3. To promote the intellectual education of its members in all ways.

4. To pursue, shoulder to shoulder with our German colleagues, the interests of the proletariat. [. . .]

§3

The goal of the association shall be achieved:

a. Through the unified organization (unification) of all workers from Russia, Lithuania, and Poland living here.

b. Through the collection of dues and collection of money for the movement in Russia.

c. By conducting regular meetings.

d. By educating and taking care of the members and thereby strengthening their solidarity and social interactions.

f. [sic] By loaning books to all local members.

§4

Any Russian-Jewish male or female worker living in Offenbach or the vicinity may become a member of the association. The condition of membership is acceptance of these statutes. The enrollment fee for male workers shall be fifty pfennigs; for female workers, twenty-five pfennigs. The weekly dues for male members shall be twenty pfennigs and for female members ten pfennigs. The membership card shall remain the property of the association and shall be returned to an officer in case of resignation or expulsion from the association.

[stamp:] Section of the General Jewish Workers' Confederation of Poland, Lithuania, and Russia in Offenbach am Main.

Bund Archives, New York, Offenbach file, n.d. (circa 1908–9).

A Clash of Ideologies—Medem versus Trotsky

Jewish students and workers formed "colonies" where intense debates raged over Jewish particularism and revolution in the name of universal ideals. The heat of ideological confrontation is captured in the description by Bundist Vladimir Medem of a debate that occurred between Trotsky and himself.

The suggestion was made to me at the time to visit several colonies and deliver a lecture on the most recent events. I repaired to the large, attractive national library at Munich where, for several weeks, I studied all the literature I could find on anti-Semitism. The first part of my lecture dealt with the general causes of anti-Semitism; the second part was devoted to the special conditions in Russia; at the close I spoke of the tasks and shortcomings of the Russian socialists. I gave this lecture first in Munich, then in Karlsruhe, Heidelberg, and Berlin.

I had an interesting encounter in Karlsruhe. Arriving there in the morning, I was met at the station by my comrades. They told me of their plan to hold a small discussion prior to my large public lecture in the evening. The discussion, open to members of the Social Democratic groups, would center on the national question and would involve a political dialogue with a recently arrived, prominent young Iskrist [Russian social democrats around the newspaper *Iskra*, The Spark]. The man? Upon hearing his name I remembered. About a year and a half before, I had served as leader of a circle in Bern composed of young female students. One of them had told me about her brother, a very able young man and an exile in Siberia at the time. It was he who had just arrived from Siberia. The girl's name was Bronstein, at present the wife of Kamenev, the prominent Russian Communist. Her brother? The now-famous Leon Trotsky.

We set out for the encounter. Not far from the house in which the discussion-debate was to be held, I observed a small group of persons on the opposite side of the street heading for the same place. "There he is," someone said to me. He was a tall, slim young man with long hair and wearing yellow shoes. The yellow shoes struck me as rather too conspicuous; in those days such shoes were simply not worn in our circles. He resembled his sister. True, her eyes were dark, his light gray; but both had something about their faces which made them look like birds of prey. It was more striking with him because of his distinctive mouth—large, curved, mordant. It was a terrible mouth.

The exchange lasted several hours. One of my comrades from Karlsruhe launched it with an enunciation of the national program of the Bund as adopted at the Fourth Congress in 1901. Then Trotsky offered a detailed critique, to which I gave the response. I can no longer remember the details of the debate, but I do recall that it was conducted vehemently and that both sides, as usual, left feeling satisfied with themselves. I must confess that I developed a dislike for the fellow at that time, and I have reason to believe the feeling was mutual. It was not until evening, however, that interest really mounted and certain characteristics became apparent. Upon the completion of my lecture, a few Zionists took the floor, as did several unaffiliated youths with erratic ideas. Trotsky spoke next. He responded to the Zionists wittily and well. But then he turned on me, taking umbrage because I had "dared" to direct some caustic remarks at the Russian Social Democrats. I had accused them of having consistently neglected the important task of fighting anti-Semitism, and I made no secret of the fact that I considered this a grave misfortune and a serious shortcoming which must be avoided in the future.

Trotsky took up the cudgels for the Russian socialists. First, he said, it wasn't true: they had fought anti-Semitism. For instance, in his hometown, Nikolaev, a leaflet had even been issued about it years before! And second, it was not necessary to fight anti-Semitism in particular. Anti-Semitism was, after all, nothing more than a consequence of the universal lack of consciousness among the broad masses. Hence the need to bring them to a state of general awareness after which anti-Semitism would fade away willy-nilly. To make the Jews a special subject of discussion among the broad masses was superfluous. This justification was highly characteristic. On a subsequent occasion, when I met Trotsky in the company of another prominent activist, David Riazanov, if I'm not mistaken, it became clear that his attempt to deny even to himself the truly severe guilt devolving on the Russian socialists was nothing more than a rationalization on his part.

> Vladimir Medem, *The Life and Soul of a Legendary Jewish Socialist:*
> *The Memoirs of Vladimir Medem*, ed. and trans. Samuel A. Portnoy
> (New York: KTAV Publishing House, Inc., 1979),
> pp. 268–69.

The Po'alei Zion and the November Revolution

The Po'alei Zion supported the November Revolution of 1918 that formed the (Weimar) Republic, in the belief that it would rid Germany not only of its old—reactionary—system, but of anti-Semitism as well.

A Proclamation of the Secretariat of the Jewish/Social-Democratic Po'alei Zion Groups in Germany

On November 12, [1918,] the secretariat of the Jewish/Social-Democratic "Po'alei Zion" groups in Germany issued a proclamation. In the first part of this proclamation, they congratulated the German socialist proletariat on the success of the revolution and greeted the Free Socialist Republic of Germany. The second part of the proclamation is directed to Jewish workers. It states:

> The defeat of the monarchist giant means that one of the great fortresses of anti-Semitism and national oppression has been destroyed. The German reactionary movement was a nest of modern anti-Jewish sentiment, the hope and pride of the international "Black Hundred" [sic]. Only in the bloody years of the World War, in destroyed cities and towns on the Eastern front, did German militarism come face to face with the broad masses of the Jewish people. Its bloodthirsty, anti-Semitic servants and deputies sucked out the last drop of blood the devilish war had left in our brothers' bodies. This encounter will be marked in red in our history! Driven by hunger and need, tens of thousands of Jewish

workers had to leave home to seek safety and bread across the only open border. Their short stay in the old Germany has been a long chain of enslavement, oppression, worry, and torture. And when growing hunger and the corrupt rule of the German military commanders forced new masses of workers to begin the same migration, the now-fallen government renewed the old medieval ghetto laws, closing the border of the country to Jewish workers in particular and, at the same time, silencing anyone who dared to groan in his suffering, so that no one outside could learn of their devilish deeds. This anti-Semitic border closing was the last "present" the dying regime gave to its victim, the Jewish workers it itself had ruined, shortly before it died! And even now sounds from the old days are heard: as the country is rebuilt on a new economic basis, the first victim is to be the immigrant Jewish worker. It is with solid trust and hope that the Jewish working class, united under the banner of the Jewish social-democratic organization "Po'alei Zion" in Germany and all over the world, looks to its German socialist comrades in the new government. As it destroys the accursed legacy of the fallen rulers, the socialist proletariat will also destroy the Jews' heavy burden of oppression and restriction. The new government must put an end to all of the laws and procedures that oppress the tens of thousands of Jewish immigrants in Germany economically, politically, and as a people. In the new state structure, being created by the supporters and servants of the socialist ideal, there should no longer be any reminders of the old ideology, which differentiated between one worker and another and sacrificed one worker's interests to those of the other.

Institute for Labor Research, Tel Aviv, 12/III 43, no. 1.

Threat of Expulsion

After the 1919 Spartacist Revolution, the Jews were blamed for the collapse of Imperial Germany. Rosa Luxemburg, Kurt Eisner, and Gustav Landauer, leading figures of the revolution, were murdered. There was growing concern about the prospect of increased Eastern European Jewish immigration, and, in the early postwar years, the threat of immediate expulsion hung over them if they made a "nuisance" of themselves or became "troublesome" in the eyes of the police.

Transcript
Recorded in Essen on October 2, 1922
Official interrogation.

Isaak Pommeranz. Profession: performing artist. Present address: Albrechtstraße no. 32, Hamborn-Bruckhausen (in Essen since

October 1, 1922). Previous place of residence: Lodz. Born:
February 26, 1893, in Konstantin, District of Lodz. Citizenship:
Polish. Married to: Rosa, née Weissbrot. Religion: Jewish
[*mosaisch*].

ad rem:
   I admit that I crossed the Imperial [German] border at Kempen
in May of this year, and that I did not possess a valid passport and
visa stamp. When I crossed the border I was neither vaccinated
against smallpox nor deloused.

> read back, approved, and signed
> [signature:] Pommeranz (Russian)
> signed as above

> signed: Kurzawski, Police Officer

Interrogated again, P. explains further:
   After I entered Germany, I first took up residence in Berlin; I
lived for three weeks at Wiesenstraße no. 55, and did not work
during that time. Later I traveled to Bochum, but since I could not
find any work there, I left immediately. After that I traveled to
Hamborn; I lived in Bruckhausen (c/o Alfinger, Karl-Albrecht-
Straße no. 9) and worked in the blast-furnace facility of the
Thyssen company. For the last week I have been living at
Albrechtstraße no. 32 in Bruckhausen. I am not officially
registered there because I possess no passport and the registration
was not accepted by the police. The two loose pieces of paper were
sold in my workplace at a price of ten marks each for agitation
purposes.

> read back, approved, and signed
> [signature:] Pommeranz (Russian)
> signed as above

> signed: Kurzawski, Police Officer

Note:
Essen, October 3, 1922
Pommeranz is a Russian-Polish Jew. Except for a membership book
from the Polish Textile Workers' Guild, he has no identity papers.
Among his belongings we found several pictures and postcards,
including some depicting Rosa Luxemburg, Marx, and Lenin. By
his own admission, Pommeranz has resided in Germany since May
of this year but has not been registered with the police. He traveled
from Berlin to the industrial area and has spent time in Bochum,
Hamborn, Bruckhausen, and Essen. On Sunday, October 1, he was

observed among the demonstrators at a demonstration of the German Communist Party [KPD] in the Burgplatz here and at another location; he was not seen acting as an agitator at the demonstration. The circumstance is reported, however, because it is not impossible that he might be a Russian agent sent to the industrial area for propaganda purposes. He was not carrying propaganda material on his person when he was arrested. A photograph of Pommeranz is included.

> signed: Emmelmann, Criminal Operations Assistant

Chief of Police,
No. I.P.711
Essen, October 5, 1922

I present the attached transcript as per the instructions issued by the subsidiary office on January 28, 1921, [. . .] regarding the presence and propaganda activity of Russian Communists in the industrial area.

Pommeranz was stopped in Essen on October 1 and arrested because he is a foreigner with no official identity papers whatsoever. Since he was carrying pictures of Rosa Luxemburg and Lenin with him, it is possible that he might be a Russian agent.

Pommeranz speaks only broken German and Polish, but fluent Russian. Today he was taken to Police Court [Amtsgericht] to be sentenced for illegal entry; I requested that Pommeranz, once he has served his sentence, be returned to my custody so that I can begin deportation proceedings.

I enclose a photograph of Pommeranz.

to
The Administrative President—C.B.11—
in Düsseldorf

> Hauptstaatsarchiv Düsseldorf, Regierung Düsseldorf 15739.

The Expulsion of Polish Jews from Germany (1938–39)

On March 31, 1938, the Polish government announced that Polish citizens who had lived abroad for more than five years had to have their passports revalidated. The Nazi government took this opportunity to order the expulsion of the approximately eighteen thousand Polish Jews residing in Germany, leading to the first major deportation of Jews.

Dear Cilli,
Our expulsion happened as follows: The day in question, the 27th October, was bad from the beginning. Early in the morning I went to the Labour Exchange to get my [unemployment] benefit

payment and was told that I would receive only RM 5.50 per week
from now on instead of RM 12.50. When I came home, the second
blow was waiting for me: a letter from the landlord, informing us
we were not allowed to have any lodgers. In the afternoon I went
to Herschberg to give him an English lesson. After we had finished
I waited while Herschberg shaved. We then wanted to go into town
together. I sat in his room while he was in the bathroom. Suddenly
the doorbell rang, and I heard Herschberg talking with two men,
whom he then brought into the room where they quietly sat
down. I continued to read my paper. Suddenly I noticed that one of
them wore a swastika and I had a dark suspicion that they might
be from the Gestapo. He remarked that "he takes a long time to
shave; he's probably tearing his hairs out one by one." He went
into the bathroom and asked Herschberg who the man in the room
was (meaning me). Herschberg gave him my name and, in answer
to the next question, mentioned that I was a Polish citizen. The
man came back, asked me for my passport (which terrified me),
and identified himself as a Gestapo-man. He asked me where I
lived; when I told him Moritzstraße 2, he said that they had been
looking for me for quite a long time. He kept my passport. In the
meantime Herschberg was ready. The officials told us to put on our
coats and come with them. In answer to our question where we
were going, they said: to Palestine, and added that we had had five
years' time [to go there].

We thought it was a joke, especially when we were told to take
along food for twenty-four hours. In answer to my objection that I
had to go home first to get the food and let my mother know, I was
told that I was going to see my mother anyway. Then we left, one
official went ahead with me, the other followed with Herschberg.
While we were walking he asked me all sorts of questions, tried
again to make me believe that we were being sent to Palestine, and
added that I could thank my co-religionists for it. We came to
Jakobsstraße and suddenly found ourselves in front of
Zweisinger's dance hall. In front of it stood a police car from which
quite a number of Jews emerged. We were led into the hall, where
many more Jews were already assembled. We talked among ourselves and speculated on what was going to happen to us. In the
meantime more and more Jews were arriving, old and young men,
women and children, accompanied by Schupos* in uniform or
plainclothes Gestapo-men. The entrance was guarded by Schupos
with guns, and many Schupos and higher police officers were wandering around the hall. One very young police officer, who seemed

---

Schupo is the abbreviation for Schutzpolizei, the uniformed metropolitan Pro-
tective Police.

to be in charge, threw his weight about and abused us (though only verbally). By then Mother had arrived, and she told me that Schupos had come to our apartment and told her to dress warmly and also to take along food for twenty-four hours. The many thousands of Jews who were rounded up in Germany on the 27th and 28th October have never been told the real reason. Miss Kind came along with Mother. The Schupos never asked about the Aptekers. It came out only gradually what was going on. I was handed a printed form, which stated that according to statute such-and-such, by order of the Reichsführer SS, we were expelled from Germany and had to leave the German Reich by 29th October. The evacuation to Poland would be regulated by the Chief of Police. That, of course, was quite a blow. To be expelled so unexpectedly, and without knowing why: without being able to take anything with us, [we were to leave] just as we were. I personally had nothing with me, not even a winter coat. I was wearing my summer coat. What was going to happen to all the assets, the factories, businesses, shops, houses, flats? The hall became more and more crowded; some people who had not been found at home the first time, were being searched for again and again. It became later and later, we sat around the table of the dance hall from which Jews had been banned and which had now become our prison.

> Letter from Julius Rosenzweig to Celia Rosenzweig, August 19, 1939, in Sybil Milton, "The Expulsion of Polish Jews from Germany, October 1938 to July 1939—A Documentation," *Year Book of the Leo Baeck Institute*, vol. 29 (1984), pp. 175–77.

Resistance against Nazism

By the late 1930s, Berlin had the largest Eastern European Jewish quarter in Germany, the so-called Scheunenviertel. Several people who were able to escape from the ghetto joined the Communist movement and armed resistance against the Nazis.

A Boy from the Ghetto

The story of our resistance struggle against fascist barbarism has many heroes. True heroes. Ruben Rosenfeld, a quiet, modest boy from the Berlin ghetto, was one of them. He was living in poverty. He would run about with torn and tattered clothing, always curious, always thirsty for knowledge. Even as a fourteen-year-old he came running after me whenever he saw me marching in a demonstration. After all, I was already seventeen. He marched along with me in formation—he wanted to be part of the march, not just to run along beside us like a small child—even then. Only rarely did he forget to ask me where there would be an assembly. I told him, and Ruben came, even if it was far from the ghetto. He came on foot—he had no money for the fare.

Still just a teenager, Ruben left home. [. . .]

He was irresistibly drawn to the workers' movement. At seventeen he was already a member of the youth organization, and at nineteen he became a member of the German Communist Party [KPD]. [. . .]

In 1933 he was one of the hunted and hounded men who were working double-time for the people's cause. But by September of that year he was already locked up in the Gestapo dungeons, living through hell on earth. When they arrested him, the SA men found a note indicating the time and place of a meeting with a comrade from the district leadership. The Nazis took him there, to the Luther monument on Kaiser-Wilhelm-Straße. They had to cross the street. At that moment, Ruben threw himself in front of an approaching car. He wanted to sacrifice his life to save that of his comrade.

Mischket Liebermann, Aus dem Ghetto in die Welt (Berlin-
Bayreuth-Zurich: Verlag der Nation, 1995), pp. 72–73.

AMSTERDAM
The Diamond Cutters' Strike

Henri Polak was the great initiator and organizer of the Algemene Nederlandse Diamantbewerkers Bond (ANDB), the General Dutch Diamond Workers' Union. He was subsequently one of the founders of the National Trade Union (Nederlands Verbond van Vakverenigingen, NVV) and of the Social Democratic Workers' Party (Sociaal Democratische Arbeiders Partij, SDAP). One of the major concerns of the ANDB was to educate and civilize the proletarian masses, including the Jews. Polak wrote many articles in the ANDB press about the way in which a modern worker should live, dealing with everything from architecture to interior design to education.

The Diamond Workers' Union was founded as early as 1868 by a few energetic men. The immediate cause for its creation was the tyranny to which the workers were exposed by the factory owners, in particular from the previously mentioned Diamond Cutting Company. This company demanded, namely, that the cutter rent a scaife for Fl. 1.65 per day if he worked with two tangs (a cutter can work with four tangs simultaneously and thus have four stones on the scaife at the same time); if he wanted to use a third tang, then the rent of the scaife was Fl. 2.47^5 per day. The use of a fourth tang was absolutely forbidden.

After a short strike, the union succeeded, through the intervention of the then mayor, Mr. C. Fock, to win a small reduction in the rent of a scaife. For the rest, it was powerless. When, however, the "Cape Era" [of prosperity] was in full swing, the council, which had not lost its head, attempted to take steps in order to maintain the high wages, due to the exceptional circumstances of the industry. It foresaw that a crash would inevitably occur if no lid were put on the recruiting of hundreds of new workers. As long as the demand for cut diamonds remained as it was, there was no need; all workers, veteran and green, could find work. But what would happen, union council members wondered, if that demand should lessen, or if it came to an almost complete halt sooner or later because of a crisis at the trade's doorstep, or due to an eventual war?

They therefore harnessed themselves to labor, as the very first order of the day, disentangled the wage chaos and established a decent pay scale. After this crucial step had been taken in 1873, they started taking precautions and proposed to the union not to accept apprentices for a period of three years; only fathers would be permitted to teach their sons and guardians their charges how to become diamond workers, and this was subject to all kinds of rather troublesome stipulations. These proposals were adopted unanimously. [. . .]

When, also in 1889–90, due to financial maneuverings on the part of the De Beers Company, the diamond industry underwent a long crisis during which over nine months almost no work or extremely little was done, it was necessary to form a committee to support the diamond workers in need. From five hundred guilders per week in 1873 to nothing in 1889—that was a fall, *with a vengeance* [sic—in English], as the British say.

The only remedy for this and similarly miserable situations, the only dam that could stem the tide of wage reductions, could only be, of course, a powerful workers' organization; yet the diamond workers wanted to hear nothing of the sort. The fate with which the pre-Cape and Cape unions met, we have already seen: they disappeared completely after 1876, or dragged themselves through an anemic existence, impotent, powerless, and unknown to the majority of workers.

In 1888, however, a renewed effort was undertaken to organize the diamond workers. The diamond workers' group, together with the Amsterdam

division of the then Social Democratic Union, formed the Dutch Diamond
Workers' Union.

> Henri Polak, *De strijd der diamantbewerkers* (The Struggle of the
> Diamond Workers) (Amsterdam: S. L. van Looy, 1896),
> pp. 17–18, 30.

The Union as a Social Relief Agency

*The following text is a report on four unemployed families of diamond
workers. They were all members of the ANDB and all Jewish, which is evident from their names and from the streets where they lived. They all
cheated and had no right to get the money they had asked for, but this is a
good example of how the trade union took care of social relief for its members.*

Civil Welfare Board
Amsterdam, June 5, 1917
At-Home Poor,
Widows' Court and Poorhouse
No.: [blank]
Enclosures: [blank]

In response to your missive with regard to checking up on the
pensions of members of the General Dutch Diamond Workers'
Union, my looking into 148 random surveys this past May came
up with the following results.

No. 350 L. Hyman, K. Kerkstraat 6; family man, wife and 4 children
ages 18, 16, 15, and 10, received Fl. 10.50 in relief and received,
according to the report, Fl. 2.50 per week in family income. Upon
investigation, it turned out that Fl. 12.20 per week was coming in. On
last May 31, word was sent per telephone to the Welfare Department of
the ANDB.

No. 1729 N. Blaugrund, N. Amstelstraat 10, man, wife without
children. He received Fl. 6 in relief from the ANDB as well as Fl. 4.90
per week from the Committee for Refugees (relief stipend). Had no
income according to the report. He was receiving money from both
organizations while he was working. On May 16 both were advised per
telephone to stop his assistance.

No. 1590 S. Croonenburg, Peperstraat 10. Man, wife and 2 children
aged 5 and 4 years. He received Fl. 8.25 in assistance and had no family
income. At inspection it turned out that he earned approximately Fl.
7.50 per week as a tailor, of which notice was given on May 16.

No. 1018 J. Waterman, Rapenburg 2. Man, wife and 4 children aged
14, 12, 10, and 2 years. He received Fl. 9.75 in relief and received,

according to the report Fl. 3.75 in family income. At inspection it turned out that both he and his wife were earning Fl. 3.75 and Fl. 5 per week, respectively, which they had not mentioned. Last May 16, notice was sent.

> Amsterdams Gemeentearchief, Archief Sociale Zaken (Amsterdam Municipal Records, Social Affairs Archive), no. 1084A.

Debate in Favor of Socialism over Zionism

The Dutch Socialists responded to the Zionist challenge in the Jewish community with a call for further integration between Jews and gentiles.

The war of 1914 certainly proved that the bulk of humanity still feels totally unsafe on the wide sea of pure internationalism; that people want to feel the borders of country and people around them. The new internationalism, to be built up after the war, will, in applying the right to self-determination, start or have to start doing exactly this on the basis of a complete recognition of nationalities. These latter will become the great building blocks of the League of Nations.

Yet, within those nations, the people themselves will have to commence the tearing down of the countless "partitions" that divide the people: of position, possession, and religion. A leveling out is neither necessary nor desired; that which is social does not at all need to be contrasted so starkly against that which is individual. Yet, we must attempt to overthrow everything that artificially cuts people off from one another so that a fresh breeze may finally blow over the world and humanity may engage in an actual, total flowering of all its forces and talents. Therefore, I would also like to see the Jewish partition fall and see a melting together, preferably as completely as possible, of the Jewish and, let us simply say, the Christian population. All the best qualities that Jews possess: their practical moral code, their generous charity, their spiritual facility, their self-sacrificing idealism, all of this they can bring into a society with other peoples and overcome through learning their faults and idiosyncrasies, which everyone shares. For each people with whom they assimilate, the benefits will be great. And so strong are their racial qualities that no one need be afraid that these will be quickly exhausted in the mingling with other peoples.

*   *   *

Still, inclination and deep-rooted prejudice on both sides—attachment to Jewish religious customs that dominate domestic life to such an extreme that the intimate living together of persons with divergent perceptions is in fact impossible—will resist a total mixing through intermarriage for a long time to come. Therefore, the emphasis here falls only on the previously indicated necessity, that one must choose, one cannot have it both ways. Zionism hereby functions as an element of purification. People will now, with this movement, be able to declare themselves in favor of the new Jewish Nation organization; yet anyone, once registered, will at the earliest opportunity have to try to settle in the country of their forefathers and divest themselves of their Western nationality. Those who are not considering this, i.e., becoming Jewish Nationalists, will have to stand as a purely interested party, as a contributor, in their relation to Zionism, but they will have to keep themselves free of the wave of Jewish Nationalism. In this way the other peoples will know whom they can count upon as their own, and on whom they will be able to rely fully. The halfheartedness of the past years, which is becoming very dangerous for Jews in the West and in the East, can hereby reach an end.

L. Simons, *Joodsch nationalisme en assimilatie* (Jewish Nationalism and Assimilation) (Amsterdam, 1925), pp. 12–13 (originally published in *De Nieuwe Gids,* September 1920; copy in Bibliotheca Rosenthaliana [Br. Ros. Ned. J 44], Amsterdam University Library).

Call of the Zionists to the Socialists

Socialists should become Zionists, responded the latter. The following article describes Dutch Zionism and Dutch socialism as parallel movements, although according to the pamphlet, a socialist society was far away, and socialism was not an answer to the specific Jewish problem.

Why should a Socialist be a Zionist at the same time? One would best be able to answer this question in the Jewish manner, with another question: Why not?

It will be more difficult to answer this last question than the first one, for there is no single argument imaginable that holds water as to why a Jew, who is a social democrat, cannot also be a Zionist.

Yet it is a fact that many Jewish Socialists, particularly in the Netherlands, still take an undecided, perhaps even hostile stand with regard to Zionism.

The explanation for this is, in the first place, to be found in history. The modern Zionist organization was founded in the last years of the nineteenth century by Theodor Herzl. The aim of the Zionist organization was formulated in the Basel Program of 1897: *"Zionism strives toward a publicly-legally guaranteed place of its own in Palestine for the Jewish People to live."* Just like every other people, Herzl reasoned, our people as well deserves to have its own country, its own statehood, in which it can be completely itself. And what other country would come to mind than the old Jewish homeland to which each Jew through age-old tradition is connected? Palestine should once again become Eretz Israel, a Jewish commonwealth.

At the same time Socialism was gaining a foothold among the working class. In 1894, a Social Democratic Workers' Party [SDAP] was established in the Netherlands. Among its founders and leaders there were and still are many Jews. They needed all their forces to make the young party flourish. The proletariat, including Jews, lived in miserable circumstances. The workday was still practically unlimited, the wages were low, the living and health situations were bad. The workers did not have political power, the right to vote. Bit by bit, step by step, in a never-ending struggle, the workers' movement—political party and trade unions—had to overcome everything that had continually been denied the working class. In so doing, it was unavoidable that the workers would concentrate all their thought, feeling, and will to working for Socialism. From disordered multitudes a power was shaped, to the glory of humanity, as a socialist song put it.

The movement was young and its followers believed unfalteringly in the coming of Socialism, which would be a cure for all social ills. And if the misery within which the wandering, scattered Jewish People lived should be pointed out to them, they would declare that it was their firm conviction that Socialism would also solve this problem.

When social democracy grew in magnitude and power, when slowly but surely shorter working hours, higher wages, better places to live, general voting privileges had been won, people began to perceive that the realization of Socialism was not as simple as its first preachers had thought in their fiery idealism. People began to understand that a capitalist society could be changed only through democratic evolution into one in which private ownership of the means of production would be able to be replaced by communal ownership. The consequences of this newly acquired insight were far-reaching. While the Social Democratic Party had initially been exclusively an opposition party, it started, wherever possible, to take on responsibility. All kinds of issues that once lay beyond its scope now had to be recognized, because party leaders understood that the solutions to these issues could not wait until the distant future when Socialism would be realized.

One of those issues was the Jewish question. The Social Democratic Party had, it goes without saying, continually stood in the breach whenever it counted to protest the injustice that had been perpetrated on the Jews in many countries. Anti-Semitism at the end of the previous century and since the beginning of this century became stronger and stronger. Pogroms, persecutions on account of ritual murder, and the withholding or taking away of citizens' rights were the order of the day. Between workers and the repressed and oppressed Jews there was a natural sympathy. The solution to the Jewish question also began to preoccupy the Socialists.

Waiting until Socialism would be realized turned out to be impossible. By far the majority of Jews lived in countries where the victory of Socialism would undoubtedly come very late in the day. Before it had gotten to that point, practically all the Jews would have been killed.

Would Zionism be able to offer a solution? Before the war, there were only a few who believed that Zionism would ever become a reality. That the Jews would ever again be able to return to Eretz Israel, ancient Palestine, which had been reduced to a wasteland under Turkish misgovernment, seemed impossible. People laughed sympathetically at the crazy, but fortunately harmless, little group that believed in such utopias.

That was the way it was particularly in Western Europe. But in Eastern Europe, where most of the Jews, including the Jewish proletariat, were concentrated, people saw it differently. While in the West the Socialists, including the Jewish ones, thought that the concept of nation was of capitalist origin and that the international solidarity of workers would overcome national differences, the Eastern Jewish proletarians were personally experiencing that they belonged to a people different from the people among which they lived. And when they were forced to leave the inhospitable country, to move to the land of promise, the United States of America, they soon noticed that they were not welcome there either, that they were considered to be wage-spoilers who threatened the American working class's standard of living. For them Zionism was an equally fantastic ideal. The founding of the Po'alei Zion, the organization of Zionist socialist workers, was the proof of the pudding. People understood that liberating the Jewish People could only be the work of the Jews themselves, just as according to Marx, the liberation of the working class had to come about through the workers themselves.

Like so many other difficult issues, the world war resolved this as well. It was enlightening in two ways.

In the first place, the war proved that workers' class consciousness was no stronger than their national feeling. Everywhere "national thoughts, national differences prevailed." The Social Democratic Party started realizing this. In our country this was brought home by the leader of the SDAP no less, Mr. P. J. Troelstra, who, in his brochure "The World War and Social Democracy," wrote: "The way to the Socialist International does not run above or beyond or against, but through socialist nations."

This opinion has since then obtained civil rights within social democracy. People have begun to understand not only the larger meaning of nationalities, but socialists everywhere now champion the right to self-determination of nations and the protection of national minorities. When, during the war, the social democrats set up an international conference for peace in Stockholm, the demand for development and protection of Jewish colonization in Palestine was included in the resolutions accepted there. [. . .]

Social democracy welcomed this declaration with joy. As early as February 1918 another international socialist conference posed the demand that Palestine become a free state, under international supervision, where the Jewish People could develop their own culture independently.

This happened. Palestine was freed from the Turkish yolk and placed under the direction of the Peoples' Union, which England appointed to govern the country as authorized agent.

The Zionist Organization is considered to be the representative of the Jewish People, until the time will have come when our People are organized strongly enough to select independent representation.

The construction of Palestine herewith became an affair of honor for the Jewish People. But certainly, and not least, for the Jewish proletarians as well. The greatest part of the Jewish population in Palestine presently consists of workers, mostly socialist workers. They are cultivating the ground and attempting to turn the land into a land overflowing with milk and honey again. This land is largely not private property, but is bought up by the Jewish National Fund, an organ of the Zionist Organization, that earmarks all its land as the inalienable property of the entire Jewish People.

> S. Mok, *Waarom moet een Socialist tevens Zionist zijn?* (Why Should a Socialist Be a Zionist?) (Amsterdam, 1928), pp. 2–6 (Brochures van den Ned. Zionistenbond, no. 1; copy in Bibliotheca Rosenthaliana [Br. Ros. Z c 41], Amsterdam University Library).

Zionist Agricultural Project for Refugees

From 1934 onward, a major Zionist project was started in one of the new polders, aimed at teaching Jewish refugees to work in agriculture. Marianne Philips was a popular leftist Jewish writer who reports here on life in the village in the late 1930s. (The village existed until 1941; its end was very brutal. Since then, some accusations have been made that its inhabitants were the first to be deported because they were not Dutch.)

Reader. When you awoke this morning, that was an "in the beginning." Nothing existed yet. Then you slowly let go of your dream and adapted yourself to the world around you. You do that every morning and it happens pretty easily, because the world is punctually awaiting you every morning. There is the little bedside rug with your slippers. You can step into the new day. There will still be a dream image shimmering in the back of your mind, but the familiar form of your closet or the hangers on which your trousers are suspended will quickly have driven that away. And so you sit up, poke your legs out of bed and let them slip down to the floor.

Stop! Now, just imagine that there is no floor to be found. Imagine that you are reaching for a spot with your toes on which you can stand in order to get ready for the coming day, *and that that place is no longer there.* You grope around in the emptiness, you sit on the edge of your bed and the floor that you expected, that had been there faithfully every day, is *gone,* has *vanished.*

No, I do not want to give you a description of a nightmare. Before I start telling you anything about Wieringen, I only want you to fathom with your body what the labor camp inhabitants went through psychologically before they arrived in Wieringen.

There the *Jugendliche,* the boys and girls, are done with school in no time. Their eyes are still filled with the dream. Father, mother, the living room table, the lamp above the white tablecloth, the usual household things, which are merely things, of course. The child's land, in which even now, even in Germany, it is still possible to dream. [. . .]

But the young people, at least if they had a chance to work for some time in the "Jewish Labor" Foundation of Wieringen and adapted to things there, accept this fact. They also accept the fact that others will temporarily take care of their material needs. They do not consider that a favor, thank god. Those who own nothing in the world but a human soul and a body are sooner disposed to consider fellow humans as brothers, of whom, if necessary, they can expect help.

And these Jewish young people, sprouted from a tribe that through all the ages considered fellow humans as "neighbors," very rightly do not consider themselves to be objects of philanthropy. They feel themselves to be young Jews, temporarily reduced to the bare simplicity of human existence, but more than ever bearers of all the potentials of Jewish soul and vitality.

This is the great difference between them and the older emigrants, the desperate outcasts, who line up at the counters of the Jewish Refugee Committee. Perhaps Wieringen touched me so deeply, gave me such a feeling of freedom, because that same morning, there at the 's Gravenhekje [Earl's Gate], I spent a short time standing among the silent, pitiful older people, people who, along with their property, had lost all feeling of safety and security. "Whenever I feel myself sinking too far into the suffering of the refugees, a visit to Wieringen is like a refreshing bath," a board member of the Refugee Committee told me. I can understand that.

Marianne Philips, *Nieuwe grond* (New Ground) (Amsterdam: Uitgave Stichting "Joodse Arbeid"/Publication of the Jewish Labor Foundation, 1938), pp. 3, 6.

Chapter 4   Culture
and Identities

Religion, tradition, and secularization confronted each other in the New Worlds. Through their societies, organizations, and political activities, as well as in their daily lives, Jewish workers (sometimes consciously, more often not) came to grips with competing cultural demands and forged often syncretic identities. They were identifiably Jewish, yet at the same time Dutch, and, for the immigrants, increasingly American, Argentine, English, French, or German.

The migration experience brought Yiddish culture to the West. Theater troupes criss-crossed Europe and then the Atlantic, delighting uprooted immigrants with the tragedy and humor of home. But local troupes were formed as well, and they helped participate in the turn-of-the-century Yiddish renaissance. New schools of Yiddish theater and poetry arose in New York, for example, with playwrights and actors explicitly aiming to rescue the Yiddish stage from the melodramatic, vulgar *shund* (trash) theater that pandered to unsophisticated audiences.

While Yiddishists also had to fend off Hebraists, on the one hand—particularly with regard to educational programs for the young—and assimilatory linguistic tendencies (often propagated by the native Jewish communities), on the other, another struggle was being waged over the soul of the Jewish workers. Newspaper articles lamented the decline of tradition. Kashrut confronted frogs' legs in France. Yom Kippur balls were the anarchists' extreme expression of secularization. Dutch Jewish leaders fought for kosher food for the Jewish poor in the municipal charity organizations. But for the most part, modernization meant smaller, daily, gradual changes of habits and customs. The busy season in the garment industry meant choosing between celebrating the Sabbath or finishing an order on time. The next generation, educated in the schools of the new country, would make an even more decisive break with tradition.

Ethnic identities developed differently in each country. Americanization, Anglicization, or Gallicization, did not all have the same effect on Jewish identity. It may have meant boxing in England or America, playing baseball in the United States, or going to hear the popular singer Mistinguett in France. But more fundamentally it meant adapting to the modes of behavior possible for a minority group in each majority environment. In Germany, there was no Yiddish revival, as the less numerous and more dispersed immigrants acculturated fairly quickly into the German Jewish *Gemeinden* (official community bodies). In Holland, the Dutch Jews defended their Dutchness with little ambiguity.

Elsewhere the Yiddish press itself was both a symbol of cultural continuity and invariably a host to the ongoing debates over identity and acculturation. Workers' groups from Paris to Buenos Aires argued about the benefits or dangers of joining the local labor movements. On a more personal level, letters to the editor asked for advice in bringing up culturally wayward children. While the intellectuals who wrote and published the workers' press cannot be considered to have incarnated a purely authentic workers' voice, the discussions they engaged in confronted issues that spoke to workers' communities while going beyond them. "Workers' culture" was in any case itself in flux during the period considered. Over time, the immigrants became "ethnics"—as the Dutch Jews already were?—and the workers became middle class. In the meantime, the specific combination of plural cultures and multiple identities forged in the modern Diaspora attested to a vibrancy and flexibility of individuals and communities.

NEW YORK
Religion and Kashrut

Rabbi Moses Weinberger, who arrived in America from Hungary in 1880, was a harsh critic of immigrant society. Disappointed in the waywardness of American religious practices, he published a Hebrew-language pamphlet in 1887 entitled Jews and Judaism in New York, *in which he openly criticized various trends in American Judaism. His writings reflect the difficulties of a transplanted traditionalism, while at the same time they helped materially bolster traditional Judaism: the proceeds of his pamphlet went to aid an orthodox Jewish school in the city.*

The story is told of one immigrant who arrived here and barely supported himself and his wife by renting a small grocery on one of the streets. Came the month of Nisan (the Hebrew month in which Passover falls) and he did as he and all faithful Jews always did: he searched through everything that might contain *chomets* (leaven) and slowly began to remove it to the basement and attic in order to make room for the Passover goods that he had ordered a month before. On the morning before Passover, the merchandise arrived all properly weighed and measured just as he had requested in his letter to the dealer. But to his great astonishment, no Passover certification appeared: not from the head of the *bes din,* not from some individual *dayan* (judge), not from anybody at all. He was brokenhearted—and furious. "Surely some horrible error has occurred," he cried angrily. "Doubtless some confused clerks are to blame." But what could he do? There was no time to go out to obtain new holiday merchandise, for customers had already gathered and were coming in. If sent away empty-handed, they would never return.

There remained but one solution: to race to the nearest grocers and to borrow the needed merchandise or actually to purchase it from them at full price. This proved impossible however. To a man, the grocers claimed that they had enough only for their own needs, and had to look out for themselves. And so, while his wife stood full of misery in the store he ran around town like a madman. Half a day passed in turmoil and confusion. Finally they closed their doors.

Four days later, even before light had dawned on the first of the intermediate days of the holiday, he was already standing at the large supply house on S——Street. Still enraged and furious, he fought with the supervisors and those higher up. They swore to have sent him everything he needed for Passover, but to no avail. They showed him a special place on the first floor where a sign on the wall read PASSOVER G(ROCERIES), and there was his name.

"But where is the Passover certification?"

Finally the owner of the supply house came out, brought him to his office, gave him a seat, and in a soft earnest voice said "I see, my friend, that you are as green as can be. You just arrived in this country, and you know nothing of its ways. Be aware of the fact that, aside from flour, there is no Passover merchandise in New York. Many Jews who would never dream of drinking c(offee) or eating s(ugar) or dried fruit on Passover, and who place in their store windows and advertisements large signs reading PASSOVER G(ROCERIES) are actually lying. The words are a deception and fraud. Since many of the storekeepers who do business with us requested it, we were forced to act as you saw. Not that it helps us any, but—as you too now understand and will know for the future—it does benefit the storekeepers in the Jewish areas."

A new year came, and he knew what lay ahead. Though snow still covered the earth, he already had a sign prepared in gold letters ready to hang in the window before the holiday. But his wife, who came from a good family in the Hungarian state, felt most distressed and argued with him daily. "How is it possible," she asked him, "to stock s(ugar) on Passover without any proper certification? Did the sages in our country dwell on this problem in vain? Did the *gaon* from Szerem waste his time troubling himself about it? And what about the dried fruits: do you know where they came from? Would the Jews back home have used them? Does America have a special Torah for itself?" Her husband listened and proceeded to burn his sign before her eyes. Now he is among those working to bring about improvements in those matters where the Torah strictly demands proper Passover supervision.

> Jonathan D. Sarna, ed. and trans., *People Walk on Their Heads: Moses Weinberger's Jews and Judaism in New York* (New York: Holmes & Meier, 1982), pp. 74–75 (copyright ©1981 by Jonathan D. Sarna; reproduced by the permission of the publisher).

Americanization and "Judaization"

The Educational Alliance, founded by the merger of several previously existing organizations in 1889, was one of the central institutions of the Lower East Side. Its five-story building on East Broadway was the setting for lectures, classes, religious services, theatrical productions, social and literary club meetings, and athletic events which drew together thousands of adults and children each week. Its purpose, as stated in the following minutes of its uptown Advisory League, was to socialize the immigrants and help further their acculturation to American life.

The fourth meeting of the Advisory League was held at the residence of Mr. Louis Marshall, No. 47 East 72nd St. on Monday evening, Feb. 26th, 1906. [. . .]

Judge Greenbaum addressed the meeting on a similar topic, speaking of the emigrant who arrives here, in a strange land with customs and language unknown and utterly different from what they have been brought up to understand; to take these men, women and their children, to teach them these things; to make them understand the political ideas and systems here,—is the work that the Alliance undertakes to do. Before the emigrant can go to a public school, he must learn English; and a preliminary course is thus necessary and is given at the Alliance and in a comparatively short time, the newly arrived emigrant imbibes the American idea of citizenship, commercial and political duties, so that when he is ready to become a citizen of the United States, he can understand and appreciate the meaning of the privilege.

Missionaries in the cause of the Alliance is the necessity of the hour. Money is badly needed, and the spreading of the knowledge of this work, even more so. He urged upon all, not only to try to get new members, but to enthuse them with the knowledge of the good work and have them become workers in the cause also.

YIVO Institute for Jewish Research, Records of the Educational
Alliance, folder 14.

Zvi Hirsch Masliansky, a preacher and organizer for the proto-Zionist Hibbat Zion movement in Russia, became enormously popular among the large numbers of orthodox immigrants in the United States. In his Friday night sermons at the Educational Alliance, Masliansky defended traditional values and religious orthodoxy even as he praised American republicanism and democracy. Masliansky sought to "Americanize the immigrant parents and Judaize their children" while at the same time preaching the Zionist message.

"And the waters increased and bore up the ark, and it was lifted up above the earth." [in Hebrew and Yiddish; Genesis 7:17] [. . .]

Hovering in the air for over eighteen hundred years, we were weakened physically. And for that very reason our fantasies became strong! We became dreamers and visionaries, enthusiasts and fantasizers! We have empty dreams and false hopes. We are neither fish nor fowl. We fly in the air, live in the sky, and strive after illusions. We are no longer what we once were. No small matter, this—living beings hanging in the air! How terrible it is! Caught in the sky on a fantastic hook, we hang from a chain of rapture in the air between heaven and earth. Severed from the earth and still far from heaven. Oh, how cruel this sort of life is for an entire nation in an ark "lifted up above the earth!". . . [. . .]

The call, "Get thee out" [Genesis 7:1], still resounds in our ears wherever we turn—in large depots and small ones, on the shores of all the seas, and at the borders of countries both great and small. We hear the call, "Get thee out," most strongly from the Russian and Romanian gendarmes at their accursed borders. And the echo reverberates in the port cities of Hamburg, Bremen, Antwerp, Rotterdam, Liverpool, and so on. And from there it reaches the tiny isle of tears, Ellis Island, in America. [. . .]

"And he brought him forth abroad." [Genesis 15:5] Then the Almighty took him out among all the nations. That is, He showed him that his children would be "exceptions," different from all the other nations. Assimilation would not affect them. They would always be his children, a "people that shall dwell alone" [Numbers 23:9]. They would remain a nation apart. [. . .]

And then the sun set, and a deep sleep came over Abraham, and a dark and terrible vision appeared before his eyes. And a cry came from the depths of his heart: "Oh, my children, my children, slaughtered, torn apart, violated, and exterminated, God!"...

And the terrible vision disappeared from Abraham, and before his eyes appeared a magnificent and enticing image of the Holy Land in all its glory, with its tall proud mountains and its green valleys. And God's strong voice resounded mightily in his ears, "Unto thy seed have I given this land [Genesis 15:18]. Behold this beautiful land. It belongs to your children. It will be their compensation for all of the afflictions and troubles that they have suffered in Exile." Amen!

> Zvi Hirsch Masliansky, *Maslianski's droshes fir shabosim un yomim-toyvim* (1908), 3 vols. (New York: Hebrew Publishing Company, 1927), 1:10, 12–13, 22–25 (reprinted by permission of the publishers, Hebrew Publishing Co., P.O. Box 930157, Rockaway Beach, NY, 11693-0157, copyright © 1927, all rights reserved).

Yiddish in America

Many of the radical intellectuals who arrived with the first wave of Jewish immigrants came with a contempt for the Yiddish language, which they regarded as incapable, even unworthy, of expressing the fine sentiments of idealism and progress which they hoped to propagate. Gradually, however, the radicals recognized the need to speak and write in Yiddish if they were to reach the Jewish masses, and, as in Russia, the Jewish socialist movement ultimately became a driving force in the development of Yiddish as a modern literary medium. Abraham Cahan, the future editor of the Forverts *(Jewish Daily Forward), was one of the first to recognize the need for propaganda in Yiddish. In 1882, he gave what is thought to be the first socialist lecture in Yiddish ever held in America.*

When I expressed the opinion that speeches for Jews should be given in Yiddish, he burst out laughing. A couple of the people standing near us laughed along with him—even those who spoke Yiddish quite well. The suggestion that one could give a speech in Yiddish seemed funny to them. Yiddish was seen as a language for the home, the traditional Jewish elementary school, and the Jewish store. They were unaccustomed to the idea that it was possible to do anything so important as give a speech in Yiddish.

"So, why don't you give a speech in Yiddish?" Mirovich asked me jokingly.

"And why not?" I answered proudly and angrily.

In short, more in fun than in earnest, the Propaganda Association rented a hall for the next Friday evening and it was agreed that I would try to give a Yiddish speech on socialism.

I spent the whole week preparing. With my own few pennies I had handbills printed in Yiddish, and Bernard Weinstein and I distributed them in the Jewish neighborhood.

The meeting took place on July 26th, in a small hall behind a German beer saloon at 625 East 6th Street.

> Abraham Cahan, *Bleter fun mayn leben*, 5 vols. (New York: Forward Association, 1926), 2:106–7.

The cellar where the meeting was held was so crowded with Russian-Jewish immigrants that it was impossible for the speakers to push their way to the platform.

Those present listened with great interest to Cahan speak in a clear Yiddish. The speaker used simple examples to explain socialism and criticize capitalism. To this day I remember the image that Comrade Cahan then painted in these words: Imagine a tall tower composed of people. Exhausted people stand on the bottom, holding the tower on their shoulders. A little bit higher stand others, for whom it is a little easier to hold up the tower. The higher the people stand, the easier it is to hold the tower, which rests on the shoulders of the exhausted people on the bottom. Then, on the very top of this tower, sit the lucky few who look beautiful, healthy, and happy. This is a picture of the present capitalist society, the speaker explained. Society rests entirely on the backs of the workers who create all wealth— those who dig the coal, plant the wheat, bake the bread, make the shoes, and sew the clothing. Meanwhile, the capitalists, who do not lift a finger, sit on top and live in luxury and ease. Then the speaker explained the teachings of Karl Marx, showing how socialism would replace capitalism, and how the socialist society would introduce freedom, equality, and brotherhood for all people who produce. [. . .]

That evening has remained etched in my heart to this day. That was the first time I really understood the doctrine of socialism.

> Bernard Weinstein, *Fertsig yohr in der idisher arbayter bavegung* (New York: Farlag Veker, 1924), pp. 44–45.

Radical intellectuals were not the only ones who struggled with questions of language and identity. Almost from the time of their arrival, the immigrants absorbed hundreds of English words and phrases into their Yiddish speech. Nevertheless, there were difficulties inherent in the process of adap-

tation, illustrated here by the great Yiddish writer Sholem Aleichem. More-over, to the immigrants' American-born children, for whom mastery of the English language represented access to American society, the immigrant generation's continued use of Yiddish seemed a badge of backwardness and isolation.

This annoys my mother. She sticks up for me and my friend Mendel. She says that we earn our bit of bread fair and square, because at dawn, before the *stand** opens, we deliver the morning *paper* to our *customers*. After-ward, we go to *school* (yes, we are already in *school*). And when we come home from *school,* we help *attend* to the *business.* That is what my mother says, in those very words. She already speaks half in the local language. She no longer uses the Yiddish words, hun and kikh. She says *chicken* and *kitchen.* So, what then? With her it comes out backward. A kikh is for her a *chicken,* and a hun is for her a *kitchen.* "I'm going," she says, "to the chicken to salt the kitchen. . . ." Everyone laughs at her. She laughs too: "Yak reydele to reydele, abi dobre meynele."** . . . Well, are you clever enough to translate that into English?!

Sholem Aleichem, *Motl Peysi dem khazn's: in Amerike*
(New York: Morgn-Freiheit, 1937), p. 179.

A Question of Identity

Over the years, the Forverts/Forward *reflected the growing acculturation of the immigrants and particularly their children. Through its famous advice column, "Bintl brief," the paper addressed daily questions of iden-tity and language.*

1933

Worthy Editor,

I am sure that the problem I am writing about affects many Jewish homes. It deals with immigrant parents and their American-born children.

My parents, who have been readers of your paper for years, came from Europe. They have been here in this country over thirty years and were married twenty-eight years ago. They have

---

*Italics, added by the translator, denote English words (written in Yiddish char-acters) in the original.
**"Say it however you like, as long as your meaning is clear."

five sons, and I am one of them. The oldest of us is twenty-seven and the youngest twenty-one.

We are all making a decent living. One of us works for the State Department. A second is a manager in a large store, two are in business, and the youngest is studying law. Our parents do not need our help because my father has a good job.

We, the five brothers, always speak English to each other. Our parents know English too, but they speak only Yiddish, not just among themselves but to us too, and even to our American friends who come to visit us. We beg them not to speak Yiddish in the presence of our friends, since they can speak English, but they don't want to. It's a sort of stubbornness on their part, and a great deal of quarreling goes on between our parents and ourselves because of it.

Their answer is: "Children, we ask you not to try to teach us how to talk to people. We are older than you."

Imagine, even when we go with our father to buy something in a store on Fifth Avenue, New York, he insists on speaking Yiddish. We are not ashamed of our parents, God forbid, but they ought to know where it's proper and where it's not. If they talk Yiddish among themselves at home, or to us, it's bad enough, but among strangers and Christians? Is that nice? It looks as if they're doing it to spite us. Petty spats grow out of it. They want to keep only to their old ways and don't want to take up our new ways.

We beg you, friend Editor, to express your opinion on this question, and if possible send us your answer in English, because we can't read Yiddish.

Accept our thanks for your answer, which we expect soon,

Respectfully,
I. and the Four Brothers

ANSWER:
We see absolutely no crime in the parents' speaking Yiddish to their sons. The Yiddish language is dear to them and they want to speak in that language to their children and all who understand it. It may also be that they are ashamed to speak their imperfect English among strangers so they prefer to use their mother tongue.

From the letter, we get the impression that the parents are not fanatics, and with their speaking Yiddish they are not out to spite the children. But it would certainly not be wrong if the parents were to speak English too, to the children. People should and must learn the language of their country.

Isaac Metzker, ed., *A Bintel Brief* (New York: Doubleday, 1971, copyright © 1971 by Isaac Metzker), pp. 156–58.

LONDON

Orthodoxy and the Immigrant Poor

The citadel of Judaism in the East End of London was represented by the Machziké Hadass, whose religious leader was Rabbi Aba Werner. In the first article given here, the Anglo-Jewish community newspaper describes the immigrant synagogue with somewhat astonished approval. In another article, six years later, an interview with the immigrant rabbi stresses that immigrants can provide a model of religious traditions for English Jewry that does not reject modernity.

The Machziké Hadass and the New Arrangement

Some account of the "Great Synagogue" in Spitalfields, of which Rabbi Werner is Minister, should prove of interest to those who are unacquainted with this remarkable place of worship. It is unlike any other synagogue in the United Kingdom. Formerly a Wesleyan chapel, the transformation which it has undergone since it came into the possession of the Machziké Hadass is, to say the least, wonderfully striking. [. . .]

[. . .] In the synagogue proper there is accommodation for about 1,000 people, 700 on the ground floor and 300 in the galleries.

It is a curious sight that this place of worship presents to a visitor at almost any hour of the day or night. From four or five in the morning until twelve o'clock at night, or later, there is always something going on. And in this respect also the Spitalfields "Great Synagogue" rather resembles a Roman Catholic place of worship, which is open to prayer all day. Some four or five separate services are held in the course of the morning. At one o'clock in the day the first *Mincha* service is held, and thus the working man is enabled to pray with Minyan [quorum of ten adult men necessary for public synagogue service], on his way to or from work, during the dinner hour. And there is a similar succession of evening services, from sunset onwards. These services are conducted at the small reading-desk by laymen who are mourners or have Jahrzeit [yearly anniversary of a death], and who are thus enabled to fulfil the strict *Din* of the *Shulchan Aruch*. It was about half-past six one evening when we found about a hundred persons assembled at one of these services. At the same time, the larger and smaller Beth Hamidrash each contained its complement of students. Some of them no doubt had turned in in order to meet their *Landsleute* for a friendly chat, using the place as a sort of poor man's club, from which smoking was not altogether excluded. But the chief object of those who attend the Beth Hamedrash [sic] is study, and the majority go through a systematic course of reading, whether in *Gemorah, En Jacob* or *Chajé Adam*, which is styled a *Shiur*. We were present at the termination of one of these *Shiurim*, when the leader of a study class finished a course in the traditional manner by reciting *Rabbonim Kaddish*.

On Sabbaths, we are informed by Mr. Feldman, the synagogue is crowded to its utmost capacity. The most popular service is *Mincha*, at which, from time to time, lectures in Yiddish may be delivered by regular or itinerant preachers. [. . .]

The subscribing members of the Machziké Hadass consist, for the most part, of the working classes. Having regard to their restricted means, the charity that they do can only be described as wonderful. No poor outcast ever presents himself at the synagogue on Friday evenings for whom Sabbath meals are not provided. And collections are constantly being made for people in distress. [. . .]

Quite as remarkable as the Synagogue and Beth Hamidrash, if not more so, is the purpose to which the adjoining house is put. Here is a Talmud Torah, at which 1,000 children receive instruction in Hebrew and Talmud, the instruction being given through the medium of Yiddish. It is a huge building, four storeys high, consisting of at least sixteen class-rooms, which would give an average of sixty children to each class. Many of the rooms are overcrowded, and though windows are opened, the atmosphere is not of the freshest. In one class boys of fourteen are studying Talmud, being initiated into the mysteries of *Baba Kama* in the sing-song style which prevails in Poland. In another class, where *Chumish* is taught, the boys shake themselves as if they were at prayer. The majority of these lads are new arrivals in this country, who speak only Yiddish. [. . .] It costs £1,400 a year to maintain this institution, which has lately got into such financial low water that for some weeks past the salaries of the teachers have not been paid. Unfortunately, the school depends for its maintenance on poor people, who subscribe their penny and twopence a week. While the kind of teaching that is given can hardly be approved of from an English standpoint, one cannot but admire the enthusiasm of the foreign poor which sustains them in the sacrifices they make to give their children what they regard as a suitable Hebrew and religious training.

The Jewish Chronicle, February 24, 1905.

A "Foreign" Rabbi

INTERVIEW FOR THE *JEWISH CHRONICLE* WITH RABBI A. WERNER

We have heard a good deal recently about the "foreign" Rabbi. He has in some quarters been represented as a ferocious fanatic, if not a religious maniac. [. . .]

Does the Rabbi think that Orthodox Judaism has recently weakened? was asked. And, in the way of a reply you have to soar with him through the historic heights of centuries of Jewish thought; you are brought upon the scene when Jews were still in Palestine, the religious tendencies of the various parties and sects, the development of the Talmud, the Gaonic period, followed by a decline, the subsequent revival in the form of eclectical Judaism, and so you stumble on the rocky paths of history—reluctantly and protestingly—till you reach the Chassidaic movement on the one side and the Haskalah or Mendelssohn period on the other side; and it is here you get your reply:

"These two movements have, in my opinion," said Rabbi Werner, "greatly weakened Judaism. From different points of view both movements made light of Jewish learning, the one being swept by emotionalism, the other by rationalism; they diverted attention from the study of Judaism."

Would you have preferred, then, that the Jew should remain in his spiritual ghetto?

"Not at all. The Jew can take an active interest in the welfare of the State without becoming estranged from Judaism; such cases are not without record in Jewish history. There is no reason why secular education should alienate Jews from their own literature.

"The weak spot of Judaism in England is the lack of study. What is the use of making reforms to strengthen Judaism if people are ignorant? The leaders of Anglo-Jewry are certainly good Jews, but they lack the historic perspective, they need knowledge of the Torah, and it is a great pity that it is not explained to them. [. . .]

"[. . .] There need be no fear for the future of Judaism in England or elsewhere if the children obtain a good Jewish education." [. . .]

[. . .] Rabbi Werner thought that Judaism in England is stronger now than it was when he came here twenty years ago. This, of course must be attributed to the influx of Russian Jews into this country. It was a pity, he thought, that the Jews who come here cannot learn quickly the English language. English Jewry would appreciate their brethren to a greater extent than they now do if the latter could make themselves understood. Judaism would also gain much, as the English Jew would be influenced by the foreign Jew who knows and understands so much better about questions concerning Jews and Jewishness.

The Jewish Chronicle, June 9, 1911.

Freethinkers

Socialist and anarchist freethinkers challenged Jewish orthodoxy. Lectures purporting to prove the absurdity of religious belief, delivered by orators such as Benjamin Feigenbaum, were often dramatic occasions. The first account is of a lecture that was given in the late 1880s or early 1890s. In the second article, we see that the disputes between freethinkers and orthodox occasionally even exploded into violence.

The large Christ Church Hall on Hanbury Street was nearly filled to capacity when they arrived, and still more men and women kept coming. Finally the meeting was opened by the chairman. After him came two speakers on "The Absurdity of Religion." Then Feigenbaum was introduced as the principal speaker of the evening, on the subject: "Is there a God?"

He was of medium height with broad shoulders and gesticulated as he spoke. [. . .]

He spoke for nearly an hour, extemporaneously, freely quoting from scripture, science and history. Mot [the writer] listened intensely, obsessed with a feeling of enthusiasm and fear. Suddenly the speaker stopped. He took out his watch from his pocket, placed it on the small table in front of him, paused for a moment and with a dramatic gesture shouted: "If there is a God and if he is almighty as the clergy claims he is, I give him just two minutes time to kill me on the spot, so that he may prove his existence." The challenge created a tense silence in the hall. Mot felt a shiver running through his body, fearing that something might happen to the speaker. The two minutes finally elapsed. The speaker in his dramatic pose exclaimed: "See, there is no God!" A thunder of applause echoed through the hall. In the meantime the music struck up the Marseillaise, the national hymn of the French Republic, at that time the revolutionary hymn throughout Europe. Then the Yom Kippur Ball was announced and the meeting was over.

Thomas Eyges, *Beyond the Horizon: The Story of a Radical Emigrant* (Boston: Group Free Society, 1944), pp. 77–78.

Day of Atonement Disturbances in the East End

A regrettable incident, which has attracted considerable attention, occurred on Monday, the Day of Atonement, in the neighbourhood of Princelet Street, Spitalfields, when a breach of the peace took place between orthodox and socialist Jews, the latter of whom have a large club in Princelet Street, close to the Princelet Street Synagogue.

STATEMENTS OF A RESIDENT IN PRINCELET STREET

[. . .] Ever since the establishment of the Club it had been a constant source of annoyance to the neighbours, most of whom were orthodox Jews, though

Christian residents had also complained. On Friday nights there were functions at the club which were continued to a late hour, and the noise was such as to disturb the rest of the neighbouring residents. On one occasion he [the resident] was compelled to remove from his ordinary bedroom and sleep elsewhere. He was taking legal advice with a view to remedying the nuisance. On Yom Kippur the Socialists paraded the streets smoking, even entering the precincts of the synagogue with cigarettes in their mouths. Food was openly partaken of at the Club, and passers-by were invited to participate. There was no possible doubt that the disturbances were deliberately provoked, and he condemned in the strongest terms the behaviour of the Jewish socialists who had acted in flagrant disregard of the feelings and sensibilities of other Jews. The club members were mostly new arrivals, and they combined with their free-thinking views an entire lack of all moral restraint.

INTERVIEW WITH A SOCIALIST LEADER

Our representative subsequently visited the Club in Princelet Street, and had an interview with Mr. S. Ellstein, organiser of the East London Branch of the Social Democratic Federation, and other managers of the Club. Mr. Ellstein emphatically denied several statements which had been disseminated in connection with the affair. For instance, he characterised as an "absolute lie" the statement that they had invited rabbis to a concert at the Club on the Day of Atonement, or that members of the Club had entered the synagogue smoking. The Jewish masses had no idea of constitutional usages, and it was the object of the socialists to uphold the banner of constitutional freedom among the Jewish workmen. It was not true that they conducted a propaganda against religion or religious observances, holding that religion was a matter of individual choice. At the same time they maintained their right to freedom of thought, and if Yom Kippur was the same to them as any other day they had a perfect right to do as they pleased in regard to eating and smoking. In reply to the suggestion that the dictates of good citizenship should induce them to refrain from offending the sensibilities of their neighbours, Mr. Ellstein replied that just as he did not raise any objection to Jews going to synagogue, however much that might conflict with his private opinions, so, too, the so-called orthodox Jews should be equally tolerant. The disturbances had really commenced on the eve of New Year when a party of young Jews had smashed the Club windows, but owing to the energetic action of the Club Managers reprisals had been prevented. The police were fully aware of the state of feeling which existed, and anticipated a renewal of the unpleasantness on Yom Kippur. The Club premises were crowded on Monday, but extraordinary decorum prevailed, and it was preposterous to allege that the disturbances were commenced by the Club members. They tried to make the Club a "People's Home," and to supply all the material and intellectual wants of the members. Thus, they had lectures and cheap meals which had been very successful, and he suspected that the jealousy of certain neighbouring restaurant-keepers had been aroused, and that they were not unconnected with Monday's riot, as there were several professional "bruisers" in the crowd. He regarded as significant the fact that no member of the Princelet Street Club had been arrested, while he considered the magistrate's remarks a great moral triumph for their cause. They naturally regretted that violence had been resorted to as they deprecated all breaches of law and order, but the blame did not rest on their shoulders. Apart from the misrepresentations of this incident, they considered that they had not been treated fairly by the English Liberal Press. Jews had helped in the general social movement, and should now be helped when they were working for their own social regeneration.

The Jewish Chronicle, September 23, 1904.

Rigoletto *in Yiddish*

Yiddish was not only a vehicle for preserving religious orthodoxy and a traditional culture but also the means by which Western European culture reached the immigrant masses. Yiddish newspapers carried translated serializations of many classics of European literature. The theater was another arena where Western secular culture was translated into a form accessible to Eastern European Jewish immigrants.

Music and Drama

"RIGOLETTO" IN YIDDISH:
A NOTABLE TRIUMPH

We are becoming so accustomed to the remarkable enterprise of the authorities of the Temple, East End Jewry's playhouse in Commercial Road, that we cease to wonder at anything they now attempt in order to entertain a fastidious public. But it was, however, with more than a feeling of indifference, that we accepted the invitation to witness the performance of "Rigoletto" last week. It was an ambitious project, this "doing into" Yiddish of Verdi's greatest opera, and the successful accomplishment of so great a task reflects all the greater credit upon those who had undertaken it. Mr. S. Alman, the musical director, once again showed his remarkable versatility, for to him was entrusted the difficult work of translating the libretto into Yiddish, a work which was beset with no ordinary difficulties, but which he accomplished with surprisingly successful results. His version appeared to fit the musical accent admirably and to run easily.

This represents the first occasion upon which "Rigoletto" has been produced in the jargon, and little did Verdi imagine, when his work was first produced in Venice in 1851, that sixty-one years later it would delight the denizens of the East End in their own tongue. But such is the march of time, and all opera lovers in search of new and refreshing experiences may be recommended to pay a visit to the Yiddish theatre in our midst. That the production, from all points of view, was a notable one goes without saying, for we already know what talent is found among the stock company at the "Temple of Art," and what a skilful batôn is wielded by the translator and composer of "King Ahaz." As a contemporary remarks, "Rigoletto" cannot sound as well in Yiddish as in Italian. "Caro nome del mio cor" becomes "Oisgekritzt in main hartz." But Mr. Alman, the composer-conductor, has evidently done his translation with poetical feeling and—as far as possible—with due consideration for vocal effect. To him and, no doubt, also to Mr. Winogradoff, the stage director, the performance owed its artistic style, its precision and forceful and captivating swing, and its dramatic sensitiveness. The drawback was the smallness of the orchestra and, to a lesser degree, that of the chorus. It is a mistake to think that the orchestral part in Verdi's opera is of little importance. However, all honour to the leader and the members of the orchestra and chorus, and the capable and eager representatives of the various lesser rôles in the opera. [. . .]

Taking all things into consideration, it is hardly surprising that the general press are so enthusiastic over the production, and we cannot help culling the following from the *Daily Chronicle,* which in the course of its *critique* remarks:—"Nowhere, except in grand opera at Covent Garden, could one hear, in England, a company of such brilliant talent as in this Yiddish Theatre, in the very heart of the East End, which has been founded by the subscriptions of rich and poor Jews, and has been built to fulfil a great racial ideal among those people who have come from all parts of the world, refugees from persecution and direst poverty, to the Ghetto in London, where they are bound together by the same faith, the same tragic history, and by that mixed language spoken by all the Jews of Europe. The performance of 'Rigoletto' in Yiddish stands by itself as one of the most notable operatic triumphs in this country. The libretto has been translated by Mr. S. Alman, the conductor, and the music, which is full of technical difficulties to any but the most highly trained singers and musicians, was performed both by the company and the orchestra, with an accuracy, a precision, and a perfect mastery, astonishing in its excellence."

The Jewish Chronicle, April 19, 1912.

Anglicization, Politicization, and Gender

Ruth Adler was born in London in 1912, but her Polish Jewish parents returned to Poland shortly before World War I, where she stayed until after the war. Returning to London at age seven, Ruth then experienced the stresses of Anglicization. The Anglo-Jewish community was haunted by anti-alienism and drove forward educational and cultural programs designed to assimilate immigrants into the mainstream of British life. This policy divided children from parents and caused long-term problems of identity. Later, Ruth became active in the Workers' Circle and the Communist Party in London. She was interviewed in 1984 by the Jewish Women in London Group.

I remember my first day at school; it was all very strange. Things were happening round me which didn't register, but I don't remember being scared. A little cousin who was six was given permission to come from her class and sit next to me and translate what the teacher was saying. I don't remember having any difficulties with the language after that. At the end of the first year I got a prize in English. I spoke only Yiddish till I was seven and a half; English is my second language. For quite a while my parents and I spoke to each other in Yiddish. But then a teacher said to me, "If you want to learn English, you must speak English, read English and dream in English." When I told this to my father, he roared with laughter. But I took her advice and stopped speaking Yiddish. Then I spoke to my parents in English and they answered me in Yiddish. This is a very common story, not only among Jews. And so we got by until my parents began to speak English too.

[I went to Stepney Jewish School. . . .] A new headmistress came when I was about 10 or 12, Miss Kate Rose her name was, and she wanted us to look like secondary school children. She didn't say so, of course, but I can now interpret it that way. She issued an edict that we were to have uniforms, navy-blue gymslips and white blouses. Well, I could go on for a week about the trouble this caused. How long can you wear a white blouse? Our parents didn't have the wherewithal to keep a stock of white blouses and give us a fresh one every day, so by the time Friday came, they were pretty grubby. The teacher would say, "You should have clean blouses on, girls, even on a Friday." But our mothers would say, "It's the last day of the week; it's not worth putting on a clean blouse." My mother couldn't face the expense of buying the new uniform so she made mine. She was handy with a needle, but this was difficult because you had to have three box-pleats in front. She found she didn't have enough material for three, so she made two. Imagine my agony, going to school with only two box-pleats—but I had to sweat it out.

[...] In the Progressive Youth Circle, which [my future husband] and another comrade set up in the late twenties, there were all sorts of young people: communists, anarchists, socialists, Zionists, and non-Party people who were interested in political matters. We used to thrash things out in lectures and discussions. It was a marvellous time for me. Up to that time I'd been buried in books. When the two young men from Poland arrived, my future husband was 19 and his friend was 17. I was 14, in short socks, and didn't even notice them. They would argue with my father about politics but I didn't really listen; I was reading my eyes out. When they introduced me into the Progressive Youth Circle I was about 16 or so. A new life opened, an intellectual life, people hammering out their ideas. It was meat and drink to me. I'd veer between Zionism and communism according to who was speaking. I can't say now whether I was intellectually convinced that communism was the right way forward because of a dispassionate examination of the facts or because the two people I was in love with, one after the other, were communists. That may have helped to swing me over. At any rate, I became a communist.

With the little education and intellectual training that I'd had, my politics were absolutely emotional. I can see it now, though I probably would have challenged it at the time. What appealed to me was the idea that all men were brothers (which of course meant "all men and women are brothers and sisters"—we didn't need to spell it out) and that we would build a beautiful world where everybody would be nice to everybody else and there would be no more war, no more poverty, no more disease, because socialism would put everything right. This was our nebulous ideal.

Jewish Women in London Group, *Generations of Memories*
(London: The Women's Press, 1989), pp. 31–33.

On Anglicization and "Real Culture"

While Ruth Adler remained in a Jewish (Communist) milieu much of her life, she had also accommodated herself to the English style of pleated skirts. The well-known Yiddishist Joseph Leftwich had a different attitude toward the Anglicization policy that developed between the wars. Reflecting, like Adler, through the prism of memory, his view of the issue is much more bitter than hers.

East End

With my background and my outlook I am not likely to be unmindful of the importance of "Anglicisation." I can be just as intolerant as the next man of the wilfully alien—Yiddish or German-speaking, who refuses to fit in to his new home and imagines he can live here isolated, excluded. [. . .]

[. . .] We Jews, by the very fact that we are Jews must refuse to partake of certain elements of the life around us. Yet things get through our pores. And the more obstinately "foreign" acquire some English—and what they despise even more—Anglo-Jewish habits and ways.

Yet a certain kind of priggish Anglicisation which our betters tried to instil into us when I was a boy could only have the effects of putting up the backs of some of us. It lingers. I was invited not long ago to a pageant showing the development of one of our Jewish boys' clubs. I know what good work the boys' clubs in the East End have done. But I resented a tendency there to present the boy coming from a "foreign" home as an uncouth creature who had to be taught the rudiments of social behaviour, and who with the acquisition of English speech and an introduction to English athletics and sports suddenly becomes a little gentleman. As though the "foreign" homes bred barbarians.

We were in our "foreign" homes and in our chedarim much closer to real culture, and certainly to Jewish culture and to a respect for Jewish tradition and Jewish values. To-day, when so much of our Anglicised East End Jewish youth is dance-mad and cinema-mad, indifferent to things Jewish and politically Communist, with little Jewish knowledge or desire for Jewish knowledge, it is distasteful to be told by Christian East End teachers and head-teachers who have through some of their East End contacts learned to respect Yiddish and Hebrew and Jewish religious and cultural values that their efforts to encourage an interest in these things among their Jewish youth are frowned on and thwarted by Jewish social workers and club leaders in the East End, who detest all this "foreignness." It is such a pity, I am told, that your own people fight against our efforts to make your youth appreciate your own traditions.

Nearly fifty years ago, when I was a boy at school in Whitechapel, the leaders of Anglo-Jewry entertained the headmasters of the East End schools, my own among them, and spoke to them of their ideas of Anglicising the children. Some of them were puzzled, my own headmaster, who became a lifelong friend of mine afterwards and told me so, among them. They could not understand why there should be this desire to smoothen out, to flatten and to neutralise all the rich colour and variety of the life which they found around them in the East End. That same puzzlement is felt by their successors to-day.

The East End world of the chedar and the Talmud Torah and the Chevra may have upset the Anglicisation dreams of some of our well-meaning and self-sacrificing Jewish social workers. But fifty years of experience should have convinced them that away from it lies something that for most of our youth is neither English nor Jewish.

> AJR (Association of Jewish Refugees) *Information* 5:10
> (October 1950): 4.

PARIS
Kashrut and Rival Polish Jewish Groups

Rather than join the French synagogues, the immigrants set up their own places of worship (private oratories) as they settled in. In time they also wanted to have a say in religious matters in Paris. In 1911, a group called Agoudath Hakehiloth appealed to the Consistoire, the official body of French Jewry, to be represented on its Committee for the Supervision of Ritual Practice. This demand sparked the ire of a rival group, which accused the Agoudath Hakehiloth of being unworthy fanatics. The issue was settled only when the Consistoire accepted one of each of the immigrants' representatives onto its board. (Later the Agoudath Hakehiloth went on to build the Guimard synagogue on the rue Pavée.)

To the Grand Rabbi J. H. Dreyfuss

President of the Religious Section, President of the Commission on Kosher Meat and Mikwés of the Association Consistoriale Israélite de Paris

Dear Mr. President,

We have the honor to inform you that we have just created an Association culturelle israélite in conformity with the law of December 9, 1905, with the name "L'Union des Communautés" (Agoudath Hakehiloth). Its headquarters is in Paris, at 32 rue de Turenne, and it is administered by a thirty-member council.

The association is made up of nine community groups spread out among nine *oratoires* [small shuls] representing the religious interests of close to one thousand (1,000) believers who are particularly attached to the religion, and the majority of whom are members of the Consistorial Association.

We believe that it would be right and just that our association be represented within those commissions of the Consistoire that are especially focused on religious observance and the overseeing of ritual prescriptions.

We wish to exercise our action in the most perfect harmony with the Consistorial Association, and we would be very happy if the support we offer you to this end would appear to you as useful as we flatter ourselves to believe it is.

We think, Mr. President, that under these circumstances, five members of our council, including the rabbi of our society, can and should be part of the religious commissions of the Consistoire— and we most sincerely hope that you will intervene favorably [on our behalf] with the Consistoire which, we hope, will share the same sentiments.

Please accept, Mr. President, the expression of our highest regard.

> For the Council,
> the President,
> J. Landau, 32 rue de Turenne

Paris, August 11, 1911

Mr. J. H. Dreyfuss, Grand Rabbi of Paris, President of the Commission on Kosher Meat, Paris

Dear Grand Rabbi,

We have learned that a delegation presented itself before you and, after having presented Mr. Herzog as the rabbi of the Russian-Polish community of Paris, asked you that he be appointed to the *schehita* section along with other delegates.

The undersigned would like you to know, Sir, Grand Rabbi, that Mr. Herzog, far from representing the totality of the community, has only a few partisans among the most fervent members of the community.

We, the oldest members of the Russian-Polish community, have M. Eischichki as our rabbi, whom we have known for many years and who is a very honest man, resistant to all intrigue. As in the past, we continue to have full confidence in the administration of the greater consistorial community which does all it can, to the extent of its power, to maintain the *kashrut*. The best proof of this is that we have publicly protested against the installation of a *schohet* by M. Brenner and Co., who are of Mr. Herzog's party, and we have declared that the meat is completely traife. Anyway, we hope that in a short time, the butcher's shop will be completely eliminated. But if the Consistorial Association wants to receive in its religious and *schehita* section someone from the Russian-Polish fraction [of the community], it should also take into account the most important and most reasonable [*calme*] element of the community that the undersigned have the honor of representing.

They are as of now already prepared to designate, with the consent of the Consistoire, those members whom they believe to be the most qualified in this respect.

In the hope that this letter will be taken into consideration, we hope that you, dear Grand Rabbi, will accept the expression of our most devoted sentiments.

> Mr. Wolf Glass, 13 rue Geoffroy St. Hilaire
> President of the Committee
> Weinstein, Vice-President; S. Sames, Secretary;
> Salmon Glass, Treasurer
> Members: Messrs. Léon Sidlowski; Lapinski;
> Tschernezki; A. Lubetzki; Gamine Sidlowski;
> C. Ratshkovski; Sacs; Prais; A. Schlomovitz
> For the Committee
> The Secretary
> Sames, 12 rue de l'Arbalette, Paris

> Association Consistoriale Israélite de Paris Archives, file B90
> (1911), "Union des Communautés."

Frogs' Legs and the Assimilation Question

While some immigrants set about preserving traditional ways, others embraced French culture more or less enthusiastically. In the semi-autobiographical novel L'Epopée de Ménaché Foïgel, *France is depicted at one point as Babylon, where it is impossible to distinguish the Jews from the goyim. Old Sarah recounts her trip to Paris to visit her son.*

He had really changed since his departure from Apukorsovo, the son of old Sarah! He had married a goy, and to be a real goy, all he needed now was the baptism.

"Can you imagine that his bakery stays open on Saturday!"

At the synagogue on the rue de l'Hôtel-de-Ville, you could have thought you were in a holy community in the Ukraine, but the faithful came there in such small numbers, barely fifteen or so, that it was a pity. And no one but old people! As for young people, they filled the streets. Freshly shaven, a cigarette between their lips, the swaggering Romeos wooed the young women. But that was nothing compared to what Sarah then came to learn.

"What else then?" said Ménaché, intrigued and amused all at once.

"In Paris there are Jewish pimps."

"Oh, pshaw!"

"Yes, and in the Hôtel-de-Ville district which is the Jewish quarter par excellence, I was shown places of debauchery kept by Jews where Jewish pensioners live and which young *shkoutzim* (good-for-nothings) call *kosher* houses. What do you say to that, young man?"

[. . .] The *goyim* themselves, they say, have a religion. They go to church, they pray, and they fear God, whereas the French Jews know neither God nor Devil.

"And more yet which would take too long to enumerate! I saw, young man, people eating frogs, cats, snails, and all sorts of filth!"

André Billy and Moïse Twersky, L'Epopée de Ménaché Foïgel,
3 vols. (Paris: Plon, 1927–28), 1:166–68.

On Yiddish

Whether people were inspired by tradition or communism, Yiddish continued to be the federating element in the Jewish immigrant community. Yiddish was the means to remaining Jewish beyond religious considerations and in the face of the secular state's integrationist attitude.

Imported Jewishness

Let us take a look at the Jewish baggage with which a Jewish child grows up in Paris.

A few words of bad Yiddish, snatched, but not grasped, from his parents and from a few cheap plays which he saw as a child at the Yiddish theater. (As an adult he will no longer attend.) A few memories of his parents' house. Sometimes a bar mitzvah celebration, which later either assumes the nature of caricature in his eyes or is forgotten altogether. [. . .]

Because he does not know enough Yiddish, he is inclined to believe that Yiddish is not even a language at all. We all know such people who murder with great pleasure even the few words that they do know, in order to demonstrate how insignificant Yiddish is in their eyes, and how contemptuously they relate to it. I have never heard of a Jewish child raised in Paris who at least felt sorry that he did not know Yiddish. On the contrary, I have found many times that young Jews like to show off their lack of knowledge of Yiddish.

This is all because we have no schools in Paris. A school is an institution that not only teaches a language but also instills respect for it in its students. As long as there is no network of supplementary schools for the Jewish child here in Paris, our Yiddish will be murdered and broken in the mouths of our children. They will relate to it in the worst way. [. . .]

We feed our Jewishness in Paris with arriving immigrants. That is all well and good, but the basis for Jewish life in Paris must not be import, but education. You can never be sure of an imported supply. What will we do if France starts, like other countries, to close its gates to the influx of new immigrants? Instead of importing Jews from other countries, we should produce Jews ourselves. As we said, you can never be sure of an imported supply. We see how they closed the borders of England. In America, Jewish life is becoming emaciated. Life there was once fat, hale, and hearty. Now responsible Jewish leaders there complain that communal life has shrunk. Why? Because they lived off of imported Jews. They did not create enough schools for their children. They depended on other countries, such as Russia, Poland, Lithuania, Latvia, and Romania, to manufacture Jews for them. They themselves did not devote themselves enough to the education of their own children. [. . .]

Let us not become tired of shouting, beating the drum, and calling:

Jews, build Jewish schools for your Jewish children!

A building must start with a foundation, and the foundation of life is the school!

Parizer haynt, October 4, 1933.

Our Supplementary Schools

Our children need joy. They get it from us. When they arrive, they do not find a second school where they must study, but a club where they feel free, surrounded by love and friendship. They immediately sense that the club is their own, and that the teacher is an older member, together with whom they will run the club. All responsibilities are placed in the children's hands.

Events of great importance take place in daily life. The children hear about them on the street and at home. They are interested but do not understand—at least not fully. The father works secretly; the right to work; expulsion. What is this all about? In school and on the street, the child often hears the phrase, "Dirty foreigner." Hitler in Germany; worker fathers fight for better wages; workers' holidays. Parents are often angry, worried. Why? The child is helpless. He searches for answers to his questions. Where are they to be found? In the public school? Impossible!

Our supplementary schools, where the teacher is a close friend, are the places where the child finds out about all the burning issues through friendly chats and readings of interesting stories on selected topics. Instead of turning his anger on his parents, he begins to understand and even to help out at home. . . .

Our supplementary schools draw the child closer to his home. We acquaint them with our writers. We teach them to speak, write, and read Yiddish. We teach very differently, however, from the way the public school teaches. We teach with song, Yiddish poetry, attractive stories, children's plays, drawing, and crafts—all drawn from working-class life.

> G. Izidor, "Nos écoles annexes," *Unzer kind* (Our Child; published in Paris by Fraynd fun arbeter-kind, Friends of the Working-Class Child), May 1936, bulletin no. 1.

Mistinguett and Victor Hugo in the Yiddish Press

Pariz, a literary and artistic weekly, dealt not only with Jewish subjects. The two following articles, relating an interview with the singer Mistinguett and the fiftieth anniversary commemoration of the death of Victor Hugo, show how the immigrant Jewish milieu of Paris was attentive to French culture, ranging from its variety stars to its most important authors.

A Talk with Mistinguett

THE CAREER OF THE FAMOUS VARIETY PERFORMER—ABOUT JEWS ON THE FRENCH STAGE—THE GORGEOUS MANSION OF MADAME DUBARRY—MISTINGUETT GIVES A SPECIAL RECEPTION FOR MAURICE SCHWARTZ AND OUR CONTRIBUTORS—MISTINGUETT GIVES HER REGARDS TO THE READERS OF *PARIZ*

"In the next few days I will be leaving for Cannes for the holidays. I will spend a couple of weeks there and then return to Paris, where I will prepare for my first sound film. Later, I will prepare for the operetta by Strauss which will be performed at the St. Martin Theater."

"Are you familiar with the Yiddish theater, and have you ever met any Yiddish actors?"

"Unfortunately, I have never had the opportunity to see any Yiddish theater, although I have heard very many good, even inspiring, things about Yiddish drama. I have, though, seen Jewish actors on the non-Yiddish stage. I had the honor to perform together with one of the greatest actresses which the modern theater in general has produced. I mean the great Sarah Bernhardt, who was of Jewish origin. In her acting, one could sense a Jewish temperament full of tragedy, and deep soulfulness—those things which, in my opinion, characterize Jews in general."

Pariz, January 1, 1935.

Victor Hugo as Man and Poet

Seldom have the ideas of a century been so clearly and obviously embodied and expressed in one person, as the 19th century in the personality of Victor Hugo.

We must not forget that if the last century prepared and realized ideas and forms generations in advance, then France was their laboratory and workshop. Everything that is now taking place in gigantic proportions in the world at large has already been tested in advance by the French people. In the course of barely 150 years, the French have had two monarchies, two dictatorships, three republics, three political revolutions, and one social revolution—the Paris Commune. [. . .]

It would be a mistake to think that Victor Hugo is obsolete, or that his work belongs to the archives of human culture. This is as false as the opinion that the French people have already carried out their historical mission and must now make way for the so-called younger peoples. One might perhaps think that way if those peoples had been able to realize and move beyond all the ideas of the 19th century. Unfortunately, we see the opposite. Instead of moving forward, Germany has gone backward to primitive savagery. Russia continues to experiment in order to realize the Paris Commune. In France also there are those who want to take away the French people's right to the future. These are the very people who want to imitate Germany or Italy, in order to demean Victor Hugo's value as a French genius— because everything for which all of humanity is now fighting, all of its hopes and dreams for the future, all of the pathos of the better part of human culture, have never found such a clear expression as in the work of Victor Hugo. [. . .]

It is the unfolding of Victor Hugo's genius that convinces us in the righteousness of his creations and in the truth of his ideas. Seldom has a writer moved with such iron logic toward his goal as he did.

Pariz, April 19, 1935.

BUENOS AIRES
For and against Religion

While Rabbi Halphon, true to his critical spirit, drew up a bitter balance sheet concerning the local Jewish community's religious practices, some of the working-class literature reflected the hold that religion and tradition still maintained over the Jewish masses. The workers' movement developed propaganda very early on in favor of a more secularized Jewish life.

Religious and Moral State of Jews in Argentina

Religion loses its sway over our brothers here each day. By the force of circumstances it is true, almost all of our coreligionists have already replaced Saturday with Sunday. This last day is dedicated to rest, but work continues not only on Saturdays but also on the other Jewish holidays. Even circumcision, which is still practiced among Israelites despite everything, is on its way to disappearing here. Mixed marriages also increase day after day among our coreligionists of the republic. Taking into account the current state of things and, furthermore, if one considers that we are not yet in the presence of a purely "Argentinean Israelite generation" (since the flood of immigration continues to bring us, without pause, the habits and the Jewish traditions of Europe), we may ask what will become of Judaism for the young Israelite generation born and raised here outside of our traditions and our history, and absolutely deprived of all religious instruction. The answer is clear: We can hardly count on having good Israelites in the future.

S. Halphon, "Rapport adressé aux membres du Conseil de l'ICA,"
July 29, 1910, pp. 210–11.

Communist propaganda against religion was the most provocative.

On Yom Kippur Eve

> There will be a grand ANTI-RELIGIOUS EVENT sponsored by
> the Jewish Communist Youth Group together with the Jewish
> Section. The place and program will be announced in the next issue
> of *Royter shtern.*
> SEPTEMBER 25TH
> in the "Augusteo" Salon
> Sarmiento 1374
> CONCERT AND DANCE
> The Yugoslav proletarian
> BALALAIKA ORCHESTRA
> will appear for the first time before the Jewish community with
> a number of Slavic folk tunes and songs of proletarian struggle.
> Details of the program—in the next issue.
> *Royter shtern* (Red Star), September 3, 1926.

The Library, Center of Social and Cultural Life

Before World War I, the library was one of the main centers of sociability for Jewish immigrants in Buenos Aires. After the war, social activities would center more around cultural and sports centers in conjunction with landsmanshaftn, *other mutual-aid societies, or political or union organizations.*

In this city there are, in effect, for an approximate total of 60,000 Jews, about thirty Israelite culture groups, which are developing with relative prosperity and an excellent measure of success. Almost all conduct business by means of libraries, nourished with good books, which are made available to the readers through all types of facilities, and by means of: periodic and regular university-supported and scientific lectures; free discussions on general and specific topics; organization of free courses of basic instruction, typically attended by students; publication of literary periodicals; and, in sum, trying everything at hand that suits their ends. In the rural areas, where there are pockets of Israelite communities, there abound centers of culture, albeit proportionally smaller ones.

The beneficial effect of these centers is evident. The worker leaves his work tools in the shop or in the factory and walks quickly, just like an employee or anyone else, to the warm hearth of the library, to delight in the reading of sound works, to acquire in night school the rudimentary and indispensable knowledge of which the ignorance or poverty of his parents deprives him, to receive from the lectures the notions of science, philosophy, or art that are forbidden to him for being unable to enroll in preparatory studies or enter the university halls; to orient himself in the questions of thought, with open discussions, free of solemnities. And all this in the midst of a pleasant and comfortable family ambiance that could not be found outside of the nucleus in which he lives, to which he feels attracted by irresistible forces, and where he can speak his language and observe his customs.

There are also cultural groups with a specific Israelite character, where one may become acquainted with modern literature in "Yiddish" [. . .] Jewish problems are commented on and discussed; theatrical productions which feature the best works of Jewish authors are performed; and, in sum, what is accomplished has a wholly Jewish aspect, but always in the cultural realm.

Without any intent to boast it should be added that this zeal for cultural activity displayed by the Jews through such clubs or societies is not seen in any other foreign community in the country. While the other colonies concentrate their social activities exclusively through relief associations or institutions of worship (when they have religious beliefs different from those of the country), or in patriotic societies, ours employs its energy in the quest for a higher level of culture, leaving aside religious preoccupations without neglecting the noble task of mutual aid and welfare.

"Actividad cultural," *Juventud*, no. 49, 1916, pp. 49–51.

Yiddishism as Seen by Bundists and Communists

The first Congress of Jewish Culture in Argentina met in 1915 at the initiative of Jewish workers' organizations, in opposition to the First Argentine Israelite Congress, organized by the Zionist Federation. Its resolutions showed how the secular organizations and leftist Jews sought to support "Yiddishism" and popular culture. By the mid-1930s, however, the Communist attitude toward Yiddishism had become much more critical.

The First Jewish Culture Congress in Argentina

In quiet and tidy La Plata, on a quiet, half-darkened street, on a quietly murmuring spring evening, in a quiet, modest hall decorated with flowers, the First Jewish Culture Congress in Argentina was opened on November 20th in loving and earnest stillness by the representative of the Max Nordau Cultural Society of La Plata.

The following delegates were present: I. A. Koriman and I. Grimberg of the Max Nordau Society, La Plata; M. Medvedoff of the Vorwärts Library, Dora Colony, Santiago del Estero; B. Traskunov of the Cultural Society, Santa Fe; A. Pinsker of the Workers' Library, Rosario; L. Shunarinsky of the Popular Library, Tucuman; V. Berditchevski of the Popular Library, Bernasconi; A. Rosenblum and M. Bloshtein of the Jewish Library, Villa Crespo; P. Pianka of the Jacob Gordin Society, Buenos Aires; M. Rosen and P. Wald of "Avangard," Buenos Aires; M. Weber and E. Shteren of the Workers' Federation, Buenos Aires; M. Fodim and A. Nabis of the Jewish Youth, Buenos Aires; M. Novik and Y. Goroditsky of the "Searchers for Truth," Buenos Aires. I. Sh. Liajovitsky of the Jewish Library in San Martin also attended.

The Jewish Culture Federation is now a fact, from which, sooner or later, in greater or lesser proportion, certain products may be expected. Meanwhile, the Jewish Congress is still an abstraction whose accomplishments are becoming ever more doubtful. This congress could still have significance to the extent that it demonstrates a general need. However, our fine householders and their staff of servants have not bothered to do this.

"Der ershter yudisher kultur-tsuzamenfohr in Argentine," *Der avangard*, no. 1, January 1916, p. 27.

The Anti-Proletarian Character of Yiddishist Culture

As a petit bourgeois cultural movement, Yiddishism flows together with the muddy stream of bourgeois culture in general. It has rejected and denounced the concept of proletarian culture, countering it with the slogan of "national Jewish culture." This concept is supposed to be holy and dear to all Jews, regardless of class.

Foaming at the mouth, the Yiddishists reject the "mire" of class affiliation imposed on Yiddish culture. The Yiddishists repeat all the old bourgeois contentions: Only the tender flowers of objective human spirit grow on the blessed fields of culture. The weeds of gray, prosaic struggle and class conflict, God forbid, have no place there. [. . .]

[As opposed to proletarian culture, Yiddishism puts forward the struggle against assimilation as the only justified social struggle for the working masses.]

Socialist in essence, national in form, that is the nature of proletarian culture, as established many years ago by the greatest follower of Marx in his argument against the "petit bourgeois nationalistic" theories of the Bund. The essence of culture, that is, must be permeated by the great working-class ideals of social struggle. This class is the only heir to all of the valuable progressive elements in human culture. It is also the creator of its own class culture, which will grow into the highest stage of human culture in the classless society. Assimilationist or exploitative tendencies are therefore foreign to proletarian culture, which, as a culture of liberation, arrives at its fullest expression in the national forms and languages of the peoples who create and build it. [. . .]

[None of the basic principles of Yiddishism are in any way original.]

What is indeed "specific" to Yiddishism is its theory of the class character of the Yiddish language—also a discovery, by the way, of Dr. Zhitlovsky. That is, because the bourgeois "tip" of the Jewish social pyramid always assimilates, it breaks with the Yiddish language and adopts the languages and cultures of the peoples among whom it lives. Yiddish therefore remains a living everyday language only among the working masses. Like Yiddish culture in general, Yiddish literature therefore automatically assumes a popular and progressive character. The Bundist and labor Zionist politicians have broadened this theory and arrived at the conclusion that since Yiddish culture is created by the Jewish working class, everything that is created in Yiddish—or almost everything—is purely proletarian. Jewish workers must therefore give it their full approval and sincerest blessing.

In reality, however, linguistic form is not a guarantee of content. The *Emes* writes in Yiddish, just as the *Forverts* sells its wares in Yiddish. Yiddish is the tempestuous revolutionary song of Itzik Fefer and Yiddish is also the mystical lament of Aaron Zeitlin. David Bergelson is a Yiddish writer, as is the Zionist David Pinski. Kushnirov's "Hirsh Lekert" is Yiddish theater, as is Mr. Shmarovoz's "Love Without a Roof." The historical cultural achievements of the broad popular masses can be recorded in Yiddish, and the scholastic casuistry of the Jewish rabbis can be collected in Yiddish. Yiddish is spoken at meetings of councils in Jewish Birobidzhan, and in Yiddish the sexton calls the faithful to penitential prayer. In short, Yiddish, like all languages, can be an instrument for playing the boldest and most exalted tones, encouraging the struggle for higher forms of life. And Yiddish can be made into a vessel for the enemy's venomous filth in order to conquer and dull the masses.

A. Grishin, "Der klasnkharakter fun idishizm," *In gang,*
February 1935, pp. 4–5.

The Census and Jewish Identification

Identities could also be an affair of state. In 1914, the Bundists launched a campaign taken up·by other community institutions in order to mobilize the Jewish population for the third national census. Their goal was to get a majority of Jews to recognize themselves as such by responding to the question on religion.

Being surrounded by the ignorance of the masses, the assimilationist spirit of the intelligentsia, obstructions from the authorities, and the indifference of the more wealthy classes, it could, of course, not be expected that the goal would be completely met. That is, that all Jews in Argentina would list themselves as Jews at a time when nationality was not even asked. It would, however, be a crime not to try to break through the wall of self-denial, ignorance, and one-sided and false accusations.

In connection with the movement against self-denial among the Jews, a note was sent to the state commission for the census calling attention to the Jewish movement and its goal, and pointing out that the census could not be complete without recognizing the Jewish presence. It had earlier been known that there would be no changes made this time in the census questionnaires. Calling attention to the defects, however, was no small matter. The following two facts demonstrate the extent to which its significance did not simply end with the Jewish movement in and of itself. They also demonstrate the extent to which Jews registered as Jews: In the ninth and eleventh districts in Buenos Aires, where Jews live in a compact mass, the census commissions took extra measures to prevent Jews from listing themselves as such. That these measures were unsuccessful is confirmed by *La Prensa* of June 2, 1914: "In order to carry out the census in the Jewish neighborhood, it was necessary to allow 'Israelite' as an answer to the question, 'In what country were you born?'" Now we have learned that the documents of the census include the following statement: "By 1914 there were 129,390 Russians in Argentina, of which the majority are Jews." This figure indicates that the majority of the 129,390 people who answered that they came from Russia said at the same time that they were Jews. Including Jews from Austria, Romania, and all other countries, who did not figure as Russians or list themselves as Jews in the census, gives one a better idea of the general number of Jews in Argentina. This is something that was absolutely impossible before. It is now possible, though not definitive.

P. Wald, "Di folks tsaytung," *Der avangard*, no. 9,
September 1916, pp. 4–7.

GERMANY
Memoirs of an Actor

Memoir literature and other firsthand accounts by immigrant Jewish workers in Germany are quite sparse compared to the voluminous works written by their counterparts in other lands. This is not surprising given the relatively small population of Eastern European Jews in Germany and their precarious living conditions. Thus, for the most part, we learn about them as the objects of government reports and German Jewish concerns. Nonetheless, Alexander Granach, who eventually became a stage actor, offers one of the rare accounts from an immigrant's perspective as he depicts his circle of acquaintances in Berlin shortly after his arrival from the East.

I got off at the end of Lothringerstraße and Schoenhauser Gate. At the corners of Grenadier, Dragoner, Mulak, and Ritter, and Schendelgaße—all of them small, crowded, dark little streets—they sold fruit and vegetables. Women with painted faces and large keys in their hands walked around the "strip" just like they did on Zoshina Volya Street in Stanislav, or on Shpitalna Street in Lemberg. There were many stores selling eggs, butter, milk, and baked goods, as well as restaurants advertising themselves as kosher. Jews hung around dressed as they did in Galicia, Romania, or Russia. If a Jew did not have his own little store, he peddled tablecloths, handkerchiefs, suspenders, garters, hair clasps, and women's underwear and stockings; or he sold pictures and furniture on installment. Still others went from door to door, calling out, "Make a deal!" and buying up old clothing, which was then sent to the "old country" by richer merchants. But the majority of them, men and women, worked in the cigarette factories of Manoli, Garbati, and Murati.

There was also community life. The more pious had their synagogues. The Zionists, Socialists, Social Revolutionaries, Bundists, and anarchists all had their respective societies. The comedian Kanapof appeared at Koenig's Café, on Muenzstraße. And a Yiddish theatrical troupe performed on a small stage at Levanthal's Restaurant at Grenadier and Muenzstraße. Posters with big letters and pictures advertised minor actors and supernumeraries from the Yiddish theaters in Russia, Romania, and Galicia as famous international stars.

My friend and I rented places to sleep on Lothringerstraße near Schoenhauser Gate. Eight people slept in one room. I found work with one Sholem Grinbaum on Lothringerstraße, and immediately made myself at home in big Berlin. Shmuel, on the other hand, was hired by a dealer in old clothes who had a small business in a cellar. My friend's job was to record what was bought and sold. His boss, an older man who dressed in European garb, lived with a daughter and son-in-law and their child. But, one day, my friend came to me in distress. The old man was locking himself up with him in the cellar, touching him and kissing him. . . At first, he thought it was a joke. But it repeated itself several times, with the old man becoming more insistent each time. He was simply scared of him. It revolted him. Shmuel even burst into tears. What was more, he had that day received a letter from his father, requesting that he come home immediately. His father had long forgiven him for taking the money; he was even sending him more money for travel expenses. This time, too, there was a separate note to me. The father begged me, for heaven's sake, to have mercy and return his helpless child to him.

"Do you want to go home?" I asked my friend.

"I can't live in a city like this," he pleaded with me.

Shmuel went home, and I stayed in Berlin all by myself.

I started to make acquaintances. I often went to Levanthal's Restaurant where a certain Bleichman performed honest, but very bad, theater with his wife, daughters, and sons-in-law. It was a real mess compared to the theater in Lemberg! Every two or three days, they produced a "new" piece. In fact, it was always one and the same piece, with the same subtitle, "A drama with song and dance." I also saw the same plays there as I saw in Lemberg. I therefore tried to compare and criticize, and to carry on debates with the young audience in the gallery. We were very unhappy with the plays and the acting, yet we continued to attend the performances. Guest stars—the Gutentags, Tshizshiks, or visitors from America—also made appearances. They used to put together their own troupes and perform in Sofien Hall, Blumen Hall (later Rezi), Wilhelm Hall, or the Prater Theater in Kastanien Allee. I never missed a performance.

One time I met a small, pale, young man with long hair and an artistic cravat. His name was Shidlover. An actor with a certain sense of social and cultural responsibility, he was also unhappy with the cheap trash and bad acting. We became friends and got together often. He believed that the theater should not just be a place of amusement and cheap jokes. Rather, it should take the place of the synagogue and the church. The stage is higher than the audience, he used to say, because it should raise the onlookers above their everyday existence. It should raise their spirits and make them feel festive. He therefore could not perform in the trashy theaters, and would rather have produced "better" pieces with young people, simple workers, who looked upon theater as he did. He acquainted me with a circle of cigarette workers, married and single, men and women, who were older than I. Most of them had fled Russia in 1905. The gave me pamphlets and stories to read, and then discussed them with me in the evening or on Sunday. I then heard for the first time words and concepts that were totally new to me. I had been raised to walk in God's path and to have pity on the rich rather than hate them, for that was the natural order of the world. But my new acquaintances thought differently. They thought that this order was not worthy of the name and had to be changed drastically. The only thing they did not know was exactly how it would be changed. So they had continued to study and learn, reading about this in various books and then discussing them. I was not yet able to take part in the debates myself, so I only listened and asked questions. We often all pitched in and ate together at the homes of the various comrades. We also all helped cook, serve, and wash the dishes. It was quite homey and cheerful. There were always a few of us without work, but we managed to get by. We believed that one should not allow himself to be exploited by the bosses. It was preferable to go without a new suit of clothes than to work a whole week so the boss could make a profit. For every mark that the worker earned, the boss made twenty-five marks. It was worth earning two marks less each week, as long as the boss lost fifty marks in the process.

Our entire circle consisted of foreigners. We were therefore forbidden to belong to any political organization. In order to spread our revolutionary ideas, however, we decided to form an "innocent" theatrical society, through which we would acquaint the Jewish people with the ideas of the non-

Jewish Rudolf Rocker. That is how the Jacob Gordin Society came into being. The actor Shidlover was the director.

Alexander Granach, *Ot geyt a mentsh* (New York: YKUF [Yidisher Kultur Farband], 1948), pp. 175–79 (© 1960/1973 by F. A. Herbig Verlagsbuchhandlung GmbH, Munich, *Da geht ein Mensch*).

Agudas Jisroel

From the beginning of World War I, orthodox German Jews tried to transfer Eastern European Jewish workers to Germany. Their primary reason was religious. The keeping of religious laws, such as kashrut and the Sabbath, were of much greater importance to them than the sociopolitical concerns or the improvement of the working and living conditions of the immigrants.

Frankfurt am Main / Berlin / Cologne / Katowice / Ostrowo
July 30, 1915

Employment Service
of the Agudas Jisroel
In cooperation with the German Central Workers' Office

Authorized by order of the Imperial [German] Civil
Administration for Poland Left of the Vistula on July 8, 1915.

Central Office:
Frankfurt am Main / Kettenhofweg 22
Telephone: Taunus Office No. 1100

Dear Sirs:

We are pleased to inform you that we are now making an effort to provide German industry and agriculture with appropriately trained *personnel* from the large, and presently impoverished, Jewish population of Russian Poland.

The service is provided with the permission of the Imperial German Civil Administration for Poland Left of the Vistula and in close contact with the Berlin "German Central Workers' Office," with which our agents are cooperating. The costs and conditions are exactly the same as those of the Central Office itself.

We, however, make a selection from among the available workers; we choose *workers with conservative religious convictions,* who observe the Sabbath and dietary restrictions and for that very reason offer a kind of guarantee in terms of moral behavior. We try to place larger groups of these workers in appropriate workplaces.

Experience has already shown in a number of cases that it can be quite easy to take the religious wishes of the Jewish-Polish workers into account, especially where there are shift changes and Sunday work. The employers are pleased to have this steady, modest element among their workers.

If you are interested in having us provide you with some of these workers, please complete the enclosed questionnaire and return it to us.

Respectfully,
for the Employment Service of Agudas Jisroel:
Leo Wreschner, President

Hauptstaatsarchiv Düsseldorf, Regierung Düsseldorf 9084.

Religious Education

This account of immigrant children is written from the perspective of a German Jewish writer who visited with her subjects to write an account of their lives. Although written sympathetically, it also betrays the patronizing stance of many German Jews involved in aiding the immigrants and expresses the belief that differences between immigrant and native Jews would disappear in the future.

The children of the immigrants do not differ in any way from those of German-born Jews with respect to their career choices. The Eastern European Jewish parents have a strong desire to see their children succeed in life. Very frequently they understand this in terms of the possibility for children to take up a trade different from that of their fathers. The children also feel ambition early on and strive for wealth and status. A school principal, who has headed a school in the Grenadierstraße neighborhood for thirty years, confirmed this for us: "Often one is surprised to see how far these children can go, considering that at first they hardly spoke any German." In his experience, the Eastern European Jewish children are intelligent and more flexible than the others. They produce excellent written work but are weaker in the sciences and quite awkward in drawing. The Russian children adapt to the school rules easily, whereas the Galician parents themselves must first be taught that their children are to come to school regularly, every day. At first, Galician children are absent quite frequently, and it is never a matter of "playing hooky." Instead, it is the parents who have kept them home to help with some activity. In the experience of this school, however, it is easier for the school to establish a connection with the Eastern European Jewish mothers than with the native-born mothers. The former show much greater interest in maintaining the home-school relationship.

Requests for children to be excused from school or from writing on Saturdays have increased at the above-mentioned institution over the last ten years. This is all the more noteworthy because religious life in general has weakened in the ghetto. Most of the Eastern European Jewish immigrants, especially those of the older generation, think and feel in a definitely Jewish-religious way. But the number of people who live by the strict orthodox rules has doubtless grown smaller. To be sure, there are certain visible traditions that the Eastern European Jews will not break away from quickly. Many who have abandoned their old beliefs still maintain a kind of religious character in their lives. The Sabbath candles are lighted every Friday night, even in families for whom Saturday has become a normal workday—and there are many of these, except among the Galician families of the ghetto. The older generation shows little interest in Zionist issues. In general, the Eastern European Jews see to it that their children learn Hebrew. Almost all of the children of the ghetto neighborhood go every afternoon for two hours to the exclusively Eastern European Jewish religious schools on Grenadierstraße and Dragonerstraße to learn about the Jewish scriptures. Many of the Eastern European Jewish children who attend high school have Hebrew tutors at home in addition to their religion classes in school. The administration of the school with a large number of Eastern European Jewish children among its students believes that the influence of the Eastern European Jewish teachers of their religion classes, the "Talmud Torahs," has become greater in recent years, which explains the increase in the number of children who are absent or will not write on Saturdays. Other schools do not seem to be having the same experience. It is not possible to determine exactly how many Eastern European Jewish children are attending a high school, but the relative number may not be small. We heard from the director of a Jewish community boys' school that many children, despite the poverty of their parents, have home tutors to help them prepare for *Gymnasium*. In the Jewish community school there is no apparent difference between the performance of the Eastern European Jewish children and that of the other Jewish pupils. In summary we can say that even the second generation, if it grew up here, is no longer a special group within the Jewish population.

Klara Eschelbacher, "Die ostjüdische Einwanderungsbevölkerung der Stadt Berlin," *Zeitschrift für Demographie und Statistik der Juden* (1923): 18–19.

The "Licht" (Light) Workers' Cultural Societies

From the early 1920s on, Eastern European Jewish Arbeiterkulturvereine were set up in many large cities, such as Berlin, and in the major Ruhr towns, in particular Duisburg, Essen, Bochum, Herne, and Gladbeck. They were federated in the Landesverband Rheinland-Westfalen der jüdischen Arbeiterkulturvereine with its head office in Essen. All workers' cultural societies in Germany, especially in the Ruhr area, also maintained relations with the Jüdisches Arbeiterfürsorgeamt in Berlin. Reading rooms, in which the most important German and Yiddish newspapers were available, along with discussions and lectures, provided the workers with numerous cultural activities.

Statutes of the Jewish Workers' Cultural Society "Licht"

1. PURPOSES OF THE SOCIETY

a. The society shall work for the intellectual and cultural advancement of its members, and if possible for the improvement of their material condition.

b. The purposes of the society shall be furthered by:

Presenting lectures of educational content and evenings of entertainment; holding classes; furnishing a workers' residence and a reading room; and establishing a library.

Providing job-finding services in cooperation with the Duisburg Jewish Employment Office.

Setting up a support fund for unemployed persons who are not in debt.

2. MEMBERSHIP

c. Membership shall be open to all gainfully employed male and female Jews. The leadership and the General Meeting shall have the right to accept unemployed persons as members in special cases.

d. The leadership shall decide on admission to membership in the society, after reviewing the candidate's personal status information.

e. The admission fee shall be three pfennigs for each member; the weekly dues, one pfennig. In exceptional cases, the leadership shall have the right to excuse members from paying all or part of their dues.

f. A member can be expelled from the society if he or she:

fails to pay the dues on time, despite repeated warnings;

is found guilty of dishonest dealings;

acts counter to the interests of the society.

The leadership shall decide on expulsion from the society; their decision can be appealed to the General Meeting.

Hauptstaatsarchiv Düsseldorf, Regierung Düsseldorf 15669.

AMSTERDAM
Chanukah, the Feast of the Poor

Meyer de Hond, the rabbi of the poor, is one of the few authors who described the ghetto and its poverty with love. Although already during his life the ghetto and its Jewish culture were disintegrating, he believed that all efforts should be made to restore tradition. Rabbi de Hond loved the solidarity of socialism but hated its secularism. In his view the warmth of Jewish traditional life had been replaced by emptiness. Jews should care for each other and cling together. In the following story, a peddler tries to find his way home in heavy fog on the eve before Chanukah.

Dedication

The sky is missing something. Maybe a cloud. That is why it is misty on earth. It's bad in the Jodenbreestraat [Jewish Broad-Street]. Two alleys are missing. With all else. Everything is thrashing around in the clouds. Carts swim along in deep, white air. Sawhorses soak in sticky steam. Boards float in wet woeful fog. Phantoms shuffle around, breath smoking. Spooks make haste in skittish shadows. Out of the sea of invisibility rise throats. Of drifting creatures clamoring for bread. On all sides. With vaporous voices. And veiled gestures. That grasp and give. They deal in mist. They barter by touch. Money for wares. The money is good. The wares hope to be.

This afternoon, mist. Tonight, Chanukah. That is the way it should be. Once such a heavy mist hung over the Jews. And Chanukah made light.

One more sale. That you would otherwise miss. Chanukah-gear. The cheapest holiness. Religion can be of any substance. From gold to wood. From silk to paper. But no matter what you take, it is expensive. A little paper tefillin costs a bundle. A woolen tallith costs paper. Now think about what a tefillin and a tallith are supposed to do. Good God. That should all be there for the *asking*. And people should be happy that you would want to have it. So you'll just have to buy in installments, says Vroom [a department store]. Religion on credit. Stupid problem. You shell out for tefillin, seven bits. Five down and two on the cuff. You blaze through Moses' five books. Genesis, paid for. Exodus, came to the door, not home. Leviticus, begged on the street. In the Wilderness, had no small change. Deuteronomy, come back in a year, my husband's out of work. Or mahzors [festival prayer books]. Pesach, break even. Shushan Purim, with three dimes to spare. The four weeks of yontef [holiday] "in a schwindel [a swindle]." Purim, don't even think about it. Costs a whole megillah. No, pride and glory of the Maccabees, they made it all right. Light conjured up in dark dearness. Cheap creed created. Chanukah you can celebrate without having paid up. Oil, a pittance. Wicks, come on. One penny for a Chanukah-burner. And a lamp, laughably cheap. A hanging lamp for only forty cents. A standing one for almost fifteen. Tin. Of course. Were you expecting platinum? Tin is the most beautiful. With your lamps [the Dutch word *blik* means both tin and look or gaze—therefore "lamps" also means eyes] you can pull somebody out of the mist. An expensive menorah is poorly dumb. A tin Chanukah-menorah is richly wise. So you learn to laud, you learn to live, you lavish love. Isn't oil the same everywhere anyway? Is light ever any different? Does the wick lament about whether it is laid in a little gold cradle? Doesn't it play just as nicely nestled in tin? Does a candle laugh louder than a lamp? Come on, that light is your soul. Your laud, life, love. And that all seems dumb in an expensive body. But in a sober body it deems itself wise. Hurrah. Hasmonaean heroes, that was your triumph! At great expense you sold your life, in order to make faith cheap!

Man, what a fog! His cart in the befogged alley. He himself has to be guessed at. His body consists only of lines. Where it ends at the top, I guess a cap. Where it starts at the bottom, I suspect clogs. Hearing does not fade in the fog, only seeing. I can hear he is wearing clogs. I believe he is shaking with shivering cold. With chilly thoughts and frozen dreams. Probably a descendant of the Maccabees. Tin rattles from a brutish collision.

"Cantcha watch where ya goin'?"

"Can I see?"

"No?!"

"So?!"

A collision between two classes. Standing and walking. The one standing has Chanukah candles. The one walking has geese. Both Chanukah-gear. Because a goose on the cutting board is also proper for Chanukah. Those without money will have to play the board-game of goose. Long live Mattathias!

A load of Chanukah candles, oh man, what a pile. Surely you are not going to sell all that! Your outlook is much too wide. That many Jews won't be lighting the day of Judas Maccabeus tonight. Look, if you can, through the fog. People avoid your "lamps," without blinking an eye. In the age of electricity, candle and oil are foolishness. The dedication of a cine-temple is certainly worth a pawnbroker's note and a crowd. But nowadays, who is going to drag themselves for a couple of nickels to the Feast of the Dedication? The sky is missing something. And how. The earth gets everything. Everybody wants this world. Heaven can be missed.

Say, little man, shouldn't you be going to the shul? Mincha, three-thirty! Dedication. You are standing in the Jewish Corner in the name of Judas the Maccabee! You are fighting for bread, armed with Chanukah candles.

Say, little man, you skipped the dedication at the shul. Shouldn't you be going home? It's almost nighttime. Shouldn't you be lighting the candles? Don't you have any children at home? A Jew who is fighting for bread has children, right? Don't you worry about God and temple, home and child? Or don't you have Chanukah candles at home? Then take one from your cart! Take a loss on your business, but not on God!

Meyer de Hond, *Kiekjes* (Amsterdam: Menno Hertzberger, 1926), pp. 29–31.

Preparing Shabbat

In the following excerpt from the memoirs of an elderly woman looking back on her early childhood after the war, the preparations for the Sabbath are described with nostalgia.

It is Friday morning 3 min. past nine the organ on the street is playing a common tune and immediately my thoughts go out to the past, but then Friday afternoon approaching shabbes, it all fit, the cake had been baked the food was simmering you would get a happy feeling, that white tablecloth my mother with a clean apron on, you were a totally happy child. There were four of us Marietje, Chellij, me, and Coenie without a K it was written with a C because my father insisted on Coenie with a C. My mother stood all day Friday in the kitchen, on Thursday the whole house was cleaned, newspapers on the thresholds, because they would have been polished and shone like a mirror. Mother often cooked her meal on oil, only on Fridays coal was used that was for the cake or kugel she baked with the best. Not with sweet butter, but simply chicken fat, we feasted, the table would be set with unbroken plates, during the week plates got damaged the difference was, during the week chips out, on shabbes chips back in, after dinner we would all sing my mother always sang a little song about the little glowworm. All the lights would be on, during the week a single lamp. We had a little apartment 2 rooms and a toilet, in the back room there was a big window, Father made a countertop there and on the side 2 shelves with lace

Mother was so tickled with it I can still remember the countertop the zig-zag parquet motif.

Private collection, Selma Leydesdorff.

Tradition among the Young

De Joodsche jeugdkrant was a weekly magazine aimed at young people, published by those who wanted to keep Jewish tradition alive (and compete with the socialist youth movement). The main editor was Rabbi de Hond.

Betsalel-Youth

1913	1928
——MAY 13——	
5673	5668 [SIC]

Betsalel Youth, a subdivision of the Jewish Betsalel Society, has been in existence for fifteen years. For fifteen years Betsalel [has] performed its beneficial work among the youth of Amsterdam: [it has] kept a large number of boys and girls aged eleven to seventeen off the streets night after night to give them instruction in elementary, intermediate, and advanced religious education, and attempted to shape this host of boys and girls into orthodox Jews. Those children who had gone through the Jewish school from beginning to end with good results discovered through Betsalel plenty of opportunity to hone their skills in Torah studies. Those who had enjoyed religious education for only a short while were able to get more acquainted with it—through Betsalel—and those who remained entirely deprived of religious education, the illiterates, received their religious education through Betsalel from the very beginning. This is not the place to elaborate extensively on the society's brilliant and difficult work. It is sufficiently well-known in this country as well as abroad and soon, when the Jubilee will be magnificently commemorated along with the 20th anniversary of the larger Betsalel this autumn, there will be occasion enough. That Betsalel stands at the center of the life of the youth of Amsterdam and has also been able to extend its efforts to all Dutch Jewish youth by means of the *Paper for Youth (Jeugd-Krant)*, is primarily thanks to the Honorable Chairman and Founder of the Society, Rabbi Dr. M. de Hond, who during these fifteen years, supported by an excellent staff of teachers, has guided instruction in such an outstanding fashion. Betsalel cannot offer the children many pleasures. A Chanukah party, a festive Awards Evening, a day in the country in the summertime, behold, this is all. For the rest it is learning night after night, and it is a joy to see with how much pleasure the children come to the evening lessons. Boys and girls elsewhere in the country, young readers of the *Paper for Youth,* you are all, in fact, also members of Betsalel Youth. For by means of the *Paper for Youth* you also profit from the lessons of Rabbi de Hond.

De Joodsche jeugdkrant (The Jewish Paper for Youth),
May 17, 1928.

Orthodox Youth Workers

Orthodox youth workers tried to keep Jewish children off the streets and teach them some religious feeling through both educational and leisure activities.

VIII. Beis Yisroël—Our Jewish House

Old-time Amsterdam Yiddish lent to the word *beis* various meanings. It meant "bad" or "angry," a bastardization of the German *böse* or else "house of," the translation of the Hebrew word *beis* or *beth.*

Anyone walking on a quiet evening through the Plantage district down the Parklaan who sees a loud group of young people and hears the word *beis* now and then in their conversations need not fear that something bad happened, that there has been an argument and that two groups of angry members are confronting each other. Anyone who has stepped closer will hear that the word *beis* is spoken with a passion which can only be sparked by something good. And indeed, when those children and youngsters in the Parklaan say the word *beis,* they are enthusiastically thinking of the good offered them by "Beis," which comes from the official name of Beis Yisroël—"Our Jewish House."

"Beis" is the youth club of the Jewish district. Night after night it opens its doors to hundreds of children and adults who, after their daily tasks, find rest in truly Jewish spirit, who come to learn or relax.

Beis Yisroël was founded in 1918 at the initiative of the late Chief Rabbi A. Asscher, then still Rabbi of Amsterdam. This was during the time that the Reformed [Church] mission preferred to perform its work among the Jews in the Jewish quarter and attempted to make proselytes particularly among Jewish children. Sensitive to the needs of the soul of the Jewish child from a working-class neighborhood, Dajan Asscher understood that if the attempts of the missionaries, who tried to coax Jewish children over to their cause with candies and comfort, were to run aground, it was essential that local premises be opened up in the Jewish quarter itself where Jewish young people could find a place of comfort in a Jewish environment.

The first meeting proved to be a huge success from the outset. No less than two hundred children showed up in search of distraction under the auspices of Beis Yisroël. Meetings were then organized at irregular times. When it became apparent that the need for this work was becoming greater and more and more children started coming, it was decided that regular courses should be arranged. At first, courses were offered in the old girls' school on Rapenburgerstraat. Later Beis was welcomed into the Rapenburgerstraat School. The work ultimately broadened to such an extent that it was necessary to find a building for Beis. For a few years now, Beis Yisroël has been located in the spacious mansion on the Plantage Parklaan, where Professor Hugo de Vries once lived and worked.

Gradually Beis's work branched out. So much so that the last annual report was able to announce 1,145 visitors per *week*! Better proof of how much Beis's work is appreciated by young and old I certainly cannot offer.

I am not mistaken when I write by young and old. For it is not only the young who visit Beis; others too, mothers and fathers of the youngsters, regularly gather there, listen to popular presentations, and receive tips that are useful in day-to-day life.

An important program at Beis is the organizing of youth services. About two hundred children come every Sabbath to attend these services. Nor should we neglect to mention Beis's seder evenings, during which many youngsters, often with their parents, observe the most solemn of family traditions.

Now that the city has grown so much and that the decentralization of the Jewish population continues to take place, Beis has also established branches in East Amsterdam and in the Indies quarter. But Beis's heart still beats in the Parklaan. Anyone who has once been counted among the visitors at Beis comes back faithfully, and it has recently happened again that a "Beis child" kept coming, even after her marriage, that the club of which she was part surprised her with a baby outfit made by the other "children" and that this "Beis child" received the right to a place in the mother's club.

Something like that typifies Beis the best. The visitors feel at home there. The foundation became what its name denoted: a Jewish "Our House," where everyone feels at ease. Anyone would be loathe to miss an evening here.

Let my readers follow my example. Go take a look some time, and I am convinced that Beis will have found one more admirer who will be overjoyed to support this necessary work.

Joseph Gompers and Fré Cohen, "Zwerftochten door Klein-Jeruzalem" (Wandering through Little Jerusalem) (Amsterdam: *Nieuw Israelietisch Weekblad*, 1935–36).

The Socialist Neighborhood and Jewish Identity

In the following interview, a child of a diamond worker discusses his family's move to the socialist neighborhood and to what extent he continued to consider himself a Jew.

No, my parents went to live in a, let me say, modern neighborhood very close to where the first housing society was in Amsterdam, the Transvaal neighborhood. There were lots of Jews there, but all were members of the modern labor movement, members of the SDAP [Social Democratic Workers' Party], who at that time certainly felt that there should not be any distinction made between race and belief, all people were the same; there was but a single humanity. There was no particular bond to any country, there was only the earth, well, the Netherlands, but the earth was why we were— the whole world.

And in that sense there was no tie with the Jewish quarter, nor a tie with the Jewish proletariat, for no small part a lumpenproletariat, and not thought very highly of. On the other hand there were still Jewish ties, but they were consciously being cut. Not with any feeling of hate, certainly not, it wasn't that, that was the old way—the new way, that was something different. [. . .]

[. . .] But I still heard from my parents that people really weren't so enthusiastic about it, even though they had come into a better apartment, that people wanted to stay in their old neighborhood. But that passed; relatively quickly, too, when they started to realize that the apartments really were better and that although the character of Uilenburg had disappeared, the neighborhood still developed its own character because the people were all from the old neighborhood so they were still able to feel at home there. [. . .]

The Jewish quarter was thus not discussed, Jewishness was not engaged in, with the exception of a white tablecloth on Friday nights. . . . That again? . . . That again, and my father usually worked the Jewish hours at the diamond factory. In the diamond industry people were able to choose between Jewish and non-Jewish hours. Those who had the Jewish hours did not work on Saturdays, but a half day on Sundays if they wanted to. And those who worked the non-Jewish hours worked a half day on Saturdays. Most of the diamond cutters worked the Jewish hours, I think.

Did that pay more or less . . . or the same?

No, in the diamond business one doesn't get paid by the hour, one gets paid according to production. One got paid per piece, per stone.

I also met diamond workers who consciously chose the non-Jewish hours because they paid more.

Polishing and cutting diamonds is piecework everywhere in the world, here [in the Netherlands] and in Belgium. With some kind of minimum wage per week, sometimes, but it gets paid according to production. [. . .]

You see, the average Jewish diamond worker was not in denial of their Jewishness, but was [part of] what is called proletarian assimilation, which was namely merging with the rest as a group. But in so doing, renouncing certain cultural characteristics. It was a—I don't know if you know about those things: the debate about the difference between proletarian and bourgeois assimilation—that [you] should inquire of Mrs. Nordheim, the wife of Prof. Dr. S. Kleerekoper, who wrote primarily on proletarian and bourgeois assimilation. And this was proletarian assimilation: as a Jewish group, not renouncing the tie with the Jewish group—on the contrary, it often existed—but wanting to merge with the whole.

Interview by Selma Leydesdorff, 1981.

Conclusion

Memory (and pride) among Jews, and stereotypes among non-Jews, have combined to highlight social mobility as one of the central characteristics of modern Jewish history. While this route has indeed most often been a successful one, memory does history a disservice in forgetting the Jewish workers' experiences of less than a century ago. Beyond remembrance, we have wanted to examine and compare the Jewish workers' lives from one city to another, from one country to another. Questions of similarity and difference arise on every page as we ask, What makes an *ouvrier juif* in the Pletzl of Paris different or not from a Jewish worker on the Lower East Side of New York, in the East End of London, in Villa Crespo, Amsterdam, or Offenbach, from the turn of the century to the 1930s?

SIMILARITIES

The similarities in experience and social structures on both sides of the Atlantic are striking. Jewish poor and Jewish workers existed everywhere. Their experiences were a function of nineteenth-century urban transformations and were mostly, but not always, concomitant with immigration. The Jewish workers settled together and formed social, religious, and political organizations that in many ways resembled each other from one city to another.

The immigrant and working-class neighborhoods created throughout the modern Diaspora were the locus of a rich cultural life, which by and large included a lively immigrant press, Yiddish theater, and café or street-corner socializing and debates. Socializing not only was informal but occurred through workers' societies and organizations that covered most aspects of the life cycle, from youth to death, from schools to burial societies.

There were tailors everywhere. Indeed, the tailor is so often the symbol of the Jewish worker that we decided it would be repetitious to have an article on the Jewish garment worker in every city. The Jewish immigrants brought skills with them, but they also entered new and expanding trades where "hands" were needed. For every Eastern European tailor or seamstress, there was a garment worker who learned to sew or treadle only in the New World. Light industry of all sorts provided opportunities for Jewish workers, but it also often meant seasonal work and precarious employment, wages, and status.

Many "workers"—as we have defined the term widely—were also peddlers. Peddling was the quintessential job of the urban poor and a particularly easy form of first employment for the newly arrived. If many pushcarts were eventually transformed into sidewalk stands or even modest storefronts, not every Jewish peddler became a department store owner, as founding myths of the latter would have us believe. Yet fluid social mobility was part of the Jewish "working-class" environment, and garment bosses worked alongside their employees, whose circumstances they themselves had been in not long before.

A Jewish labor movement appeared throughout the world and lent its tone to the poor Jewish neighborhoods. At first reenacting or continuing debates started in Eastern Europe, Jewish immigrant workers began to organize in their new homes over local issues as well. They formed sometimes enthusiastic, sometimes uneasy alliances with local labor movements, infusing a measure of internationalization into those movements while coming to grapple in varying degrees with issues already familiar to the Dutch Jews: participation in the local labor movement and in local politics meant a certain amount of acculturation. But nowhere did acculturation occur—in the labor movement or outside of it—without debate.

Finally, then, questions of ethnic and national identities confronted the Jews everywhere in the modern Diaspora. These issues were not the province of either Jewish workers or Jewish immigrants alone, but within the working-class and largely immigrant Jewish communities, economic constraints and various strategies for survival accompanied and complicated the acculturation process.

DIFFERENCES

If we can identify a basic framework within which to examine the Jewish workers around the world, the similarities are but a starting point for understanding important differences which raise fundamental questions about the Jewish experience in the modern Diaspora. In what ways did the formation of Jewish workers' communities in each locality fit into the economic opportunity structures of each city? Were all Jewish garment workers alike? How did specific political and labor laws affect working-class organization and militancy?

Some major differences explain the way in which we organized the documents. New York, London, Paris, and Buenos Aires belong together because they were all areas of urban concentration where Eastern European immigrants settled in ethnic neighborhoods and engaged in light industry and small commerce. While Germany presents a similar situation of Eastern European immigration, for legal and economic reasons there was no mass concentration of Jews there, with the exception of the small community in Berlin. The Jewish immigrant community in Germany thus remained more disseminated and more rural, with a smaller working-class population. In Amsterdam, in contrast, we have the case of an indigenous Jewish working class. Descended from the Sephardic immigration of the fifteenth and sixteenth centuries, by the late nineteenth century the Dutch Jews were basically a native group of workers who, while forming specifically Jewish charitable and other organizations, were well integrated into the Dutch polity and the Dutch socialist movement.

The different political cultures of each country affected Jewish workers' communities in different ways. To be an immigrant worker in New York was not the same as being one in Paris or Germany. The notion of foreignness had different connotations in all countries. Even the cultural Jacobinism that was more prevalent in Argentina, France, England, and Germany—and which distinguished these countries from the more pluralistic American case—did not mean that the process of becoming Argentinean, French, English, or German was the same in each case. Attitudes toward citizenship, nationality, and minorities, or the presence of relatively strong Socialist, Social Democratic, or Communist movements at different times affected the climate in which the Jewish worker or immigrant minority adapted.

Forms of political organization also differed from city to city. Jews helped found the General Dutch Diamond Workers' Union (ANDB), the International Ladies' Garment Workers' Union (ILGWU), and the Argentinean Communist Party. The diamond workers' union was founded as a Dutch union, not a Jewish one, whereas in New York, the Jews built the ILGWU in their image, and the first meeting reports and constitution were drawn up in Yiddish. In Britain and France, where national unions already existed, Jewish boot makers and garment workers could organize separately, but they generally did so within the framework of the national labor movement. The Jewish union movement in Paris, for example, consisted of

Yiddish sections of the Confédération Général du Travail that were joined by an umbrella Intersyndical Commission. Each case reflects the constraints and possibilities of politicization within the host societies as much as the needs of the immigrant workers themselves.

For Jewish workers in general, immigrants or not, jobs in the early-twentieth-century cities were as much a function of economic opportunity as a result of imported skills. The fortunes of Dutch Jews rose and fell with the diamond industry. The Jews of New York, London, and Paris entered and transformed the growing ready-to-wear industries. Where the industry was less important, as in Germany, so was the Jews' place in it. There were relatively more boot and shoemakers in London and a notable concentration of Jewish cap makers in Paris. And if there were many Jewish cigarette makers in London and cigar makers in New York, there were virtually none in Paris, where tobacco was a state monopoly. Similarly, white slavery has been better documented in Buenos Aires than elsewhere, but prostitution accompanied both poverty and migration, and this may be a "false difference," a function of the state of our sources. Furthermore, the short experience of Jewish miners in Germany shows that Jewish workers have not always been engaged in light industry alone.

Some of the specific differences among Jewish workers in the modern Diaspora are thus due to political, cultural, or economic factors.[1] Different immigration legislation resulted in different timing and composition in the construction of the Jewish workers' communities around the world.[2] The earlier cutoff of immigration in England probably led to earlier Anglicization, even though the new social historians have warned us not to dismiss the immigrant and working-class experience there too quickly.[3] In Germany, in contrast, Germanization was the result of administrative, regional immigration policy, rather than federal law. This led to both selection and dispersion of the Eastern European Jews and helped facilitate their more rapid integration into the native Jewish community.

Finally, then, we must ask whether these differences contradict the notion of the "Jewish worker" as a distinct category. Clearly the answer is no. The "Jewish worker" is an identifiable group albeit with abundant diversity. We perceive a similarity, a community of interests and activities across boundaries, often reinforced by immigrant status and a culture of difference. At the same time, we have found a vibrant variety of experiences, a heterogeneity that seems to defy historiographic pigeonholing. After all, American Yiddish picked up *alrightnik* while Parisian Yiddish added *morte-saison* to its vocabulary. From the diversity of left political organizations alone[4] to divergences in the lingua franca of the Jewish immigrants, the documentation of variety over time and across space must be a stimulus to further analysis of these workers' communities within a comparative perspective. This project would have been impossible if we had not sensed that the similarities in experience, at a general level of interpretation, make these texts eloquent testimony to the possibility of studying the modern Diaspora as a "unified" concept. But by giving voice to the Jewish workers of the past, we also recognize the multiplicity of those voices.

NOTES

1. Nancy L. Green, "The Modern Jewish Diaspora: Eastern European Jews in New York, London, and Paris," in Dirk Hoerder and Leslie Page Moch, eds., *European Migrants: Global and Local Perspectives* (Boston: Northeastern University Press, 1996), pp. 263–81.

2. Jack Wertheimer, *Unwelcome Strangers: East European Jews in Imperial Germany* (New York: Oxford University Press, 1987), pp. 176–81.

3. David Cesarani, ed., *The Making of Modern Anglo-Jewry* (Oxford: Blackwell, 1990).

4. Tami Manor-Friedman, ed., *Workers and Revolutionaries: The Jewish Labor Movement* (Tel Aviv: Beth Hatefutsoth, 1994).

Selected Bibliography

GENERAL

Arkin, Marcus. *Aspects of Jewish Economic History.* Philadelphia: Jewish Publication Society, 1975.

Baron, Salo. *The Russian Jew under Tsar and Soviets.* [1964] Revised edition. New York: Macmillan, 1976.

Berger, David, ed. *The Legacy of Jewish Migration: 1881 and Its Impact.* New York: Brooklyn College Press, 1983.

Bristow, Edward J. *Prostitution and Prejudice: The Jewish Fight against White Slavery, 1870–1939.* London: Oxford University Press, 1982.

Bunzl, John. *Klassenkampf in der Diaspora: Zur Geschichte der jüdischen Arbeiterbewegung.* Vienna: Europaverl., 1975.

Burgin, H. *Di geshikhte fun der idisher arbayter bavegung in Amerike, Rusland un England* [History of the Jewish Labor Movement in America, Russia and England]. New York: Fareynigte idishe geverkshaftn, 1915.

Caestecker, Frank. *Ongewenste Gasten, Joodse Vluchtelingen en Migranten in de Dertiger Jaren.* Brussels: VUB Press, 1993.

Dubnow, Simon. *History of the Jews in Russia and Poland.* 3 vols. [1916] Reprint. New York: Ktav, 1973.

Frager, Ruth A. *Sweatshop Strife: Class, Ethnicity, and Gender in the Jewish Labor Movement of Toronto, 1900–1934.* Toronto: Toronto University Press, 1992.

Frankel, Jonathan. *Prophecy and Politics: Socialism, Nationalism, and the Russian Jews, 1862–1917.* New York: Cambridge University Press, 1981.

Green, Nancy L. "The Modern Jewish Diaspora: Eastern European Jews in New York, London, and Paris." In *European Migrants: Global and Local Perspectives.* Edited by Dirk Hoerder and Leslie Page Moch. Boston: Northeastern University Press, 1996.

Gross, Nachum, ed. *Economic History of the Jews.* New York: Schocken, 1976.

Kahan, Arcadius. *Essays in Jewish Social and Economic History.* Edited by Roger Weiss. Chicago: University of Chicago Press, 1986.

Lestschinsky, Jacob. "Jewish Migrations, 1840–1946." In *The Jews*. Edited by Louis Finkelstein. 2 vols. New York: Harper and Row, 1955.

Levin, Nora. *While Messiah Tarried: Jewish Socialist Movements, 1871–1917*. New York: Schocken, 1977.

Mahler, Raphael. "The Economic Background of Jewish Emigration from Galicia to the United States." *YIVO Annual of Jewish Social Science* 7 (1952): 255–67.

Manor-Friedman, Tami, ed. *Workers and Revolutionaries: The Jewish Labor Movement*. Tel Aviv: Beth Hatefutsoth, 1994.

Mendelsohn, Ezra. *Class Struggle in the Pale: The Formative Years of the Jewish Workers' Movement in Tsarist Russia*. Cambridge: Cambridge University Press, 1970.

Mishkinsky, Moshe. "The Jewish Labor Movement and European Socialism." In *Jewish Society through the Ages*. Edited by H. H. Ben-Sasson and S. Ettinger. New York: Schocken, 1969.

———. *Sotsyalizm Yehudi U-tenu'at Ha-po'alim Ha-yehudit Ba-me'ah Ha-19* [Jewish Socialism and the Jewish Labor Movement in the 19th Century]. Jerusalem: The Historical Society of Israel, 1975.

Reutlinger, Andrew S. "Reflections on the Anglo-American Jewish Experience: Immigrants, Workers, and Entrepreneurs in New York and London, 1870–1914." *American Jewish Historical Quarterly* 66, no. 4 (June 1977): 473–84.

Rubinow, Isaac. *Economic Condition of the Jews in Russia*. New York: Arno Press, 1975.

Sanders, Ronald. *The Shores of Refuge: A Hundred Years of Jewish Emigration*. New York: Holt, 1988.

Shepherd, Naomi. *A Price below Rubies: Jewish Women as Rebels and Radicals*. Cambridge, Mass.: Harvard University Press, 1993.

Soloweitschik, Léonty. *Un Prolétariat méconnu*. Brussels: Henri Lamertin, 1898.

Tobias, Henry. *The Jewish Bund in Russia from Its Origins to 1905*. Stanford: Stanford University Press, 1972.

Weinstock, Nathan. *Le Pain de misère: Histoire du mouvement ouvrier juif en Europe*. 2 vols. Paris: La Découverte, 1984.

Wertheimer, Jack, ed. *The Modern Jewish Experience: A Reader's Guide*. New York: New York University Press, 1993.

Wischnitzer, Mark. *A History of Jewish Crafts and Guilds*. New York: Jonathan David, 1965.

Wistrich, Robert. *Revolutionary Jews from Marx to Trotsky*. London: Harrap, 1976.

NEW YORK CITY/UNITED STATES

Antonovsky, Aaron. *The Early Jewish Labor Movement in the United States*. New York: YIVO, 1961.

Barkai, Avraham. *Branching Out: German-Jewish Immigration to the United States, 1820–1914.* New York: Holmes & Meier, 1994.

Baum, Charlotte, Paula Hyman, and Sonya Michel. *The Jewish Woman in America.* New York: New American Library, 1975.

Brandes, Joseph. "From Sweatshop to Stability: Jewish Labor between Two World Wars." *YIVO Annual of Jewish Social Science* 16 (1976): 1–149.

Cahan, Abraham. *The Rise of David Levinsky.* New York: Harper and Brothers, 1917.

Cohen, Naomi W. *Encounter with Emancipation: The German Jews in the United States, 1830–1914.* Philadelphia: Jewish Publication Society, 1984.

Epstein, Melech. *Jewish Labor in U.S.A. (1882–1952).* 2 vols. New York: Trade Union Sponsoring Committee, 1950–53.

Ewen, Elizabeth. *Immigrant Women in the Land of Dollars: Life and Culture on the Lower East Side, 1890–1925.* New York: Monthly Review Press, 1985.

Feingold, Henry. *A Time for Searching: Entering the Mainstream, 1920–1945, The Jewish People in America.* Baltimore: Johns Hopkins University Press, 1992.

Fraser, Steven. *Labor Will Live: Sidney Hillman and the Rise of American Labor.* New York: Free Press, 1991.

Fried, Albert. *The Rise and Fall of the Jewish Gangster in America.* [1980] Revised edition. New York: Columbia University Press, 1993.

Glenn, Susan A. *Daughters of the Shtetl: Life and Labor in the Immigrant Generation.* Ithaca: Cornell University Press, 1990.

Gorelick, Sherry. *City College and the Jewish Poor: Education in New York, 1880–1924.* New Brunswick, N.J.: Rutgers University Press, 1981.

Goren, Arthur. *New York Jews and the Quest for Community: The Kehillah Experiment 1908–1922.* New York: Columbia University Press, 1970.

Gurock, Jeffrey S. *When Harlem Was Jewish, 1870–1930.* New York: Columbia University Press, 1979.

Hapgood, Hutchins. *The Spirit of the Ghetto.* [1902] Reprint. Cambridge, Mass.: Harvard University Press, 1967.

Heinze, Andrew. *Adapting to Abundance: Jewish Immigrants, Mass Consumption, and the Search for American Identity.* New York: Columbia University Press, 1990.

Herberg, Will. "The Jewish Labor Movement in the United States." *American Jewish Yearbook* 53 (1952).

Hertz, Jacob Sholem. *Di yidishe sotsyalistishe bavegung in Amerike.* New York: n.p., 1954.

Howe, Irving. *World of Our Fathers.* New York: Harcourt Brace Jovanovich, 1976.

Hyman, Paula. "Immigrant Women and Consumer Protest: The New York City Kosher Meat Boycott of 1902." *American Jewish History* (September 1980): 91–105.

Joselit, Jenna Weissman. *Our Gang: Jewish Crime and the New York Jewish Community 1900–1940.* Bloomington: Indiana University Press, 1983.

Kahan, Arcadius. "Economic Opportunities and Some Pilgrims' Progress: Jewish Immigrants from Eastern Europe in the U.S., 1890–1914." *Journal of Economic History* 38 (March 1978): 235–51.

Kessner, Thomas. *The Golden Door: Italian and Jewish Immigrant Mobility in New York City, 1880–1915.* New York: Oxford University Press, 1977.

Kosak, Hadassa. "The Rise of the Jewish Working Class, New York, 1881–1905." Diss., City University of New York, 1987.

Kugelmass, Jack, ed. *Between Two Worlds: Ethnographic Essays on American Jewry.* Ithaca: Cornell University Press, 1988.

Kuznets, Simon. "Immigration of Russian Jews to the United States: Background and Structure." *Perspectives on American History* 9 (1975): 35–124.

Leviatin, David. *Followers of the Trail: Jewish Working-class Radicals in America.* New Haven: Yale University Press, 1989.

Levine, Louis. *The Women's Garment Workers.* New York: B. W. Huebsch, 1924.

Liebman, Arthur. *Jews and the Left.* New York: John Wiley and Sons, 1979.

Moore, Deborah Dash. *At Home in America: Second Generation New York Jews.* New York: Columbia University Press, 1981.

Orleck, Annelise. *Common Sense and a Little Fire: Women and Working-class Politics in the United States, 1900–1965.* Chapel Hill: University of North Carolina Press, 1995.

Riis, Jacob. *How the Other Half Lives.* New York: Charles Scribner's Sons, 1890.

Rischin, Moses. *The Promised City: New York's Jews 1870–1914.* New York: Corinth Books, 1962.

Sanders, Ronald. *The Downtown Jews.* New York: Harper and Row, 1969.

Schofield, Ann. *"To Do and To Be": Ladies, Immigrants, and Workers, 1893–1986.* Boston: Northeastern University Press, 1997.

Sorin, Gerald. *The Prophetic Minority: American Jewish Immigrant Radicals 1880–1920.* Bloomington: Indiana University Press, 1985.

——— . *A Time for Building: The Third Migration, 1880–1920.* Baltimore: Johns Hopkins University Press, 1992.

Soyer, Daniel. *Jewish Immigrant Associations and American Identity in New York, 1880–1939.* Cambridge, Mass.: Harvard University Press, 1997.

——— . "Landsmanshaftn and the Jewish Labor Movement: Cooperation, Conflict, and the Building of Community." *Journal of American Ethnic History* 7:2 (spring 1988): 22–45.

Stein, Leon, ed. *Out of the Sweatshop.* New York: Quadrangle, 1977.

Tcherikower, Elias. *Geshikhte fun der yidisher arbeter-bavegung in di Fareynikte shtatn.* 2 vols. New York: YIVO, 1943–45.

Weinberg, Sydney Stahl. *The World of Our Mothers: The Lives of Jewish Immigrant Women.* Chapel Hill: University of North Carolina Press, 1988.

Weisser, Michael. *A Brotherhood of Memory: Jewish Landsmanshaftn in the New World.* New York: Basic Books, 1985.

Wenger, Beth. *New York Jews and the Great Depression.* New Haven: Yale University Press, 1996.

LONDON/ENGLAND

Black, Eugene. *The Social Politics of Anglo-Jewry, 1880–1920.* Oxford: Blackwell, 1988.

Buckman, Joseph. *Immigrants and the Class Struggle: The Jewish Immigrant in Leeds, 1880–1914.* Manchester: Manchester University Press, 1983.

Cesarani, David. "The East End of Simon Blumenfeld's *Jew Boy.*" *London Journal* 13, no. 1 (1987): 46–53.

——— , ed. *The Making of Modern Anglo-Jewry.* Oxford: Blackwell, 1990.

Feldman, David. *Englishmen and Jews: Social Relations and Political Culture, 1840–1914.* New Haven: Yale University Press, 1994.

Fishman, William J. *East End Jewish Radicals, 1875–1914.* London: Duckworth, 1975.

Gartner, Lloyd P. *The Jewish Immigrant in England, 1870–1914.* 2nd edition. London: Simon Publishing, 1973.

Kershen, Anne. *Uniting the Tailors.* Ilford, Essex: Frank Cass, 1995.

Kushner, Tony, ed. *The Jewish Heritage in British History: Englishness and Jewishness.* London: Frank Cass, 1992.

Lipman, V. D. [Vivian David]. *A History of the Jews in Britain since 1858.* Leicester: Leicester University Press, 1990; and New York: Holmes & Meier, 1990.

Pollins, Harold. *Economic History of the Jews in England.* Fairleigh Dickinson University Press. East Brunswick, N.J.: Associated University Presses, 1982.

White, Jerry. *Rothschild Buildings: Life in an East End Tenement Block.* London: Routledge and Kegan Paul, 1980.

Williams, Bill. "'East and West': Class and Community in Manchester Jewry, 1850–1914." In *The Making of Modern Anglo-Jewry.* Edited by David Cesarani. Oxford: Blackwell, 1990.

——— . *The Making of Manchester Jewry 1740–1875.* Manchester: Manchester University Press, 1976.

PARIS/FRANCE

Altman, Patrick. "Les Conséquences de la crise économique des années 30 sur la population juive immigrée de Paris." Master's thesis. 1985.

Benveniste, Annie. *Le Bosphore à la Roquette: La communauté judéo-espagnole à Paris, 1914–1940.* Paris: L'Harmattan, 1989.

Boyarin, Jonathan. *Polish Jews in Paris: The Ethnography of Memory.* Bloomington: Indiana University Press, 1991.

Green, Nancy L. "Class and Community: *Der idisher arbayter.*" In *The Press of Labor Migrants in Europe and North America, 1880s to 1930s.* Edited by

Christiane Harzig and Dirk Hoerder. Bremen: Universität Bremen Labor Newspaper Preservation Project, 1985.

———. *The Pletzl of Paris: Jewish Immigrant Workers in the Belle Epoque.* New York: Holmes & Meier, 1986.

Hyman, Paula. *From Dreyfus to Vichy: The Remaking of French Jewry.* New York: Columbia University Press, 1979.

Marrus, Michael. *The Politics of Assimilation: French Jewry at the Time of the Dreyfus Affair.* New York: Oxford University Press, 1971.

Morin, Edgar. *Vidal et les siens.* Paris: Seuil, 1989.

Roland, Charlotte. *Du Ghetto à l'Occident: Deux générations yiddiches en France.* Paris: Editions du Minuit, 1962.

Szajkowski, Zosa. *Etyudn tsu der geshikhte fun ayngevandertn yidishn yishev in Frankraykh.* Paris: Fridman, 1936.

———. *Di profesyonele bavegung tsvishn di yidishe arbeter in Frankraykh biz 1914.* Paris: Fridman, 1937.

Weinberg, David. *A Community on Trial: The Jews of Paris in the 1930s.* Chicago: University of Chicago Press, 1977.

BUENOS AIRES/ARGENTINA

Avni, Haim. *Argentina and the Jews: A History of Jewish Immigration.* Tuscaloosa: University of Alabama Press, 1991.

Bilsky, Edgardo. "Ethnicité et classe ouvrière: Les travailleurs juifs à Buenos Aires (1900–1930)." *Le Mouvement social,* no. 159 (April-June 1992): 39–56.

———. *La Semana Trágica.* Buenos Aires: CEAL, 1984.

Centro de Documentación e Información sobre Judaísmo Argentino "Marc Turkow." *El movimiento obrero judío en la Argentina,* vol. 4 of *Bibliografía temática sobre Judaísmo Argentino.* 7 vols. Edited by Ana E. Weinstein. Buenos Aires: AMIA, 1987.

Elkin, Judith. *Jews of the Latin American Republics.* Chapel Hill: University of North Carolina Press, 1980.

Mirelman, Victor. *Jewish Buenos Aires, 1890–1930: In Search of an Identity.* Detroit: Wayne State University Press, 1990.

Sofer, Eugene. *From Pale to Pampa: A Social History of the Jews of Buenos Aires.* New York: Holmes & Meier, 1982.

GERMANY

Adler-Rudel, Schalom. *Ostjuden in Deutschland 1880–1940.* Tübingen: J. C. B. Mohr (Paul Siebeck), 1959.

Aschheim, Steven E. *Brothers and Strangers: The East European Jew in German and German Jewish Consciousness.* Madison: University of Wisconsin Press, 1982.

Heid, Ludger. "East European Jewish Workers in the Ruhr, 1915–1922." *Leo Baeck Institute Yearbook* 30 (1985): 141–68.

———. *Maloche—nicht Mildtätigkeit: Ostjüdische Arbeiter in Deutschland, 1914–1923*. Hildesheim: Olms Verlag, 1995.

Maurer, Trude. *Ostjuden in Deutschland 1918–1933*. Hamburg: Hans Christian Verlag, 1986.

Richarz, Monika. *Jüdisches Leben in Deutschland*. Stuttgart: Deutsche Verlags-Anstalt, 1976.

Weill, Claudie. *Etudiants russes en Allemagne, 1900–1914*. Paris: L'Harmattan, 1996.

Wertheimer, Jack. *Unwelcome Strangers: East European Jews in Imperial Germany*. New York: Oxford University Press, 1987.

AMSTERDAM/THE NETHERLANDS

Bloemgarten, Salvador. *Henri Polak: Sociaal democraat, 1868–1943*. The Hague: Sdu, 1993.

Boekman, E. *Demografie van de Joden in Nederland*. Amsterdam: Hertzberger, 1936.

Bregstein, Philo, and Salvador Bloemgarten, eds. *Herinnering aan Joods Amsterdam*. Amsterdam: De Bezige Bij, 1978.

De Jong Edz, Frits. *"Van ruw tot geslepen": De culturele betekenis van de Algemene Nederlandse Diamantbewerkers Bond in de geschiedenis van Amsterdam*. Amsterdam: N. V. V., 1955.

Gans, M. H. *Het Nederlandse jodendom, de sfeer waarin wij leefden, Karakter, traditie en sociale omstandigheden van het Nederlandse jodendom voor de Tweede Wereldoorlog*. Baarn: Bosch en keuning, 1985.

Heertje, Henri. *De Diamantbewerkers van Amsterdam*. Amsterdam: Centen's Uitgevers-Maatschappij, 1936.

Hofmeester, Karin. *Van Talmoed tot statuut: Joodse arbeiders en arbeidersbewegingen in Amsterdam, Londen en Parijs, 1880–1914*. Amsterdam: Stichting beheer IISG, 1990.

Kleerekoper, S. E. "Het joodse proletariaat in het Amsterdam van de 19e Eeuw." *Studia Rosenthaliana* 1 (1967): no. 1, 97–109; no. 2, 71–85.

Leydesdorff, Selma. "'A Shattered Silence': The Life Stories of Survivors of the Jewish Proletariat of Amsterdam." In *International Yearbook of Oral History and Life Stories*. Edited by Luisa Passerini et al. Vol. 1, *Memory and Totalitarianism*. Oxford: Oxford University Press, 1993.

———. *We Lived with Dignity: The Jewish Proletariat of Amsterdam, 1900–1940*. Trans. Frank Heny. Detroit: Wayne State University Press, 1994. (*Wij hebben als mens geleefd: Het Joodse proletariaat van Amsterdam, 1900–1940*. Amsterdam: Meulenhoff, 1987).

Contributors

PATRICK ALTMAN received his master's degree in history at the Université de Paris–I (Sorbonne) in 1985 for a thesis entitled "Les Conséquences de la crise économique des années 30 sur la population juive immigrée de Paris." He is currently President-Director of Edispher, a publishing house in Paris.

EDGARDO BILSKY has received degrees from the Ecole des Hautes Etudes en Sciences Sociales and the Université de Paris–VII. He is the author of *Histoire du mouvement ouvrier et social argentin: Sources documentaires dans la région parisienne* (1983); *La Semana trágica de 1919* (1984); *Esquisse d'histoire du mouvement ouvrier argentin des origines aux années 30* (1987); and *La Fora: 1900–1910* (1985).

DAVID CESARANI is Parkes-Wiener Professor of 20th Century European Jewish History and Culture at Southampton University and Director of the Wiener Library, London. His publications include *Justice Delayed* (1992), *The Jewish Chronicle and Anglo-Jewry 1841–1991* (1994), and as editor, *The Final Solution* (1994), and as co-editor, *Citizenship, Nationality and Migration in Europe* (1996).

DAVID FELDMAN is Senior Lecturer in History at Birkbeck College, University of London. He is the author of *Englishmen and Jews, 1840–1914* (1994) and co-editor (with Gareth Jones) of *Metropolis London: Histories and Representations since 1800* (1989).

NANCY L. GREEN is Directeur d'Etudes at the Ecole des Hautes Etudes en Sciences Sociales in Paris and author of *The Pletzl of Paris: Jewish Immigrant Workers in the Belle Epoque* (1986) and of *Ready-to-Wear and Ready-to-Work: A Century of Industry and Immigrants in Paris and New York* (1997).

LUDGER HEID, Dr. Phil. Habil., is Lecturer at the Universities of Duisburg and Potsdam and Vice-President of the Salomon Ludwig Steinheim-Institute for German-Jewish History. He has published *Deutsch-jüdische Geschichte im 19. und 20. Jahrhundert* (1992) and *Maloche—nicht Mildtätigkeit: Ostjüdische Arbeiter in Deutschland, 1914–1923* (1995) and is the co-editor of *Menora: Jahrbuch für deutsch-jüdische Geschichte.*

SELMA LEYDESDORFF is Professor at the Universeit van Amsterdam and Director of the Belle van Zuylen Instituut for comparative and multi-cultural gender studies. She is the author of *We Lived with Dignity: The Jewish Proletariat of Amsterdam, 1900–1940* (1994) (published in Dutch, German, and English) and has served as an editor of the *International Yearbook of Oral History and Life Stories.*

DANIEL SOYER is Assistant Professor of History at Fordham University in New York. He is the author of *Jewish Immigrant Associations and American Identity in New York, 1880–1939* (1997) and of several articles on Jewish and immigrant history in the United States. In 1996–97 he was a resident fellow with the Sweatshop Project, a Rockefeller Foundation Humanities Institute, co-sponsored by the Lower East Side Tenement Museum and UNITE.

JACK WERTHEIMER is Provost and the Joseph and Martha Mendelson Professor of American Jewish History at the Jewish Theological Seminary of America. He is the author of *Unwelcome Strangers: East European Jews in Imperial Germany* (1987) and *A People Divided: Judaism in Contemporary America* (1993).

Index

Compositor: Braun-Brumfield, Inc.
Text: 10/13 Aldus
Display: Aldus
Printer and binder: Haddon Craftsmen, Inc.